RELIGION ACROSS BORDERS

RELIGION ACROSS BORDERS

Transnational Immigrant Networks

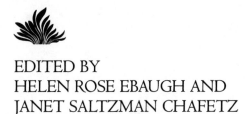

EDITED BY
HELEN ROSE EBAUGH AND
JANET SALTZMAN CHAFETZ

8/03

ALTAMIRA PRESS
A Division of Rowman & Littlefield Publishers, Inc.
Walnut Creek • Lanham • New York • Oxford

ALTAMIRA PRESS
A Division of Rowman & Littlefield Publishers, Inc.
1630 North Main Street, #367
Walnut Creek, CA 94596
www.altamirapress.com

Rowman & Littlefield Publishers, Inc.
A Member of the Rowman & Littlefield Publishing Group
4720 Boston Way
Lanham, MD 20706

PO Box 317
Oxford
OX2 9RU, UK

British Library Cataloguing in Publication Information Available

Library of Congress Cataloging-in-Publication Data

Religion across borders : transnational immigrant networks / edited by Helen Rose Ebaugh and Janet Saltzman Chafetz.
  p. cm.
  Includes bibliographical references and index.
  ISBN 0-7591-0225-2 (alk. paper) — ISBN 0-7591-0226-0 (pbk. : alk. paper)
  I. Immigrants—Religious life—United States. 2. United States—Emigration and immigration—Religious aspects. I. Ebaugh, Helen Rose Fuchs, 1942– II. Chafetz, Janet Saltzman.

BL2525 .R445 2002
200'.86'910973—dc21   2002005748

Printed in the United States of America

∞™ The paper used in this publication meets the minimum requirements of American National Standard for Information Sciences—Permanence of Paper for Printed Library Materials, ANSI/NISO Z39.48-1992.

Contents

Prologue
Lessons from American Immigrant Congregations

JANET SALTZMAN CHAFETZ AND HELEN ROSE EBAUGH

In our original study of immigrant religious institutions in Houston (RENIR I), thirteen congregations were examined in considerable depth, using common research instruments across sites (for details on research methodology and the individual congregations, see Ebaugh and Chafetz 2000b). In that project, we focused on how immigrants re-create and adapt their old-country religious institutions and practices to their new home in Houston. At that time, members and leaders were asked questions concerning their perceptions of differences and relationships between home country congregations and those with which they are affiliated in Houston. In addition, when discussing other issues (e.g., roles and status of women, the role of the clergy, secular/social services provided by the congregation), such comparisons sometimes spontaneously emerged. Findings from that phase of the research piqued our interest to examine, in a more focused and sustained way, the reciprocal relationships between Houston-based immigrant congregations and their home country counterparts, that is, the RENIR II project, the findings of which constitute the basis of this volume. Before we turn to them, however, we review here the insights gleaned from RENIR I concerning immigrants' perceptions of (1) changes in and differences between organizational structure and religious practice in their home country religious institutions and those they have developed or joined in Houston and (2) the nature of the relationships they maintain (and in some cases newly create) with religious institutions abroad.

Adaptive Change Processes
Eleven of the religious institutions we examined in depth were created by immigrants; the other two changed in composition from overwhelmingly Anglo to mostly immigrant members during the 1980s and early 1990s. Those founded by

immigrants sought initially to reproduce both their religious heritage and their ethnically specific cultures through the establishment of their own places of worship (see Chafetz and Ebaugh 2000b, esp. chap. 19). However, in the process of adapting to a new setting, most eventually instituted various kinds of changes in institutional organization and religious practice.

Fenggang Yang (who was a postdoctoral fellow on the RENIR I project) and Ebaugh use data from the thirteen congregations to demonstrate three broad processes of change that immigrant congregations, especially those that are not Christian, typically undergo as they adapt to their new environment (Yang and Ebaugh 2001b): (1) congregationalism (also discussed in detail in Ebaugh and Chafetz 2000b:chap. 17, 2000c); (2) pristinization, or a return to theological fundamentals; and (3) inclusion of ethnically and religiously diverse peoples.

Yang and Ebaugh describe changes in both organizational structure and ritual formality that they subsume under the rubric of congregational development (2001b:273–78) and suggest are rooted in Protestant practices long characteristic of American places of worship. Unlike practice in most of their native countries, especially in the cases of non-Judeo-Christian religions (in our sample Hindu, Buddhist, Islamic, and Zoroastrian), immigrant congregations provide far more scope for lay involvement in congregational life. First, membership becomes voluntary rather than simply ascribed at birth, and members must make an active effort to attend their mosque, temple, or church (on commuting distances, see also Ebaugh, O'Brien, and Chafetz 2000). In many cases, places of worship are ubiquitous in their home countries (e.g., "a mosque on every street"), and people give little thought to their status as members of a dominant, sometimes government-sponsored, religion. Because membership becomes a conscious choice in the United States, immigrant religious institutions must actively recruit members. Second, because immigrants build their congregations from scratch, they assume leadership roles that often do not exist for the laity in the old country. Most non-Judeo-Christian (and some Christian) religious institutions abroad are traditionally managed entirely by clergy. In immigrant congregations, lay boards of trustees participate in (and occasionally monopolize) decision making, and lay committees perform numerous functions. In addition, partly in response to tax codes and other legal requirements in the United States, "the division of labor and functions of each administrative department are defined in writing; legislative procedures are followed with a written constitution and bylaws" (Yang and Ebaugh 2001b:275). The third structural change involves the expansion of services provided by religious institutions, which assume a variety of functions in addition to those that are strictly religious. They become community centers that provide social services, secular as well as religious classes (e.g., general equivalency diploma, English as a second language, and citizenship), and recreational centers, and they become the locus of member social life and ethnic reproduction. The last type of organizational change involves the development of regional, national, and international organizational networks, some comprising new denominations, others more loosely structured around limited common interests (e.g., the Texas Buddhist Council, which links temples from diverse traditions and nationalities). Because this phenomenon stands at the heart of the RENIR II project, we will devote more attention to it in the next section.

At the same time that they are developing new organizational structures to acclimate to the U.S. environment, immigrant religious institutions are also altering several aspects of formal ritual practice, again especially in non-Christian faiths. First, in lieu of the traditional cycles of worship and sacred holiday celebrations, non-Christian congregations adopt those that are embedded in the traditionally Christian culture that surrounds them. Major worship ceremonies are moved to Sundays, and the celebration of major holidays is delayed until weekends to accommodate members' work weeks, which in turn are rooted in a Christian calendar. In addition, customs related to the practice of worship begin to borrow from Christianity, for instance, the use of pews to replace floor sitting, the introduction of preaching and of responsive recitation, and the use of a choir. Language of worship is almost always a contentious issue in these congregations (see Ebaugh and Chafetz 2000a, 2000b:chap. 20), but almost all have introduced English services, at least for the second generation. Many congregations include more than one native language group (e.g., Chinese Protestants who speak Mandarin and Cantonese; Hindus who speak four distinct regional languages; Muslims who speak Arabic and Urdu; a Catholic church with seven nationality groups, most with at least one non-English native language; and a Protestant church whose members speak fifty-nine native tongues). Often, English is their only common language. Finally, in many cases the role of the clergy broadens beyond the traditional one of ritual and scriptural expert. They are sought for counseling and to perform house blessings, weddings, and other "new" forms of ritual and are expected to visit the sick and receive guests from abroad. In other words, they are assuming the kind of pastoral work traditional to Christian but not most other clergy.

Ironically, at the same time that they are changing to increasingly resemble American Protestant churches, immigrant religious institutions are returning to their theological foundations, a process of "pristinization" (Yang and Ebaugh 2001b:278–81). This occurs in part because of the need to justify and legitimate many of the changes discussed previously. Thus, for instance, Muslims come to rediscover that, at the time of Muhammad, mosques served as community centers as well as religious sites. Pristinization also occurs because, in multiethnic congregations, co-religionists discover that their ways of "doing religion" can be quite different from practices originating in other nations. They return to foundational sources to discover which practices inhere in the faith and which have been added over the centuries by specific cultures. The Muslims in Houston refer to this as seeking "acultural" Islam. Finally, those whose religions are strange and new to the surrounding community are frequently pressed to explain their faith, leading many members to devote more study and attention to the basic meaning of their faith than they had in a typically more religiously homogeneous homeland (see also Yang and Ebaugh 2001a). As a result, non-Christian congregations develop classes for adults (as well as children) in which members can learn more about their religion; such congregations also stock religious libraries on their premises, and the clergy devote time during worship services to explaining the meaning of texts, all practices absent in the home countries from which the immigrants come.

The third major change process identified by Yang and Ebaugh (2001b:281–83) involves increasing inclusiveness of membership in immigrant congregations. In their homelands, nearly all these people had attended ethnically homogeneous places of worship. In order to establish a mosque, a Hindu or Buddhist temple, or a Chinese or Argentine Evangelical church, a critical mass of people and resources is required, a feat that may be unrealizable by a small group of co-ethnics. The result is that many such institutions comprise members from different nations (e.g., the mosque and both the predominantly Argentine and Chinese Protestant churches we studied) or from different regions of the same country that are nonetheless culturally very different and express their common faith in highly diverse ways (the Hindu temple). For the first time in their lives, immigrants worship with co-religionists who are culturally, including in many cases linguistically, quite different from themselves. Many faiths, such as Christianity and Islam, seek converts, including native-born Americans, and often this too brings new members from different backgrounds. With only a couple exceptions, the congregations we examined in Houston incorporate people from more than one national/cultural background.

Yang and Ebaugh (2001b:283–85) conclude by looking to the published literature to suggest that many of the changes just discussed are occurring elsewhere in the world. They hypothesize that these changes may in part reflect the influence of immigrant communities on their homeland institutions:

> The transnational impacts of religious immigrants in the United States are possible because of the influence of the United States as a core country in the world-system, the tangible and intangible resources of contemporary immigrants, and the social and cultural experiences of immigrants living in modern, pluralist

America. . . . [Immigrant religious institutions] provide immigrants with experiences and resources that enable them to exert leadership in attempting to maintain doctrinal purity, influence organizational affairs within the religious system, and use their resources to spread the faith. (285)

Among other issues, RENIR II has tried to explore the extent to which the immigrants' religious innovations are being exported back to their homelands and the mechanisms by which this is being accomplished.

Transnational Religious Ties

During RENIR I, information was explicitly sought concerning immigrants' ongoing ties with their native lands. Because we knew that a new project would be exploring this topic from the dual vantage points of Houston-based and country-of-origin religious institutions, we chose not to analyze this data in our major work on the initial project (Ebaugh and Chafetz 2000b). In this section, we present some of the data from the thirteen Houston congregations studied in RENIR I concerning religiously relevant, transnational ties. Not surprisingly, we find that by far the most frequent link between immigrants and their community of origin is kin and that the most frequent resources that flow from Houston to kin abroad are money and material goods. We will ignore this phenomenon unless there is an explicit connection to religious institutions or practices in Houston or abroad.

When immigrant congregations are first founded, influence and resources typically flow from the nation of origin to Houston. For instance, many immigrant congregations import at least their first, and in some cases continue to import, clergy from abroad (e.g., the Chinese Buddhist temple and Protestant church, the mosque, and the Hindu temple). Money from abroad sometimes contributes to new congregations' ability to build their own facility (e.g., the Zoroastrian Center and the Chinese Buddhist and Hindu temples). Religious practices are imported because immigrant practitioners want to reconstruct their traditional ways of "doing religion," because clergy come from abroad, and sometimes because of strict hierarchical structures of religious authority (e.g., the Greek Orthodox church, which is ultimately governed by the patriarchate of Constantinople, and the Mexican Protestant church, given the pseudonym *Iglesia de Dios* in RENIR I but discussed in detail in chapter 2 by its proper name, *Luz del Mundo*, which is governed by the church leader in Guadalajara, Mexico). The Hindu temple has, since its inception, chosen to consult with several highly respected priests in southern India before making major decisions.

Over time, as immigrants adapt to their new environment and both they and their religious institutions acquire more financial stability, flows of monetary resources, religious personnel, and influence often reverse or become two way. This process is expedited by modern media of communication and forms of travel that are most readily available to residents and institutions in wealthy industrialized nations (e.g., e-mail, websites, fax, audio- and videotapes, phones, and air travel).

In several cases, we find that Houston congregations and/or their individual members send money to religious institutions abroad. For instance, the Korean Protestant church supports five rural churches in Korea from donations by its immigrant members. A wealthy immigrant family that belongs to the Chinese Buddhist temple gives donations to temples in mainland China, finances scholarships for Buddhist novices, and otherwise quietly works to reestablish Buddhism in that nation. The Hispanic Department of the multiethnic Assembly of God church brings clothes and other supplies to Mexican churches during an annual visit, and their Filipino counterparts raised more than $50,000 for an Assembly of God college in their homeland. The multiethnic Catholic church supports 117 Vietnamese orphans in conjunction with a parish in that country, and many individual Vietnamese members of this church and the Vietnamese Buddhist temple send money for the reconstruction or building of temples and churches in their home communities. Filipinos in this Catholic church have begun to do likewise.

Money also finds its way to overseas congregations in many nations through payment for religious rituals that immigrants wish to have conducted in their home communities. These range from memorial services for the dead (and sometimes funeral services for those who wished to have their remains shipped home for burial) to holding life cycle events, such as baptisms, weddings, or *quincenieras* (fifteenth birthday ritual for Hispanic girls), or holiday celebrations (e.g., a Mexican Christmas *posada*) in a home country congregation. The latter occur almost entirely within the Western Hemisphere (indeed, mostly in Mexico), probably because of proximity to Houston. Another mostly Mexican immigrant phenomenon is making pilgrimages to religious shrines in the country of origin; these filter dollars earned in Houston back to home country religious sites as well. In RENIR I, two congregations are virtually entirely Mexican, one Catholic and one Protestant, and the two large, multiethnic congregations (also one Catholic and one Protestant) each have a separately organized Hispanic Department/Community that includes a substantial number of Mexicans. In all four cases, regular, if not frequent, trips home, devoted at least in part to religious purposes, are reported by members.

Other means by which religious institutions in Houston channel resources to other nations are to send abroad and financially support missionaries and other religious personnel and to support visiting religious personnel and students from abroad. The Chinese Protestant church has established a mission in Kazakhstan that it continues to support and has sent missionaries (including students on short-term assignments) to various Latin American, Asian, and European nations. Likewise, it has funded members to attend seminaries in Hong Kong, Taiwan, and Singapore. The multiple and complex transnational ties involving this congregation are explored in detail in chapter 7. In a similar manner, the predominantly Argentine Brethren church in Houston (the subject of chapter 3) has sent missionaries to Spain, Honduras, and even back to Argentina. The multiethnic Catholic church occasionally recruits foreign priests visiting the United States to come and celebrate mass in their native language, and for three years it hosted a Filipino priest who was seeking asylum in the United States. The Mexican Catholic church (called St. Mary's in RENIR I but by its proper name, Immaculate Heart of Mary, in chapter 5) sent a lay missionary to Mexico through the auspices of its youth group, while a group of Greek Orthodox youth who perform traditional folk dances was invited to perform in Greece, where they were perceived as "Greek Orthodox . . . ambassadors of those . . . faithful who had left their homeland . . . yet could not forget their Greek roots."

Ongoing ties between foreign-born clergy and other religious leaders in Houston with religious institutions and personnel abroad are maintained and expanded by international travel. For instance, one of the monks in the Chinese Buddhist temple was given the title of abbot at a Taiwanese temple while on leave there from Houston for medical treatment. He is required to visit the temple twice a year and often goes with the abbot of his own Houston temple. Other Buddhist leaders have come to the Houston temple to lead retreats and deliver talks, including the Tibetan Dalai Lama and several monks from Taiwan. The pastor of the Chinese Protestant church in Houston also serves as the dean of a seminary in Singapore, where he frequently travels to give talks and lead meetings. He also returns to a Hong Kong church to which he belonged as a youth to lead revival meetings and retreats. Conversely, the president of the Hong Kong seminary that the pastor and some other members of the Houston church attended years ago came to Houston seeking students and financial contributions. From the beginning, Argentine Brethren preachers frequently traveled to the Houston church to give sermons and advice on church matters. In more recent years, Houston church leaders travel to Argentina to a retreat camp that they developed and that is substantially funded by the Houston congregation, a place where new ideas are shared and a general revitalization of church members occurs.

Less than half the congregations we studied are closely linked to international, hierarchically organized denominations, but even those that are not typically have at least some ties to organizations that span national boundaries. For instance, the Brethren congregation, which is not controlled by a denominational hierarchy, belongs to the Stewards Foundation, Christian Missions in Many Lands, Interest Ministries, and the Messiah Project, all international organizations designed to provide aid and information to local Brethren congregations and to support and encourage their missionary activities. The Chinese Protestant church made a self-conscious decision to organize as a nondenominational church and instead belongs to two worldwide Chinese Christian associations—Chinese Christian Congress of World Evangelism and Evangelism Explosion III—which provide literature, seminars, and other information to Evangelical Christian congregations. The Houston Zoroastrian Center is a member of both the Federation of Zoroastrian Associations of North America and the World Zoroastrian Organization, whose Seventh World Congress was held in Houston in 2000. Membership in the mosque we studied automatically brings membership in the Islamic Society of North America (ISNA), which in turn is linked to a global network of religious and relief organizations. Indeed, because Houston pioneered the development of a geographically based, zonal mosque system (akin to Catholic parishes), an organizational form subsequently adopted widely in North America, it has become one of the most influential Islamic communities in ISNA.

It is clear that clergy, lay religious leaders, and even ordinary members of Houston immigrant congregations develop and maintain ties that span international borders, with clergy, individual congregations, and other types of religious bodies abroad. Together with rapid and often relatively inexpensive travel by air (and for Mexico, by bus, van, and car), modern means of communication constitute the arteries through which information, new ideas, and material resources flow, linking people and institutions in diverse nations. A few examples suffice to demonstrate the importance of e-mail, websites, audio- and videotapes, phones, and fax. The youth group at the Mexican Catholic church has strong ties with a counterpart group in a Guatemalan parish. Young people from Houston travel frequently to Guatemala to bring material aid—travel that is coordinated via e-mail. Indeed, the two groups keep in close, ongoing contact via the Internet. The Zoroastrian community numbers only about one-quarter million people worldwide and the Houston congregation only about 200 families. Their communities are spread around the world, but members can choose from at least four Zoroastrian websites to keep in touch, learn the latest news, and debate theological issues. Because the small number of children of any given age in each community know each other as if they are siblings, they must seek a mate from elsewhere to conform to religious pressure to marry within the faith. There are now several worldwide Zoroastrian "matchmaking" or "soul mate" Internet sites, and at least two Houston marriages have resulted from them (one to a person in New Zealand). At the multiethnic Catholic church, respondents tell of sending tapes of baptisms, confirmations, and *quincenieras* back to godparents in the home country. Chinese Buddhists frequently send tapes of temple talks, rituals, and services to Taiwan, and some are even circulating clandestinely in China. In fact, a Taiwanese television station reported a New Year's Eve celebration that took place at the Houston temple. Buddhists often tape weddings and funerals to share with relatives in Vietnam to demonstrate that they are still observing traditional customs. One recent Argentine immigrant, a convert to the Brethren church, recalled how her aunt sent her and other family members audio- and videotapes from Houston, speaking about her newfound faith. Moved by the message, they all ended up converting. The congregation in Argentina sends videos to the one in Houston to show how wisely it is using the money being sent to support it. Information about events and travelers circulates quickly via phone and fax, with news of births, illness, and death learned about almost simultaneously in the Houston and Argentine congregations. In addition, speakers and seminars that involve people in both locations are arranged entirely by fax.

There are some tantalizing hints in the RENIR I data to suggest that these dense webs of two-way communication across borders, combined with regular travel in both directions, spur the spread of religious innovation. Recall that as specifically immigrant congregations, those we examined often develop practices new to their faiths as part of the process of adaptation to a new environment. Therefore, the main flow direction for innovation in religious practice and institutional structure ought to be primarily from Houston to home country congregations and/or immigrant congregations elsewhere. Thus, for instance, the mosque in Houston is part of—indeed, was central to the creation of—a parishlike (zonal) system controlled and coordinated by a citywide organization called the Islamic Society of Greater Houston. This innovation has now spread to immigrant Moslem communities elsewhere in North America. The Argentine Brethren congregation began to send missionaries back to Argentina about fifteen years after the first migrants left there for Houston. These missionaries have developed a new institution for Argentine Brethren, the retreat camp, which helps revitalize the religion there. Houston and Argentine youth regularly mix at the camp, exchanging liturgical and ministerial ideas, songs, and so on (as well as not infrequently acquiring a spouse from the other country). Some respondents at the multiethnic Assembly of God church report that, in the Caribbean, clothing norms for religious services are becoming more informal because of the influence of U.S. congregations. Specifically, women are beginning to wear pants, jewelry, and makeup and to forsake a head covering when in church. These examples are suggestive, but the extent to which innovations in Houston congregations affect religious life elsewhere cannot really be studied from the vantage point of Houston. Only by conducting research in the communities and congregations of origin is it possible to see to what, if any, extent such influence is being exerted, and this is part of the reason for the RENIR II project.

Conclusion

"Transnational linkages" was one of nearly two dozen topics explored in RENIR I, and it was not among the most central. Moreover, only one side of such linkages could be explored at all in a Houston-based study. Despite these limitations, several findings are suggestive of issues to explore in more detail from the dual vantage points of congregations in Houston and religious institutions and communities in members' homelands:

1. Initial flows of resources and influence tend to be from religious institutions in immigrants' home countries to those in Houston.
2. Over time, immigrant congregations develop innovative religious structures and practices as adaptations to their new home.
3. Over time, the flow of material resources reverses, and the flow of religious personnel and innovation may reverse or at least become bilateral.
4. Transnational networks relevant to religious practice may connect units at many levels: individual laypersons, religious leaders/clergy, religious institutions, and international organizations.
5. These network linkages and the resources that flow among units within them are substantially dependent on modern technologies of communication and transportation for their development and growth.

These are some of the issues we explore in more depth in the rest of this volume. Five of the original thirteen congregations constitute starting points for the RENIR II studies, and two new transnational religious communities have been added. Chapter 1 describes the details of the RENIR II project.

References

Ebaugh, Helen Rose, and Janet Saltzman Chafetz. 2000a. "Dilemmas of Language in Immigrant Congregations: The Tie That Binds or the Tower of Babel?" *Review of Religious Research* 41:432–52.
———. 2000b. *Religion and the New Immigrants.* Walnut Creek, CA: AltaMira Press.
———. 2000c. "Structural Adaptations in Immigrant Congregations." *Sociology of Religion* 61:135–53.
Ebaugh, Helen Rose, Jennifer O'Brien, and Janet Saltzman Chafetz. 2000. "The Social Ecology of Residential Patterns and Membership in Immigrant Churches." *Journal for the Scientific Study of Religion* 39:107–16.
Yang, Fenggang, and Helen Rose Ebaugh. 2001a. "Religion and Ethnicity among the New Immigrants: The Impact of Majority/Minority Status in Home and Host Countries." *Journal for the Scientific Study of Religion* 40:367–78.
———. 2001b. "Transformations in New Immigrant Religions and Their Global Implications." *American Sociological Review* 66:269–88.

Introduction

HELEN ROSE EBAUGH AND JANET SALTZMAN CHAFETZ

Much of the migration literature prior to the past two decades presented immigrants as individuals who uprooted themselves from one society to settle and become incorporated into a new land (Handlin 1973; Herberg 1960; Smith 1978). This earlier sociological research usually predicted that ethnic attachments would weaken and then fade as immigrants gradually became assimilated into the United States and their American-born children reached maturity. Subsequent research, however, showed that ethnicity remained salient for many immigrants and that religion often served as an "identity marker" (Williams 1988:29) that helped immigrants maintain an ethnic identity. The work of Basch, Glick Schiller, and Szanton Blanc, which culminated in *Nations Unbound: Transnational Projects, Postcolonial Predicaments, and Deterritorialized Nation-States* (1994), presented clear evidence that many immigrants who invest socially, economically, and politically in U.S. society continue to participate in the daily life of the society from which they emigrated. The image of migrants as transnationals, that is, as "people with feet in two societies" (a phrase that Basch et al. borrowed from Chaney 1979:209), became the guiding metaphor for a new perspective. Transmigrants, as they are sometimes called, take actions, make decisions, and develop identities embedded in networks of relationships that connect them simultaneously to two or more nation-states. Focusing on the fact that a significant proportion of immigrants maintain ties with their home countries while becoming incorporated into a new host society, Glick Schiller (1999) has proposed transnational migration as a new "paradigm" for the study of migration across nation-state borders.

Transnational migration did not begin with the "new immigrants" who came to the United States after the 1965 Immigration Act. The "old" European and Asian

immigrants also maintained ties with their countries of origin through high rates of
return migration (Bodnar 1985; Foner 2000; Morawska 1987, 2001), seasonal labor migration (Foner 2000; Jones 1992; Morawska 2001), financial remittances
sent back to the home country (Bodnar 1985; Wyman 1993), and continued communication via travel, letters, and couriers (Jones 1992; Wyman 1993). Transnational ties among the more recent immigrants, however, is posited as having distinctive characteristics due not only to changes in transportation and communications
technologies but also to broader transformations in the processes by which capital is
accumulated, expanded, and organized (Glick Schiller 1999; Portes, Guarnizo, and
Landolt 1999). Portes et al. (1999) argue that what is new about contemporary
transmigrants is the high intensity of exchanges, the new modes of transacting business, and the multiplication of activities that require cross-border travel and contacts
on a sustained basis. Levitt (2001:23) vividly describes how contemporary technologies impact the daily transnational lives of people: "Receiving a letter every two
weeks . . . is not the same as being able to pick up the phone at any moment of the
night or day. . . . It gives migrants the ability to be involved in the day-to-day decisions of the households they leave behind." Furthermore, with jet air travel, physical
movement is easier, faster, and more common than earlier migrants could accomplish with their new technology of steamships. Today, migrants often go back home
for a long weekend without missing much work, and family from the homeland can
readily come to the United States for a visit. Such ease of transportation facilitates
the maintenance of transnational ties.

The Transnational Literature

The concept *transnationalism* is a blurry one, a catchall notion that can include references to globalization (Beyer 1992; Held et al. 1999; Kearney 1995; Robertson
1992; Sassen 1991), diasporas (Cohen 1997; Vertovec 1997), transnational social fields (Basch et al. 1994; Fraser 1991; Mahler 1998), transnational communities (Goldring 1998; Nagengast and Kearney 1990; Rouse 1992; Smith 1997),
transnational social circuits (Rouse 1992), and binational societies (Guarnizo
1994). As a general descriptive term, transnationalism has been used to delineate
so many different activities and connections at so many different levels that it has
lost much of its analytical power. As Portes et al. (1999) point out in their introduction to a special issue of *Ethnic and Racial Studies* on the topic, transnational migration studies form a highly fragmented, emergent field that lacks a well-defined
theoretical framework and analytical rigor. Frequently, studies use disparate units
of analysis and mix diverse levels of abstraction.

In an attempt to bring intellectual order to the field of transnational migration studies, Portes et al. (1999) limit the concept of transnationalism to occu-

pations and activities that require regular and sustained social contacts over time across national borders for their implementation. For methodological reasons, they define the individual and his or her support networks as the proper unit of analysis when considering transnational activities. From data on individuals, they argue, it then becomes possible to delineate the networks that make transnational enterprises possible, to identify the transnational entrepreneurs' counterparts in the home country, and to garner information to establish the aggregate structural effects of these activities. Smith and Guarnizo (1998) suggest that transnational activities take place both on the level of the everyday, grounded practices of individuals and groups ("transnationalism from below") and on the level of global institutions and actors ("transnationalism from above") and that both levels of analysis are important in understanding the dynamics of transnational interactions. Levitt (2001) insists that the intermediate level of transnational communities is also important in mediating between "high" and "low" levels of transnationalism. When individual actors identify and organize themselves as transnational communities, a response from "above," by the state or an international organization, is more likely. Likewise, when home country national political, economic, or religious leaders reach out to local-level immigrant communities, they encourage its members to maintain loyalties across borders.

In addition to the need for specifying levels of analyses, both Levitt (2001) and Vertovec (1999) argue for more empirically grounded, multisite studies that enable the researcher to make comparisons between groups on a number of variables. Most of the existing transnational migration studies are in-depth descriptions of transnational relationships among migrants from one particular home country locale living in one host country community (e.g., Levitt 2001; Massey et al. 1987; Menjívar 2000; Popkin 1999). As a result, we have an increasing number of data-rich field studies of specific transnational communities that are not comparable to one another. The next step in developing the study of transnational migration is to conduct comparative research on a variety of transnational communities from different types of home countries with the goal of specifying conditions that influence the processes and outcomes of transnational migration.

A multisited approach to the study of transnationalism requires not only the inclusion of multiple transnational communities but also that these sites represent variation in terms of geographic proximity to the United States, the immigration history of the migrant population, migrants' levels of human and economic capital, and their immigration status in the United States. The bulk of existing studies of transnational groups focus on immigrants from Mexico, Central America, and the Caribbean, all countries located relatively near the United States. In order to determine the impact of distance on transnational networks, it is important to expand studies beyond nations proximate to our borders. Likewise, the inclusion of immigrant communities with higher levels of human and economic capital than is characteristic of the Western Hemisphere's migrant populations is essential to an understanding of the relationship between socioeconomic status and the formation of transnational ties.

Most case studies of transnational migrants focus on the "new immigrants," that is, relatively recent migrants to the United States. As a result, focus is almost entirely placed on the first generation of those who came to this country, with only limited attention to children born in the home country who were raised in the United States (i.e., the 1.5 generation), not to mention those born in the United States (i.e., the second generation). Only recently are there even sufficient numbers in the second generation to make their study feasible (see Portes 1996; Portes and Rumbaut 2001). In many cases, members of the second generation now are beginning the process of making the types of life decisions that could potentially reflect identification with their parents' home countries. A major question centers around such decisions and whether transnational ties will continue beyond the life spans of the original migrants. If they do, in what ways will such ties differ from those of the parental generation whose lives were lived in two countries?

Religion and Transnational Migration

While studies of transnationalism have increased in the past several decades, one dimension of the process has been virtually neglected: the role of religion. Basch et al. (1994), in their studies of immigrants from St. Vincent, Granada, the Philippines, and Haiti, mention religion in very general terms as they list organizations that helped unify the immigrant communities. However, they provide little detailed data on the role that these religious groups play in promoting transnationalism among the immigrants. Glick Schiller's (1999) article on transmigrants in the major overview of the international migration literature does not even mention religion.

The work of Cohen (1997) and Vertovec (1997) on the role of religion in diasporas is important in emphasizing the spread of religious practices from home communities to myriad groups around the world. However, neither focuses explicitly on transnational practices. Likewise, a number of globalization scholars (Casanova 1994; Robertson 1992; Rudolph and Piscatori 1997) describe the role of religion in creating and sustaining global structures and relationships among immigrant communities. However, there are relatively few case studies that trace transnational religious beliefs, practices, and networks between host and home communities of specific immigrant groups. Levitt's (1998, 2001) study of Dominican immigrants from Miraflores who settled in Boston is one of the first that describes transnational religious ties. Her rich data describe the beliefs and practices that Miraflorenos brought from their home country and adapted to the United States as well as the impact that the Boston community has had on changes in religious beliefs and customs in Miraflores. She carefully traces the networks of transnational religious influence involving lay individuals, clergy, and institutional church agencies. Subsequently, Levitt (1997) studied transnational religious ties between a Hindu Gujarati immigrant community in Boston and their home country communities in Baroda and Anand, India. While Levitt's studies are truly transnational, she focuses on only one type of transnationalism, namely, ties among closely knit immigrant communities whose members also share one or two identifiable locales in their home society, or "transnational villages," as she calls them (Levitt 2001). The question remains whether her findings will generalize to transnational groups whose members are less closely bound geographically and socially.

Based on her studies, Levitt (2001) has begun to articulate a model for the transnational study of religion that emphasizes research in both the receiving and the sending countries. She outlines the need for studies of transnational religious practices that focus on both individual and collective manifestations of religion in both institutionalized and noninstitutionalized settings. She proposes that studies of transnational religion examine the everyday, lived practice of religion in both home and host countries. The horizontal ties linking individuals, leaders, institutions, and religious social movement actors should then be situated within the context of other types of regional, national, and global cross-border connections.

Menjivar (2000) describes Catholic and Protestant evangelical immigrants from El Salvador who settled in Washington, D.C., as transmigrants. She found the immigrant Catholic church in Washington far less supportive of transnational activism than the evangelical churches. The Catholic church was concerned with creating a panethnic identity among Latino immigrants and therefore emphasized common projects and discouraged the development of ties to specific home country localities. Evangelical churches, on the other hand, encouraged homeland-oriented activities. Given the fact that she studied only a small number of churches in the same locale, it is difficult to determine whether it is, in fact, theological differences between Catholic and evangelical churches that mainly influence the intensity and types of ties that immigrants maintain with their home communities or whether specific characteristics of the congregations and members explain the differences she describes.

McAlister's (1998) work on Haitians describes ways in which a New York City community uses religious practices to maintain connections with family and friends in Haiti. Religious pilgrimages, processions, and rituals on "sacred" days both reflect customs brought from Haiti to the United States and spiritually unite immigrants with their home community that is simultaneously engaged in the same religious activities. The mixture of Catholicism and voodoo learned in Haiti and continued in New York provides a unique sense of ethnic identity and connection between Haitians in the United States and those with whom they identify in Haiti. Many Haitian immigrants live transnational lives as they work to support households in Haiti, send their children to Haiti for schooling, return often to visit family there, and carry religious objects back and forth for ritual practice.

In their study of Christianity, social change, and globalization in the Americas, Peterson et al. (2001) include three chapters that concern religious transnationalism in varying degrees. Baia's chapter examines religious linkages between individuals in two brotherhoods, one located in Paterson, New Jersey, and the other in the home community of Peruvian immigrants. Gomez and Vasquez's chapter on youth gangs shows how they operate transnationally and the ways in which pentecostal churches that seek to convert gang members must follow their potential converts across national borders. Peterson and Vasquez's chapter on the Catholic Charismatic Renewal in El Salvador and Washington, D.C., is a broadly comparative study of the ways in which the charismatic movement evolved differently in the two countries, with few direct influences from one to the other.

With the exception of the few case studies mentioned in this section, transnational religious ties have been ignored in the literature on transnationalism. Comparative studies that provide the opportunity to study variation among transnational groups that originate in widely varied geographic locations, have different immigration histories, consist of varied levels of human and financial capital, and practice different religious traditions do not exist. This lacunae in the transnational migration literature is what prompted us, with the financial support of the Pew Charitable Trusts, to launch the RENIR II project in 1999.

Overview of the Study

As described in this volume's prologue, our Religion and Transnationalism project (which we call RENIR II) was an outgrowth of fieldwork we conducted in RENIR I (Ebaugh and Chafetz 2000) in which we interviewed members of thirteen immigrant congregations in Houston, Texas. In talking with immigrants about their daily lives and with congregational leaders about religious networks in their congregations, it was clear that religious beliefs and customs follow a circular path. Immigrants bring with them many religious practices from their home countries that they subsequently adapt to their lives in the United States. Likewise, as they communicate with family and friends left behind in their homelands, they influence religious structures and practices there. Not only does this reciprocal pattern change religious customs in the immigrants' countries of origin, but it prepares future migrants for what awaits them in religious institutions in the United States.

The cost involved in conducting field studies cross nationally prohibited the inclusion of all thirteen congregations from RENIR I in our transnational study. We knew that we had the resources to study five or six groups. Given the bias in the immigration literature toward studying Mexican, Central American, and Caribbean populations and given the fact that the only case study on religion and transnationalism at the time we began was Levitt's (1998) work on Boston–Dominican religious connections, we judged it important to include a diverse set of sites in order to compare the impact of geographic proximity, more diverse religious traditions, and ethnic variations. We resolved from the very conception of our study to include some of our original Asian congregations as well as some in Mexico and Central and South America.

Levitt's (1998) study tracing religious remittances between Miraflores, the Dominican Republic, and the United States focuses on one type of transnational community. In this type, members of a local immigrant community all share a specific place-based community of origin, usually rural, where residents tend to know one another personally and therefore, as migrants, their social lives continue to be entwined with kin and friends across national borders. From our work in Houston congregations, we realized that some groups form transnational networks that are not limited to specific home country places and whose remittance pathways are more diverse than those that characterize closely bound communities. In her later work that appeared after we began our study, Levitt (2001) expanded her notion of transnational community to include other types that are less personally bound by cross-border family and kinship ties. We had arrived at this conclusion empirically during the RENIR I project and determined not to limit our study in RENIR II to only one type of transnational religious community.

We selected five congregations that provided variation in geographic proximity of communities of origin, immigration history, faith, socioeconomic status of immigrant population, and the extent to which immigrants come from a tightly bounded geographic area. On the basis of these criteria, we selected the following congregations from RENIR I: the Argentine Brethren church (*Iglesia Cristiana Evangelica* in RENIR I); *Luz del Mundo*, an evangelical Mexican church (*Iglesia de Dios* in RENIR I); a Catholic immigrant church with roots in Monterrey, Mexico (St. Mary's Catholic Church in RENIR I); a Chinese Christian nondenominational church (Chinese Gospel Church in RENIR I); a Vietnamese Buddhist Temple (Center for Vietnamese Buddhism in RENIR I); and Vietnamese Catholics who compose a mission attached to a Catholic church (St. Catherine's in RENIR I).

In the course of the project, we added two additional research sites that were not part of RENIR I : three evangelical churches in Houston whose members are Maya who migrated from a specific area in the highlands of Guatemala and Chinese Protestant immigrants in two New York City congregations who came from the province of Fuzhou. In the first case, a colleague in the Sociology Department at the University of Houston, Jacqueline Hagan, had conducted an earlier study of the Mayan immigrant community in Houston that included their evangelical churches (Hagan 1994). She had previously visited their home community in Guatemala and still had valuable contacts there. Building on her previous research, she was able to reenter the community and focus on their transnational religious networks.

Well into the project, we learned about the research that Kenneth Guest was conducting of Fuzhou immigrants in Chinatown in New York City. His research included an examination of two Protestant churches they attend as well as churches in Fuzhou from which they migrated and with which they maintain close ties. Unlike the Chinese Protestants whom Yang studies (see chapter 7), who tend to be middle- to upper-middle-class professionals, the Fuzhou Chinese are, by and large, poor undocumented immigrants. The fact that they come from one locale in China and are more like Levitt's "transnational villagers" provides an interesting comparison with the Chinese Gospel Church in Houston. We therefore invited him to write a chapter for this volume (see chapter 8).

Taking a cue from Levitt's (1998) study of U.S.–Dominican religious ties, we were convinced of the importance of tracing, in addition to financial resources, those that she describes as social remittances (i.e., religious ideas, behaviors, identities, and social capital) in a systematic and grounded fashion by examining the various networks through which they circulate. Levitt (2001) argues that social remittances, unlike "world-level institutions and global culture," have a number of unique characteristics. First, they travel through identifiable pathways whose source and destination are clear. Second, they are transmitted systematically and intentionally such that immigrants can usually articulate what remittances are sent and in what ways. Third, remittances are usually transferred between individuals who know one another personally or who are connected to one another by mutual social ties. Fourth, there is a timing sequence to remittances such that macro-level global flows, such as exposure to U.S. society through the media, usually precede social remittances. We were convinced that the first three characteristics, in particular, called for carefully tracing resource flows between home and receiving communities while attending both to what is being sent and to the pathways through which it is sent. In addition, we resolved to investigate the impact these exchanges have, on both the individual and the organizational level, in the immigrants' home and host communities.

In January 2000, the research team met for two days of orientation. In particular, we discussed a network approach to the project and emphasized dimensions of networks that would guide the research and provide a unifying theme across the research sites. The goal was to send all the researchers (except Hagan, who joined the project the next year) to the home countries during the summer of 2000. However, Yang had to postpone his trip to China until the following summer because of political unrest in mainland China, and Ha was never able to conduct research in Vietnam. By means of e-mail, the four researchers who went abroad in the summer of 2000 sent us periodic field notes so that we kept abreast of their findings and could offer comments and advice as their field research proceeded. On the basis of their detailed field notes, each researcher prepared a paper to deliver at a special session at the Society for the Scientific Study of Religion (SSSR) meetings in Houston in October 2000.

During the summer of 2001, while Yang conducted research in several Asian sites and Hagan did so in the highlands of Guatemala, the others returned to the congregations in Houston to follow up on issues and themes that they had discovered in the immigrant home communities. Given the fact that transnational networks were not the primary focus in RENIR I, this summer research was essential for tracing specific transnational religious resources, the pathways through which they traveled, and the impact of these resources on the Houston congregations.

The Plan of This Volume

The seven chapters that follow describe transnational religious ties between members of Houston congregations (with the exception of chapter 8 on New York City Chinese immigrants) and individuals, groups, and congregations in their sending communities. Chapter 2 describes a tightly knit evangelical religious community whose members migrated in the early 1960s from the highly centralized mother church in Guadalajara, Mexico, and established the first of several churches in Houston. *Luz del Mundo* is an international religious organization with members scattered throughout the world. Its headquarters are located in *Hermosa Provincia*, a residential area on the outskirts of Guadalajara where many of the church members live within a ten-mile radius of the ornate temple. This neighborhood and church serve as both a governing center and the "heart" of the community. Each summer, about 300,000 followers of *Luz del Mundo* travel to the sacred place in *Hermosa Provincia* to attend *Santa Cena*, their most important religious ceremony. Dense personal ties exist within the local congregation and between members of the Houston church and their kin, friends, and fellow church members in Guadalajara. These ties exist on the level of clergy, lay leaders, and ordinary church members. Religious resources flow readily through these closely bound networks.

Chapter 3 is an analysis of religious networks that link *Iglesia Cristiana Evangelica*, an Argentine evangelical church in southwest Houston, with its home congregation in Mendoza, Argentina. The church in Houston was founded by Argentine immigrants from the Mendoza church in the late 1960s. Today, it links congregations and retreat centers in at least three locations in Argentina and one each in Spain and Honduras. Dense family and kinship networks between the Mendoza and Houston congregations in the early years of the migration stream provided the pathways whereby religious resources circulated across the two borders. Eventually, the Houston church sent lay missionaries to other areas in Argentina as well as to west Texas, Honduras, and Spain. These missionaries became important nodes in the transnational religious circuit that was established in the church. Over time, *Iglesia Cristiana Evangelica* emerged as the central influence within the network in terms of religious remittances to other countries.

Chapter 4 lays out the religious ties that have emerged among Protestant evangelical Maya, many of whom migrated from the highlands of Guatemala to settle in Houston, where they established three ethnic churches. The ties that exist between the home community and members of the Mayan churches in Houston are entirely interpersonal. Clergy and church members use couriers to exchange religious remittances through these personal networks, but no direct ties exist between specific churches in the Guatemalan highland community and the churches in Houston. Rather, there are dense individual ties within and across congregations in the two communities.

The Houston–Monterrey Catholic network that is described in chapter 5 also lacks institutional ties between specific churches in each country despite the international character of the Catholic Church. Rather, personal networks and local, parish-level activities of individuals in both Houston and Monterrey serve as conduits for sharing religious resources across borders. Sandoval found little contact between clergy in Houston and Monterrey; rather, dedicated laypersons serve as important bridges encouraging religious involvement in Houston and among migrants' family and friends in Monterrey.

Unlike the previous cases, Ha's study of Vietnamese Buddhists and Catholics in chapter 6 highlights the fact that almost all transnational ties involving both Buddhist temples and Catholic churches exist on the institutional level, either between religious institutions themselves or between individuals in one country (the United States) and institutions in the other (Vietnam). Immigrants, including ordinary members of temples and churches and clergy, often send monetary remittances to aid temples and churches in Vietnam. Likewise, Vietnamese Catholic churches in Houston routinely send remittances to churches in Vietnam to assist in building projects and the provision of social services to the needy. Vietnamese Buddhist temples in Houston are much less likely to send money to temples in Vietnam primarily because they are still in the process of building their own temples as well as paying off debts. An interesting feature of Ha's chapter is her discussion of the changes in the conduits for remittances sent by Vietnamese immigrants in Houston to individuals and institutions in Vietnam; these changes evolved in recent years as Vietnamese Americans realized the dire social conditions of the Vietnamese living under a Communist regime and sought charitable and social service groups in Vietnam who could distribute money and goods to the needy. They came to trust religious institutions as the safest way to deliver needed remittances to those who needed help. Temples and churches, therefore, became the major recipients of aid from American Vietnamese.

The Chinese Christian Church described in chapter 7 displays transnational religious networks that have characteristics very different from the previous cases. Rather than clearly delineated ties between immigrant members in the Houston church and family, friends, and co–church members in one or a few home congregations, transnational networks involve ties with clergy, institutions, and ordinary church members spread over many countries. These ties follow the pattern characteristic of many immigrant Chinese, especially well-educated professionals who disperse to a variety of nations rather than settle in one community in one receiving country. The Houston Chinese Church, in an attempt to evangelize, has sent missionaries to a number of Asian countries. Likewise, clergy in Taiwan, Singapore, and Hong Kong have attended the same seminaries as Houston clergy and served in many of the same churches. Strong transnational attachments and ties among these clergy result in preaching in one another's churches, cooperation in raising money for religious causes, and sharing religious reading materials and tapes. In addition, the Houston Chinese Church belongs to various international Chinese Christian organizations that create ties among clergy and lay leaders of member churches around the world.

As mentioned previously, we added chapter 8 on the Fuzhou–New York Protestant churches because of the contrast between the types of networks established by mostly poor and undocumented Chinese Protestants in New York's Chinatown and the middle-class, largely legal immigrants in Houston's Chinese Christian Church. In both cases, clergy are principal nodes in the religious networks. However, in the case of the Fuzhou immigrant churches, clergy are bridges between the churches in Fuzhou and those established in Chinatown. As Fuzhou immigrants enter the world of New York's Chinatown, they routinely seek out clergy in the local Fuzhou immigrant churches both to bring news and goods from Fuzhou to the churches in Chinatown and to seek help in getting established in the new country. Likewise, clergy in Fuzhou assist their members in preparing for migration and introducing them to fellow clergy in the immigrant Fuzhou churches in New York who might assist them when they arrive. In return, Fuzhou immigrants remit funds for the rebuilding of home community churches.

In chapter 9, we analyze the variety of transnational religious networks described in the seven case studies. In particular, we focus on four issues pertaining to these networks: (1) types of actors and ties, (2) kinds of remittances that flow between network members and their paths and directions, (3) variables that might explain why transnational religious networks differ in the ways they do, and (4) changes over time that religious networks experience. We conclude the chapter by emphasizing the importance of transnational religious networks and with the hope that religion will be included with the other social institutions (e.g., politics, economics, and family) in future studies of transnationalism.

References

Basch, Linda, Nina Glick Schiller, and Cristina Szanton Blanc, eds. 1994. *Nations Unbound: Transnational Projects, Postcolonial Predicaments, and Deterritorialized Nation-States.* Amsterdam: Gordon and Breach.

Beyer, Peter. 1994. *Religion and Globalization.* London: Sage.

Bodnar, John E. 1985. *The Transplanted: A History of Immigrants in Urban America.* Bloomington: Indiana University Press.

Casanova, Jose. 1994. *Public Religions in the Modern World.* Chicago: University of Chicago Press.

Chaney, Elsa. 1979. "The World Economy and Contemporary Migration." *International Migration Review* 13:204–12.

Cohen, Robin. 1997. *Global Diasporas: An Introduction.* Seattle: University of Washington Press.

Ebaugh, Helen Rose, and Janet S. Chafetz. 2000. *Religion among the New Immigrants: Continuities and Adaptations in Immigrant Congregations.* Walnut Creek, CA: AltaMira Press.

Foner, Nancy. 2000. *From Ellis Island to JFK: New York's Two Great Waves of Immigration.* New Haven, CT: Yale University Press.

Fraser, Nancy. 1991. "Rethinking the Public Sphere: A Contribution to the Critique of Actually Existing Democracy." In *Habermas and the Public Sphere,* edited by Graig Calhoun. Cambridge, MA: MIT Press.

Glick Schiller, Nina. 1999. "Transmigrants and Nation-States: Something Old and Something New in the U.S. Immigrant Experience." In *The Handbook of International Migration: The American Experience,* edited by Charles Hirschman, Philip Kasinitz, and Josh DeWind. New York: Russell Sage Foundation.

Goldring, Luin. 1998. "The Power of Status in Transnational Social Spaces." In *Transnationalism from Below: Comparative Urban and Community Research,* vol. 6, edited by Michael P. Smith and Luis Guarnizo. Rutgers, NJ: Transaction.

Guarnizo, Luis. 1994. "Los Dominicanyorks: The Making of a Binational Society." *Annals of the American Academy of Political and Social Science* 533:70–86.

Hagan, Jacqueline. 1994. *Deciding to Be Legal: A Maya Community in Houston.* Philadelphia: Temple University Press.

Handlin, Oscar. [1951] 1973. *The Uprooted: The Epic Story of the Great Migrations That Made the American People.* 2nd ed. Boston: Little, Brown.

Held, David, Anthony McGrew, David Goldblatt, and Jonathan Perraton. 1999. *Global Transformations.* Stanford, CA: Stanford University Press.

Herberg, Will. 1960. *Protestant-Catholic-Jew*. New York: Anchor.

Jones, Maldwyn Allen. 1992. *American Immigration*. 2nd ed. Chicago: University of Chicago Press.

Kearney, Michael. 1995. "The Local and the Global: The Anthropology of Globalization and Transnationalism." *Annual Review of Anthropology* 24:547–65.

Levitt, Peggy. 1997. "From Gujarat, India, to Lowell, Massachusetts: Localized Transnational Hinduism." Paper presented at the annual meeting of the Association for the Sociology of Religion, Toronto, August.

———. 1998. "Local-Level Global Religion: The Case of the U.S.-Dominican Migration." *Journal for the Scientific Study of Religion* 3:74–89.

———. 2001. *The Transnational Villagers*. Berkeley: University of California Press.

Mahler, Sarah. 1998. "Theoretical and Empirical Contributions toward a Research Agenda for Transnationalism." In *Transnationalism from Below: Comparative Urban and Community Research*, vol. 6, edited by Michael P. Smith and Luis Guarnizo. New Brunswick, NJ: Transaction.

Massey, Douglas S., Rafael Alarcon, Jorge Durand, and Humberto Gonzalez. 1987. *Return to Aztlan: The Social Process of International Migration from Western Mexico*. Berkeley: University of California Press.

McAlister, Elizabeth. 1998. "The Madonna of 115th Street Revisited: Vodou and Haitian Catholicism in the Age of Transnationalism." In *Gatherings in Diaspora: Religious Communities and the New Immigration*, edited by R. Stephen Warner and Judith G. Wittner. Philadelphia: Temple University Press.

Menjivar, Cecilia. 2000. *Fragmented Ties: Salvadoran Immigrant Networks in America*. Berkeley: University of California Press.

Morawska, Ewa. 1987. "Sociological Ambivalence: The Case of Eastern European Peasant-Immigrant Workers in America, 1880s–1930s." *Qualitative Sociology* 10, no. 3:225–50.

———. 2001. "The New-Old Transmigrants, Their Transnational Lives, and Ethnicization: A Comparison of 19th/20th- and 20th/21st-Century Situations." In *Immigrants, Civic Culture, and Modes of Political Incorporation*, edited by Gary Gerstle and John Mollenkopf. New York: Russell Sage Foundation.

Nagengast, Carol, and Michael Kearney. 1990. "Mixed Ethnicity: Social Identity, Political Consciousness, and Political Activism." *Latin American Research Review* 25:61–91.

Peterson, Anna L., Manuel A. Vasquez, and Philip J. Williams. 2001. *Christianity, Social Change, and Globalization in the Americas*. New Brunswick, NJ: Rutgers University Press.

Popkin, Eric. 1999. "Guatemalan Mayan Migration to Los Angeles: Constructing Transnational Linkages in the Context of the Settlement Process." *Racial and Ethnic Studies* 22, no. 2:267–89.

Portes, Alejandro, ed. 1996. *The New Second Generation*. New York: Russell Sage Foundation.

Portes, Alejandro, Luis Guarnizo, and Patricia Landolt. 1999. "Introduction: Pitfalls and Promise of an Emergent Research Field." *Ethnic and Racial Studies* 22, no. 2:217–38.

Portes, Alejandro, and Ruben Rumbaut. 2001. *Legacies: The Story of the Immigrant Second Generation*. New York: Russell Sage Foundation.

Robertson, Roland. 1992. *Globalization, Social Theory and Global Culture*. London: Sage.

Rouse, Roger. 1992. "Making Sense of Settlement: Class Transformation, Cultural Struggle and Transnationalism among Mexican Migrants in the United States." In *Towards a Transnational Perspective on Migration: Race, Class, Ethnicity, and Nationalism Reconsidered*, edited by Nina Glick Schiller, Linda Basch, and Cristina Szanton Blanc. New York: New York Academy of Sciences.

Rudolph, Susanne Hoeber, and James Piscatori, eds. 1997. *Transnational Religion and Fading States.* Boulder, CO: Westview Press.

Sassen, Saskia. 1991. *The Global City: New York, London, Tokyo.* Princeton, NJ: Princeton University Press.

Smith, Michael Peter, and Luis Guarnizo, eds. 1998. *Transnationalism from Below: Comparative Urban and Community Research*, vol. 6. New Brunswick, NJ: Transaction.

Smith, Robert. 1997. "Transnational Localities: Community, Technology, and the Politics of Membership within the Context of Mexico-U.S. Migration." In *Transnationalism from Below: Comparative Urban and Community Research*, vol. 6, edited by Michael Peter Smith and Luis Guarnizo. New Brunswick, NJ: Rutgers University Press.

Smith, Timothy L. 1978. "Religion and Ethnicity in America." *American Historical Review* 83:1155–85.

Vertovec, Steven. 1997. "Three Meanings of Diaspora Exemplified among South Asian Religions." *Diaspora* 6, no. 3:277–99.

———. 1999. "Conceiving and Researching Transnationalism." *Racial and Ethnic Studies* 22, no. 2:447–62.

Williams, Raymond Brady. 1988. *Religion of Immigrants from India and Pakistan: New Threads in the American Tapestry.* New York: Cambridge University Press.

Wyman, Mark. 1993. *Round Trip to America: The Immigrants Return to Europe, 1880–1930.* Ithaca, NY: Cornell University Press.

The *Santa Cena* of the *Luz Del Mundo* Church   2
A Case of Contemporary Transnationalism

PATRICIA FORTUNY-LORET DE MOLA

It was in July 2000, during the Sunday morning service at the Central congregation in Houston, Texas, that Pastor Oscar Gonzalez read a special letter written some years before by the apostle Samuel, the head of the *Luz del Mundo* (The Light of the World) church, inviting the religious community throughout the world to attend the *Santa Cena* (Holy Supper) in Guadalajara, Jalisco, Mexico, on August 14. Pastor Gonzalez said,

> The words of the Apostle do not have to be authorized by any Biblical Society, because His words come from God and do not need to be approved by "the world." We have to understand how important is this invitation. Why are we going to Guadalajara and more specifically to *Hermosa Provincia*? We are not going for fun, nor to see our families . . . we are going to build up our memory. We are going to remember the sacrifice of Jesus Christ. We all know that in Guadalajara there is "a man of God" who is praying for us. The *Santa Cena* allows us to get together and renews our covenant.[1]

That same evening, I attended the Sunday service at the Magnolia congregation in Houston where a layman was preaching. Again, his main concern was the imminent trip to Guadalajara. This preacher used a straightforward technique to transmit his message. With an emphatic tone, he said, "Everybody must go to the *Santa Cena*, even those members who are illegal. No matter the risk they take, it will be worthwhile. The only believers who should stay are those waiting for their papers, just these individuals will be exempted from going."

These vignettes demonstrate the central place that the religious ceremony of *Santa Cena* occupies in the process of transnationalism among Mexican members of the *Luz del Mundo* church. They also show the diverse approaches that religious congregations use to reinforce the need to attend the ritual, which in this case entails traveling to Mexico. On the one hand, Pastor Gonzalez, who has many years of experience as a minister, points out the relevance of the letter and at the same time legitimates its message and sender. The rhetoric used concerning the weakness and blindness of the Biblical Society and of "the world" functions to identify two adversaries of God, who is the only source of Samuel's words; an unquestionable agent, the spirit of God, legitimizes Samuel's power and authority. Consequently, travel to Guadalajara becomes a call from God Himself. Instructions, prohibitions, and norms by which to abide are also presented to the believers. While strengthening a transnational activity, at the same time the church establishes clear limits to those activities. The minister also explained the symbolic meaning of the ceremony and the spiritual benefits that members would gain by attending. Pastor Gonzalez has therefore given to the members many reasons to attend the ceremony in Guadalajara. On the other hand, the lay preacher strongly exhorts the members to travel to Guadalajara regardless of personal circumstances because they will be spiritually compensated. Those members who are doubtful about traveling because of their undocumented legal status will have to make a decision. If the church, however indirectly, backs an illegal activity, it must be worth the risk. Traveling to Guadalajara becomes imperative.

The type of transnationalism that is illustrated in these two vignettes reflects one side of the process, the institutional level, and it could be seen as what Smith and Guarnizo (1998) term transnationalism "from above." However, this chapter also presents data concerning the other type, transnationalism "from below" (Smith and Guarnizo 1998).

Introduction

Transnational migration has been characterized as a process that involves economic, political, social, and cultural activities that transcend the borders of one nation-state, a process that "includes actors that are not states, but are shaped by the policies and institutional practices of states" (Glick Schiller 1999:96). What makes transnational migration different from other social processes is that the migrants maintain and sustain close ties with their sending country. The empirical case of *Luz del Mundo*, described in this chapter, shows that religion plays a fundamental if often ignored role in transnational activities that maintain, nourish, and intensify social, cultural, and economic ties between migrants and their sending country. Transnational activities are directly related to annual pilgrimages, and these religious activities are neither random nor accidental but constitute part of a cyclical movement of migrants who are involved in constant border crossings between the United States and Mexico.

Although the central festivity analyzed here takes place in August, there is a large annual cycle of rituals: the birthday of the apostle Samuel (February 14); the foundation of the church (April 6); the death of the founder (June 9); Mexican Independence Day and the birthday of Samuel's wife, Sister Elisa (September 15); and New Year's Eve. Each one of these dates implies its own sequence of civic and religious events, most of which take place in *Hermosa Provincia*, headquarters of the church in Guadalajara.

The number of people who participate in the annual August pilgrimage to Guadalajara represents 94 percent (forty-seven) of the fifty members I interviewed in 1999 and 2000 in three sites: Houston, Guadalajara, and Monterrey. Two of those who did not attend said that they could not afford travel expenses, while the remaining person was awaiting her green card. Forty percent of my sample who do travel cross the U.S./Mexican border more than three times a year, 29 percent go to Guadalajara twice a year, and 25 percent do so at least once a year, in August. Among the thirty-six members interviewed solely in Houston, 81 percent meet their relatives in Guadalajara every year, and 42 percent have several relatives, such as grandparents, parents, siblings, aunts and uncles, or cousins, living in *Hermosa Provincia*. Among those with several relatives, six out of seven travel to their sending country more than twice a year. Thirty-nine percent of the members interviewed in Houston no longer have relatives residing in Guadalajara because they have all emigrated, mostly to the United States. However, they always see their relatives during the religious festivities, which facilitate family reunions precisely because everyone gathers in the same place at the same time. Among the migrants who do not have relatives in Guadalajara, I found at least two families who have a house in *Hermosa Provincia*, although it is uninhabited most of the year. Even among those with no remaining relatives, five out of seven travel to *Hermosa Provincia* two or more times annually. Through informal interviews, however, I found that some migrants with a low level of resources are unable to travel to Guadalajara until three or four years after they arrive in the United States.

The data presented and analyzed in this chapter are based on a multisite ethnography carried out with church members in three different cities and two countries: Houston, Texas, in the United States, and Guadalajara, Jalisco, and Monterrey, Nuevo Leon, in Mexico. Between 1999 and 2000, I spent three and a half months in Houston, where I conducted thirty-six in-depth personal interviews; I spent ten days in Monterrey in November 2000 and conducted seventeen personal or family interviews. In *Hermosa Provincia*, I interviewed local and international authorities of the church and relatives of some of the Houston migrants. Besides the long tape-recorded interviews, I talked informally with members in each of the three locales. In November 1999, I administered a questionnaire to a small group of young people in *Hermosa Provincia* regarding their views of the

United States, and in October 2000, together with a member of the church (Lic. Sara Pozos), I designed and administered a long questionnaire to a larger group of youngsters asking about their experiences and views concerning migration and other issues. I attended more than sixty religious events in the three cities. From August 8 to 14, 1999, I remained continuously in *Hermosa Provincia*, just like the pilgrims do, and was able to apply the ethnographic method.

There are 1,200 members of the *Luz del Mundo* church scattered throughout the city of Houston: 600 belong to the oldest group, known as the Central congregation; 300 have joined the Magnolia congregation; and the remaining 300 churchgoers attend small missions in diverse parts of the city. The study described in this chapter is based on the membership of the two congregations, all of whom are of Hispanic origin; 45 percent were born in the United States, another 45 percent were born in Mexico (mostly in the western states of Jalisco and Michoacán), and the rest come from Central American countries, mainly El Salvador. The men work in the construction industry and forestry and as electricians, technicians, and employees in big firms such as Southwestern Bell; a few own small businesses, such as a satellite dish company and an interior decoration business. Women are employed as receptionists, nurses, salespersons, baby-sitters, cleaners, and the like. Adults speak mostly Spanish, and this is the dominant language used during religious activities. The second generation is achieving a better education, as well as better jobs than their parents, and are able to speak both languages fluently.

I have chosen to use the term *transnational community* rather than other terms[2] because religion is the central feature that defines the group and keeps it together. It operates as a "moral community" (in Durkheimian terms), firmly built on a system of shared meanings, norms, practices, loyalty, and, above all, a strong collective identity. In addition, in Mexico, the *Luz del Mundo* has a subordinate position vis-à-vis the still dominant Catholic Church, which claims to be the sole owner of the national identity. To confront the Catholic Church, *Luz del Mundo* has built a strong Mexican identity, which is embedded in its origin myth (Fortuny-Loret De Mola 1995; de la Torre 1995). In order to effectively differentiate itself from Catholicism, the *Luz del Mundo* has to re-create on a daily basis discourses and practices of group identity that separate it from others.

Glick Schiller (1999:97) rejects the term *community* employed by Kearney (1986, 1991, 1995), among others, because community "left unmarked the exploitative class relations, and division of wealth and status that stratify a population." I disagree with Glick Schiller because it is precisely the subordinate political, economic, and social position that migrants experience in the receiving country that drives them to create and reinvent an "imagined community" (as in Anderson 1993) modeled after their homeland. When a group of people exists outside its place of origin, it becomes even more essential to construct bonds with their place of origin. The term *community*, as employed here, does not deny social, political, and economic differences between its members or the relations of power existing between the church elite and ordinary members. Applying the notion of community to a religious group is indeed more adequate since it implies a strong collective moral consciousness that acts as the main integrating force encompassing members on both sides of the border and transcends unequal political, economic, and social conditions. In addition, in the case of the *Luz del Mundo*, the majority of members share not only the same faith but also a regional culture, that of the central-western region where Jalisco is located, and a regional culture entails constructing frameworks and communications within and between the different identity groups (Lomnitz-Adler 1992:72).

To illustrate the production and reproduction of a transnational community, I use a specific ceremony, the *Santa Cena*. *Luz del Mundo* members regularly travel from Houston, as well as from cities and countries around the world, to Guadalajara, Jalisco, primarily to attend religious festivities. However, they do so not only because of religious reasons; economic, cultural, and social factors also contribute to strengthening and intensifying contacts and to frequent border crossings. Although it is central in their lives, religion serves to enhance preexisting social networks among the migrant population from the western region of Mexico. Most transnational studies have missed large-scale religious movements, such as the *Luz del Mundo* church, which are responsible for high-intensity cultural exchanges and a diverse number of activities requiring cross-border travel on a sustained basis (Portes et al. 1999). The social bonds that members establish between Houston and Guadalajara are constantly reproduced and diversified by their social networks (family and church). This case serves to illustrate that "the activities of interest are not exceptional, but possess certain stability and resilience over time" and that the process encompasses "individuals, their networks of social relations, their communities, and broader institutionalized structures" (Portes et al. 1999:219, 220). At the institutional level, the *Luz del Mundo* should be considered a *transnational church*, a term that "refers to any religious system whose organization transcends frontiers and weaves over and above national, political and cultural specificities a network of *ideologically unified communities* linked to a single seat of government" (Hervieu-Léger 1997:104; emphasis added). The highest authority of the religious community is embedded in the dual nature of Samuel, who holds simultaneously two types of titles: a sacred title as "Apostle" and a secular one as "International President of the *Luz del Mundo* Church." Through a select group of administrative and religious men, Samuel makes decisions, appoints ministers, gives instructions, organizes major events, negotiates with governments when necessary, defines religious doctrine and practice, and generates necessary changes. Samuel's "seat of government" has its specific locale in *Hermosa Provincia*.

Although there exist sharp inequalities between Mexico and the United States concerning political, military, economic, and social power, this empirical case challenges the general assumption that cultural flows move mostly from advanced and powerful nations to smaller and weaker ones (Levitt 1998). Power is concentrated in Guadalajara and not in Houston, and it is personified by higher church authorities located in the sending country. Although there are cultural, economic, and social factors that originate in the receiving country and exert some influence over the sending country, power and control originate in Mexico, from where they are transmitted and extended to the United States. The *Luz del Mundo* case demonstrates that most of the "social remittances," defined by Levitt (1998) as the ideas, identities, images, norms, and even some kinds of social capital, flow from sending- to receiving-nation communities. This is substantially explained by the authoritarian nature of the church, which pursues the faithful reproduction of doctrine and practice wherever individual congregations are located.

This chapter has six sections in addition to this introduction. In the first, I provide a context in which to place the specific group of migrants with whom I am dealing by describing some of the most important features concerning Mexican migration to the United States. In the second section, I focus mainly on the history of the church and its doctrine, norms, and practices; I also explain the remarkable success of *Luz del Mundo* through U.S. immigration as well as other factors. In the third section, I describe the institutional church structures that provide the broader framework for crossing international borders; I also show some of the effects of the electronic media used by the church and analyze the type of transnationalism (from above and below) that result from institutional activities and policies. In the fourth section, I focus on the transnational mobility of the religious community and demonstrate the ways by which members accumulate and use social capital through their family and church networks. This is illustrated through a discussion of the everyday activities in sending and receiving countries of one transmigrant family. In the fifth section, I analyze from a Durkheimian perspective the religious ceremony that takes place in *Hermosa Provincia*. The ceremony is important not only in sacred terms but also because it relates to the profane field of migration and transnationalism related to the *Santa Cena*. Finally, I complement the analysis of transnationalism by explaining this case as a diaspora migration. The religious community studied in Houston is characterized by a sense of living in one place while simultaneously remembering, desiring, and yearning for another. Immigrant church members share a history of dispersal, myths, and memories of their homeland. They feel and think of *Hermosa Provincia* as their "Promised Land," a destination to which they all want to return temporarily or, if possible, permanently.

Mexico/U.S. Migration: A Unique Case

The history of Mexicans in the United States is a long one. First, there were those who, without leaving their country, became residents of the United States when Texas, California, New Mexico, and Arizona were annexed between 1846 and 1848. Later, during the Mexican Revolution (1910–23), thousands of nationals left the country and went to "The North." With the *bracero* program (1942–64), a pattern of labor migration was established between the two countries, and about five million Mexican agricultural workers were temporally mobilized for work in the United States (Durand, Massey, and Zenteno 2001). In the past three decades, migration to the United States has not stopped despite border restrictions; in fact, it has increased, and many new types of migration have emerged. For example, groups of computer and electronics engineers go to Silicon Valley in California to work in big U.S. computer firms (Alarcón 1999). Throughout their long history in the United States, Mexican migrants have contributed considerably to the economy, including the construction of the U.S. railroad system, the development of agriculture and manufacturing, and recently the growth of the urban service economy (Roberts, Frank, and Lozano-Ascencio 1999:238). One of the leading scholars on the subject, Douglas S. Massey, states that the specific case of Mexico/U.S. migration is the "largest sustained flow of immigrants anywhere in the world." He also asserts that many theoretical ideas about migration have been based on empirical studies of Mexican migration (Massey 1999:47). Despite the fact that there are hundreds of political borders in the world, it is the Mexican-U.S. political boundary that has become the model for research on other borders (Alvarez 1995:449).

In recent years, according to Roberts et al. (1999), the number of documented and undocumented Mexicans in the United States "has dwarfed immigration from any other country." Mexicans make up 14 percent of all legal immigrants and as much as 40 percent of undocumented immigrants (quoted in Roberts et al. 1999; see also Gelbard and Carter 1997). The U.S. Bureau of the Census estimates the foreign-born Mexican population in 1997 to be more than seven million, or 27 percent of the total foreign-born population (U.S. Bureau of the Census 1997). One of the many explanations of Mexican migration to the United States is the sharply different levels of economic development in the two nations.[3] The increasing number of immigrants has resulted in greater diversity among them. In the 1980s, migrants were mainly low skilled and came from rural backgrounds and areas of Mexico. Since the 1990s, a growing number of highly skilled, white-collar workers of urban origin have started to migrate as well. The 2,000-mile Mexican/U.S. border seems to be one of the busiest in the world and will probably remain so for the foreseeable future.

One feature that distinguishes Mexican migration from that of other nationalities is the fact that the process of transnationalism among Mexican immigrants
has always existed. The pioneer studies done at the beginning of the twentieth century by Paul Taylor (1970, reprinted from 1928) and Manuel Gamio (1930)
found transnational ties a long time ago, and they continue to be documented by
contemporary studies (Durand 1996; Kearney 1986, 1991, 1995; Roberts et al.
1999; Rouse 1991).

Mexican migration to the United States not only constitutes the largest migrant
stream but also has shown continuity from the nineteenth century to the present.
It has been dominated in terms of sending region by the western states of Mexico,
namely, Guanajuato, Jalisco, and Michoacán (Durand et al. 2001), since as early as
1900, when the railroad in Mexico was connected to rail systems north of the border. Because the northern states of Mexico were relatively unpopulated in those
times, Mexican workers were recruited from the more densely populated states of
Jalisco, Guanajuato, and Michoacán.[4] After World War I, U.S. businessmen could
not rely on migrant labor from southern and eastern Europe because of restrictive
immigration laws, so they turned to Mexican labor, which continued to come
"from just three states: Guanajuato (10 percent), Jalisco (14 percent), and Michoacán (9 percent), which together accounted for roughly a third of all movement
during the period" (Durand et al 2001:109). During the *bracero* program, from
1942 to 1964, the three most important sending states were again those of the
western region, a trend unaltered from 1960 to 1980 (Durand et al. 2001).

Based on these data, it should come as no surprise that many members of the
church interviewed in Guadalajara have continued to take the same route north
that has historically characterized this region. In the following section, I describe
how the very first adherents to this church were recruited from among Mexican
migrants who were returning from the United States during the Great Depression.
Today, among the inhabitants of *Hermosa Provincia* (most of them church members), 75 percent say that they have one or more relatives in the United States, in
response to a questionnaire administered during the autumn of 2000.[5] This finding underlines the close relationship between *Hermosa Provincia* and U.S. congregations and demonstrates that we are indeed dealing with a religious transnational
community in motion.

Rodriguez (2000) describes two major waves of Mexican migration to the city
of Houston. The second wave began in the mid-1970s, when a worldwide oil
shortage resulted in exceptional economic growth for the city that calls itself "the
oil capital of the world." "The growth of the major international and national oil
companies located in Houston, the development of nearly 500 other oil and gas
companies and hundreds of support firms, created a huge labor demand in the
Houston economy which, by 1979, involved 1.5 million workers" (Rodriguez

2000:32). It was at this time that the initial *Luz del Mundo* mission in Houston was founded. In the 1990s, Mexicans represented nearly 70 percent of all Hispanic immigrants in Houston and accounted for almost half of all immigrants in the city (Rodriguez 2000). Mexican men and women were employed in the formal and informal labor markets. Men found jobs producing steel products for the oil companies, in the construction industry, as well as in the service sector. Mexican women were employed as cleaners and cooks and also in manufacturing companies (Rodriguez 2000:33). The end of the economic boom in Houston by the mid-1980s brought widespread unemployment; many Mexican migrants had to enter the informal sector of the economy, taking very low paying jobs and lacking protection from their employers or from the state (Rodriguez 2000:34). The stories that I have heard from my informants reflect the economic context depicted by Rodriguez, and their jobs mirror those that Rodriguez identifies as most common among Mexican immigrants to Houston.

La Luz Del Mundo Church

In Mexico, *Luz del Mundo* is the second-largest religious body after the Roman Catholic Church, with approximately one and a half million adherents. It is also the largest (non-Catholic) minority church in Guadalajara with approximately 50,000 churchgoers living in twenty neighborhoods. At the very center of the *Hermosa Provincia* (Beautiful Province) neighborhood in Guadalajara lies the greatest temple of all, not only in size but also in symbolic meaning for the group. Beyond constituting the central symbol of the religion, the temple is the international headquarters and a local congregation, with a membership of approximately 15,000 congregants.

The church was founded in the late 1920s by Aarón Joaquin Gonzalez, a man of peasant origin who was a native of the western region of Mexico. After the Mexican Revolution (1910–20) and during the years of the Great Depression in the United States, many poor Mexican migrants left the United States and returned to Mexico. Aarón recruited his first followers from among such poor displaced people and established his church in Guadalajara, Jalisco, a state characterized by its powerful Catholicism.[6] The rise of the *Luz del Mundo* movement also coincided with a revival of Pentecostalism in the United States (1920s–30s), which in turn was exported to Mexico via returning migrants. Like most Pentecostal leaders, Aarón did not enjoy any previous sacred legitimation; he propagated a Bible-based Protestant religion in a context dominated by an all-embracing, intransigent, anti-Protestant Catholicism that did not favor the use of the Bible. He represented a counterideology attractive to people who possessed little and were dissatisfied with their social condition. One of the main achievements of Aarón's new faith was to break the Catholic clergy's monopoly over the production and distribution of sacred goods.[7]

During the 1950s, Aarón established a special type of settlement for members by creating the first *Hermosa Provincia* in Guadalajara. *Hermosa Provincia* is a "total institution" (Fortuny-Loret De Mola 1995; Goffman 1988) that entails living and, if possible, working and studying in the same place where the church (or temple) is located. Members tend to live within the same neighborhood, attend the same temple, go to school together, shop in local establishments often run by members, recreate together, and in general create their own world within the religious community. This model has been reproduced in several Mexican cities, including Tepic, Nayarit, Tapachula, and Chiapas, and in cities in other countries (e.g., Costa Rica, Colombia, El Salvador, and Spain). In all these places, the neighborhoods have been called *Hermosa Provincia*, following the same original model and, therefore, transcending the nation-states in which they reproduce their transnational religious communities. In the United States, they have not been able to achieve the ideal *Hermosa Provincia* because of high land prices. Nevertheless, the general tendency is to live close to one another and to the church. Many members of the Central congregation in Houston live on the same street where the present temple is located. In fact, there is only one house in the vicinity inhabited by a gentile (nonmember). The new facilities of this congregation will be located about three miles from the present church, and several members are buying or planning to buy property close to the future temple.

Aarón died in 1964, and his son, Samuel Joaquin Flores, succeeded him as head of the church. Samuel undertook a new stage in the church's development. The expansion and educational advancement of the membership continued, hierarchies were redefined, relations of cooperation and negotiation with the Mexican government were formalized, and a majestic temple was erected (between 1983 and 1991) in Guadalajara to serve as international headquarters. Under Samuel's leadership, the *Luz del Mundo* became a more solidly transnational church. However, at present, membership is concentrated in Mexico, the United States, El Salvador, and Colombia.

The church's myth of origin and development centers on these two charismatic male leaders: Aarón and Samuel. The doctrine is a combination of Pentecostal norms and theology and regional Catholic culture. Members of *Luz del Mundo* consider their church to be the restoration of the primitive Christian church; thus, they see themselves as the "chosen people." God elected the apostles Aarón and Samuel to keep his church alive in the modern world. Church members are Christians who follow the Bible and believe that Jesus Christ is the savior of humanity. Nevertheless, salvation will be achieved only by following the two apostles, Aarón and Samuel. In this church, women do not have access to the priesthood, which includes bishops, pastors, deacons, and *encargados*, all of whom are anointed in a special ceremony at which the apostle Samuel must be present.

Women can only be *encargadas*,[8] which literally means "in charge," and *obreras*, which means "workers" but in this case is equivalent to evangelizers or missionaries, who are at the bottom of the hierarchy. They are also granted broad roles in the administration, coordination, and organization of their communities. Concerning norms, women wear long full skirts or dresses, long hair, and veils on their heads during religious services and are banned from wearing jewelry and makeup. In contrast, male members are not expected to change their appearance from that of other males in the community. During religious services, women sit on the left side of the temple and men on the right. Since its very beginnings, the church has instituted an exclusively female prayer service directed by women.

In Mexico, *Luz del Mundo* operates as a minority church, not only because of its small number of adherents relative to Catholicism but more important in terms of its subordinate position vis-á-vis the dominant religion of the larger society (Catholicism). The church's lower social status is expressed through hostile stereotypes, prejudice, and intolerant attitudes by nonmembers. The testimony of a migrant female who has lived in Houston since 1997 illustrates the socioreligious discrimination that believers can experience in Guadalajara: "In the United States, there is respect for difference [referring to Muslim women's clothes]. Here, the aggression is not against the long skirt that we wear; the aggression is against our doctrine. That kind of thing does not exist in the U.S.; there is more freedom there."

In order to understand the low social status of *Luz del Mundo*, the general religious context of Mexico should be examined. According to the last national census, 89 percent of Mexicans consider themselves Catholic. However, Catholics are not distributed evenly across the country. In the southern states (e.g., Chiapas, Campeche, Tabasco, and Quintana Roo), about 30 percent of the population claim to belong to a Christian religion other than Catholic, and some northern states (e.g., Baja California) follow a similar pattern. At the same time, the western and central states of the country, including Jalisco, have the lowest percentages of non-Catholics (less than 2 percent). Thus, although it has attained a degree of religious diversity, Mexico has not yet achieved widespread pluralism and religious tolerance. In theory, there is freedom of religion, as in the United States, but in fact the Catholic Church and its clergy still exert significant, indirect, and direct hegemonic power. Therefore, most of the "other" Christian and non-Christian religions, like *Luz del Mundo*, occupy a marginal position, and their followers can be thought of as second-class citizens. This situation affects the way minority churches and their members tend to behave. They employ a more rigid system of norms, and members have to continuously demonstrate a high level of moral and ethical behavior. They publicly proclaim that they have improved their level of education, attained better health facilities for their community, and developed other social services in order to legitimate themselves in the eyes of the Mexican state and the larger (mostly Catholic) society.

Expansion through Networks

During the formation of the church (1926–44), propagation of doctrine was undertaken through personal testimonies. Aarón himself visited prisons and hospitals and did public preaching, which he carried out in open spaces, such as markets, parks, and even the atria of Catholic churches. He also initiated missionary work beyond Mexico's borders. Around the mid-1950s, he went to Los Angeles and in the early 1960s traveled to San Antonio, Texas, to evangelize. It is interesting that the founder went first to "The North" (the United States) rather than to Central America to preach the gospel. Geographic proximity between Jalisco and Texas can only partly explain this choice. More important, as discussed earlier, migration of Mexicans from the western states to the United States had been a traditional pattern since the last part of the nineteenth century. Only years after first traveling to the United States did Aarón go to Central American countries. In the 1990s, proselytism became more organized, and missionary groups are now composed of *obreros* who go out to preach in pairs or groups of three. In Mexico, several members in each congregation are missionaries and have chosen one day a week to devote to this task. Missionaries do not receive any stipends. If a family moves to another country, its members automatically become missionaries for the church there, which is how the Houston connection arose.

The first congregation (Central) in Houston began to take shape in the early 1960s. The first members came from San Antonio, where Aarón had personally traveled years earlier. Between 1965 and 1967, the Fernandez brothers and their families moved from San Antonio to Houston and began the mission. While Pastor Gonzalez was telling me this story, he produced some old photographs of the first members in Houston. In one, dated 1969, the apostle Samuel appeared (very young then), surrounded by twenty believers, including a group of members from Guadalajara who were visiting the Houston mission. At first, the temple was only a small house where members gathered for prayer. It was replaced years later by the present temple. At present, the church has bought land and is building new facilities, which will have a basement, a projection hall, offices, classrooms for children, a library, the pastor's house, and a temple that can accommodate at least 4,500. Although the style is very different from the temple in *Hermosa Provincia*, the diverse spaces and their use coincide very much with that of the mother church. Members are planning to finish it in the next four years. Pastor Gonzalez said, "This project will make Houston the city with the biggest temple in the United States. Now, the biggest is in Los Angeles." For resources to build the new facilities, the church relies on voluntary work from members; those who cannot do construction work make offers. Youngsters collect money doing weekend car washes, and female members sell food and roses. Throughout the world, each independent congregation is responsible for raising funds to construct its own temple.

The Magnolia congregation, located in the oldest Mexican *barrio* in Houston, was founded in the late 1970s, when some members from the Central congregation moved to Magnolia. It has 300 active members and is also responsible for four other area missions: in Victoria (ten members), Rosenberg (fourteen members), Texas City (nine members), and the Woodlands (twenty-eight members). In 1998, the membership bought an old cinema and transformed it into an elegant and functional temple that they finished remodeling in the summer of 2000. Magnolia, like all congregations, operates as an independent church, with its own minister and its own missions.

The fact that both of Houston's congregations (as well as the one in Monterrey) have built or are building new temples reflects the rapid growth of the church. Pastor Oscar Gonzalez explained the expansion of the church: "The main growth in membership happened at the same time as the amnesties given by the United States government (such as IRCA in 1986). It was during those years when a lot of people emigrated from Mexico to the U.S. However, there are also some isolated believers who come independently by crossing the Rio Bravo." The church does not openly or officially support illegal migration. When leaving Mexico, members ask for a reference letter from their congregation so that they can be acknowledged as members at their destination church. However, this official permit will not be given if the members do not have proper visas to enter the United States.

According to official church sources, during the past five years the annual growth in membership in Houston has been 18 percent. Despite the increasing number of members, in neither Houston congregation is there any formal evangelizing because the lifestyle of immigrant workers does not allow them time to do so. Therefore, membership growth is due mainly to migration. Brother Carlos Montemayor (head of the public relations office in the United States and presently minister of a congregation in Phoenix, Arizona), an experienced minister who has been in charge of congregations in more than eight different cities in America, explained church growth:

> Look, I have so much work to do with the church and the members that already exist that I do not have any more time to look for new ones. When I was in Chicago, I was responsible for at least five congregations in various different nearby cities. I was also visiting a mission in the state of Michigan. Therefore, I could not afford to leave my people. The members themselves, those who are

obreros, they go and visit new converts. These *obreros*, however, have their own secular jobs, and a busy life; they do missionary work only once a week. When the *obreros* have a group of people who want to listen to the doctrine, they then ask me and I will visit them. But, I never go visiting people that I do not know. Many times, people who need advice (concerning their legal status, about their marriage or something else) visit me, and they come back to the church and ask for their baptisms afterwards. Every month we have baptisms there. Just before I left Chicago in July, we had eleven adults baptized, and then seven more and it is like that each month.

Although the majority of Houston members were already part of the church before they migrated, some were converted in Houston; even they, however, are usually immigrants. During my fieldwork, I met only one recent convert, a young man from Mexico city who learned about the faith from a co-worker who was a member of the Magnolia church. Natural increase is another important source of church growth because members tend to marry quite young (women at the age of fifteen and men at the age of eighteen), and they tend to have more than two children.

Apart from migration and births, the dramatic growth of the church in the United States can be explained partly by the manner in which congregations are developed, as occurred in Houston. A congregation begins with a small number of members or families (five or ten) who represent the first stage, called *obrita* (small work), or a mission, located wherever a few members happen to be living. At this stage, they usually gather to pray at one member's home. In the second stage, members ask a minister or sometimes a layman from a nearby congregation to celebrate services in their own place. Occasionally, the original small group goes out to do missionary work, visiting people related to church members in Mexico. The group increases through new migrants and perhaps new converts, and once it has reached about 100 to 150 members, it can request its own minister, who must have achieved at least the rank of *encargado*.

The trajectories of most ministers are similar. To illustrate the formation and training of church spiritual leaders, I draw on an example from Houston. Jose Licea was the *encargado* (man in charge) of the Magnolia congregation in Houston from 1997 to February 2000, when he was killed in a car accident in Tlaquepaque, Jalisco. Jose was born a Catholic in Cananea, Sonora, Mexico, in 1969. When he was fourteen years old, at the request of his father he went to live in Tucson, Arizona, to attend high school, where he earned a license as an electrician. Soon after his arrival, he became a Baptist through an aunt who was a member of that church. Three years later, a cousin from Cananea introduced him to the *Luz del Mundo* mission in Tucson. Following Jose's conversion, his parents and four brothers became part of the church. Later, he got married and became an *encargado* of a congregation in Long Beach, California, where he and his wife lived from 1994 to 1997. The Long Beach congregation increased from 79 to 181 members during Jose's ministry. He was then assigned as *encargado* of the Magnolia congregation in Houston, where he arrived in 1997. Jose had the ideal profile of a minister in the United States. He was a legal citizen, spoke English, and had lived long enough in the United States to understand the culture and legal system. His role as *encargado* of a congregation went beyond religious duties and affairs related to the institution. Members could rely on him when they had problems concerning their integration into the host country.

As in many other Pentecostal churches, there exist two apparently contradictory principles: (1) the discretionary power coming from the head of the church who assigns religious positions and anoints new ministers and (2) a high degree of flexibility that allows more natural development at the local level. The reproduction of congregations creates a network in which various congregations generate missions that become new congregations and so on. This pattern can be seen in the Central congregation of Houston, which has been a central actor in the formation of other congregations, not only in metropolitan Houston (such as the Magnolia, Pasadena, and Bellaire congregations) but also in places such as Dallas, Rosenberg, Port Arthur, and Nacadoches, Texas; Atlanta; New Orleans; and Orlando, Miami, and Bradenton, Florida. Missionaries from the Houston Central congregation have spread the doctrine in all these cities. In addition, a Palestinian female member of the Houston church went to Nazareth, Israel, and founded the first congregation in that country.

Institutional Framework

What are the institutional strategies that encourage border crossing? What does the church provide to Mexican migrants from *Hermosa Provincia* besides spiritual satisfaction? What is the role of the electronic media in this case of transnationalism? Can the institutional aspect of the social process be classified as transnationalism "from above"? In this section, I focus on the answers to these questions.

Every August, about 300,000 followers of *Luz del Mundo* church travel from multiple locations in the United States and Central and South America to their most sacred place in Guadalajara in order to attend their most important religious ceremony. The *Santa Cena* celebrations (which began in the 1940s) involve a series of rituals performed from August 8 to 14. In fact, this date begins the religious calendar of the church. The ritual cycle takes place in the *colonia* (neighborhood) *Hermosa Provincia* and simultaneously in other urban *colonias* of Guadalajara, such as *Bethel* and the *Aarón Joaquín*. While staying in Houston during the summer of 2000, I was able to witness firsthand the special atmosphere of expectation and anxiety related to the pilgrimage in August. As demonstrated in the vignette at the beginning of the chapter, special preaching was orchestrated in order to underscore the symbolic reasons for attending the annual ceremony. Ministers discuss religious meanings of the *Santa Cena,* laypeople refer to previous *Santas Cenas* and the blessings that they have provided to the faithful, and preachers in general exhort everyone to cross the border.

Throughout July, members attend religious services more frequently than usual as they seek to be spiritually cleansed for the *Santa Cena.* Special prayers take place every evening. It is a time of meditation, conciliation, and forgiveness. The occasion entails not only acquiring the necessary documents but also the practice of an intense set of religious activities to prepare members to receive the sacred meal, exemplifying Durkheim's (1976:341) insight: "Man sanctifies himself because the food he consumes in the ritual has sacredness." They prepare as well for the physical encounter with their "Man of God," Samuel, whose charisma extends to *Hermosa Provincia,* which is called with solemnity *ese lugar* (the place). Special hymns are dedicated to the saintly atmosphere that pervades the international headquarters of the church, commonly known by members as *La Provincia.* Sermons and testimonies enhance the sacred nature of their *Ciudad Santa,* which is evoked many times by those who have been to *ese lugar* in the past. This message is repeated over and over, intensifying the desire to be there.

Earlier, I mentioned the multiple reasons, embedded within the belief system, that move members to travel in August. Some of the strategies used by the church can be perceived as a type of direct or indirect coercion, although no matter how authoritarian an institution may be, individuals can always exert their agency. Moreover, as the voyage is one of cultural consumption, "where there is consumption there is pleasure, and where there is pleasure there is agency" (Appadurai 1996:7). However, there will always be members throughout the world who cannot afford such a trip, which is why Samuel continuously travels to other countries, such as El Salvador and Colombia, and to different cities in the United States in order to perform the *Santa Cena* for those members who missed it in the *Hermosa Provincia.* He thus re-creates ritual across space.

Apart from producing a sacred atmosphere and religious meanings, the church also provides shelter and food for those of its poorest members who spend a week in Guadalajara for the August celebration. Probably 90 percent of the membership come from a low social class (indigenous people, peasants, and members of the working class), and most of them cannot afford their expenses in Guadalajara. They all travel with extended family members in large groups that include neighbors from the same congregation and others from the same town or city. There is an official church committee that organizes accommodations for visitors. A few weeks before the event, those in charge visit the local members of *Hermosa Provincia* and of *Bethel*[9] and decide how many pilgrims can be allocated to each house. The majority of the affluent church members have built or renovated their homes with the August festivities in mind. During our stay in *Hermosa Provincia* in August 1999, Celia[10] and I noticed that the five houses that we visited had a peculiar pattern of construction. We were told that they had been built specifically to accommodate many people during the church festivities. They were two-story houses with kitchens and bathrooms on the upper as well as the lower floor. During the religious fiestas, the family who owns the house moves to the second floor, leaving the other section of the house for visitors. The church has also constructed facilities that can be used as shelters and has repaired old buildings for the same purpose. In *Hermosa Provincia* and in *Bethel*, most poor pilgrims are given rooms, schools, stadiums, and other public facilities where they can cook, wash their clothes, and sleep during the entire week.

Through official church networks, visiting U.S. immigrants organize public meals for the poorest pilgrims during the religious feast. I have reliable information that the Houston and Dallas congregations, as well as many others from Texas, California, and other southern states, provide three free meals every day to approximately 3,000 of the poorest members. Members from U.S. congregations are responsible not only for collecting the necessary money and buying the food but also for preparing and serving the meals.[11] Poor visitors also receive free meals from church foundations, such as *La Fundacion Elisa.* There is no doubt that a substantial contingent of U.S. immigrants provides many of the economic resources that make the festivities possible. In 1999, local newspapers reported not only the number of pilgrims (300,000) but also the fact that the visitors had brought approximately $90 million into the local economy. There are four big hotels in downtown Guadalajara (four and five stars) that had most of their rooms taken by affluent members, mostly from the United States.

Religion Connects the World

During the *Santa Cena* celebrations, the church is able to compress time and space so that believers from outside Guadalajara can participate in the festivities. Technological interconnections and interdependence between congregations in the United States and the mother church are substantial and serve to facilitate this time/space compression. The flow of advanced electronic equipment and knowledge goes from the United States to Mexico. Feliciano, a young member from the Houston Central congregation who was born in *Hermosa Provincia*, claims to play a central role in telecommunications during the summer ritual. He narrated with pride what he and his team had achieved during those hectic days:

> It is us [the migrants] who lead the team in Guadalajara. They [the Guadalajaran church technicians] rent the equipment but we fix and install it. Two days before

the *Santa Cena* the situation becomes really critical and we hardly have time to eat. It is a lot of responsibility and many things have to be done. We also have to arrange things to show the *Santa Cena* via satellite to other countries in the world. I was sent last December to install the satellite dishes in Brownsville and in other places so that they can be ready in August to receive the signal. They watch the *Santa Cena* in all of the countries where they have satellite dishes, like Colombia, Honduras, or cities like New York. In *Hermosa Provincia*, I was in charge of calling a whole list of places to give them the code so they can catch the signal. The whole ceremony of the *Santa Cena* can be transmitted live (sound and image). They only do it with the *Santa Cena* because satellite time is very expensive; occasionally they do show the Welcome Ceremony as well.

Electronic media are no longer the monopoly of the state (Appadurai 1996); they now serve to enhance the power of this religious institution. Electronic mediation and mass migration lie at the center of a world in motion, "where moving images meet deterritorialized viewers" (Appadurai 1996:4). In this case, both viewers and images share a religious community circuit, linking followers of the same faith in more than two countries. The moving images, scripts, and texts carried by the electronic media to distant audiences of the same circuit intensify the sense of community belonging, the collective religious identity, and the power of the religious institution. In 1999, Feliciano and the rest of the team from Houston, San Antonio, and *Hermosa Provincia* worked very hard in various *Luz del Mundo* neighborhoods, such as *Bethel, Aarón Joaquin,* and *12 de Octubre* temples. Feliciano's job includes returning the images from the send-ing to the receiving country and therefore strengthening social and cultural connec-tions between them. He later explained to me, "What I recorded in Guadalajara of the *Siervo de Dios* I showed here [in Houston] with Pastor Oscar." Mexico, rather than the United States, is the site of origin for a "world system of images" in which audi-ences are reacting to their own imagined religious community. This empirical case can be seen as an example of decentralized loci of power that challenge the unilineal par-adigm of center–periphery. *Luz del Mundo* demonstrates that cultural flows move not only in one direction but in several simultaneously. While many doctrinal and ritual instructions flow from Guadalajara to congregations throughout the world, at the same time certain cities, such as San Antonio, Houston, and Phoenix, are continu-ously sending technological knowledge and equipment to the headquarters in Guadalajara and to other congregations throughout the world. In other words, this is a multicentered social phenomenon in which cultural messages, ideas, and images flow to diverse audiences all belonging to the same religious circuit.

Does This Case Exemplify Transnationalism "From Above"?

Portes et al. (1999:221) define transnationalism from above as those activities di-rected by powerful institutional actors, such as multinational corporations and states. Those activities initiated by grassroots groups formed of immigrants are conceptualized as transnationalism from below. The former is characterized by substantial levels of organization and resources, although it lacks the grassroots intensity of involvement. The same authors present a typology that combines low- and high-level institutional activities performed within three sectors: economic, political, and sociocultural (Portes et al. 1999:222). In this framework, religious institutions are included in the sociocultural sector. However, the *Luz del Mundo* case fails to be adequately accommodated by this typology. The multiple transnational activities in this case entail a wide spectrum of individuals and organizational levels: ministers, laypersons who play formal church roles, church committees, charity foundations, organizations at the congregation level, and ordinary members on both sides of the border. Although all are subsumed by the same institutional framework, they can act with varying degrees of autonomy, and they create their own strategies to obtain resources. The final objective of all these varied agents (some more institutional than others) is to strengthen the links between the sending and receiving countries and religious communities.

Following Sikkink (1993), Mahler (1998) argues that elites should not always be thought of as traditionally conservative; under certain circumstances, they can act as transformers of power relations rather than as reinforcers. *Luz del Mundo* can be seen as an example of a situation in which transnationalism from above serves at the same time as transnationalism from below and religious elites both reinforce and change the status quo. On the one hand, the authoritarian nature of the church reproduces the established system of hierarchy (bureaucratic and religious) and therefore acts as an elite vis-á-vis ordinary believers; on the other hand, it acts as a social movement working to reconfigure existing social hierarchies by empowering the grassroots level of a traditionally excluded population (Mahler 1998). Members of Mexican immigrant religious communities in the United States constitute a population that historically has been marginalized at the social, political, and economic levels. They also have been constructed by Mexican Catholics as the inferior "Other," the non-Mexican, the ignorant. In its everyday life, the *Luz del Mundo*, at both the institutional and the grassroots level, fights powerful elites, including the Mexican Catholic Church, the Mexican state, and a relatively biased mass media. Its transnational religious communities allow the church to transcend its original Catholic-hegemonic nation-state and exist within the most pluralist and powerful nation in the world. In Mexico its status is that of a minority church, "a sect" in the pejorative sense, while in the United States it has obtained the status of a denomination with the same rights as any other religious organization. This status gain in the United States is transformed into social capital that can be used in Mexico in order to counterbalance the system of power. The constant return of Mexican migrants to their country of origin can be seen by the larger society as an accomplishment that consequently gives them a higher social status. Mexican migrants do not like to consider themselves superior to nonmigrant church members. "We are all part of the same family and of the same chosen people." They say that nonmigrant members therefore gain higher social status by sharing the same social capital as their co-members from the United States. As a result of this, both migrant and nonmigrant church members have been able to transform the relations of power within the larger Mexican society. In this sense, we are talking of transnationalism from below and not only from above.

Religious Community in Motion: Church and Family Networks

Mobility constitutes a centerpiece of transnationalism, specifically in the case of Mexican transnationalism stressed by Mahler (1998:76), and the Mexican immigrants studied in Houston confirm this statement. For the Houston members of *Luz del Mundo*, traveling to Guadalajara does not entail great difficulties; depending on their income and on the number of days they can get off work, some members fly, others drive their own vehicles, and those with lower earnings rent buses, for which, in 2000, they paid only $100 for the round-trip between Houston and Guadalajara.[12] Members organize their bus trips efficiently and safely. Often, a driver from a local company belongs to the congregation, so it is easy to make arrangements. As they have been making this trip for some time now, they know the best way to do it in order to obtain low prices and good service. Those who fly are also well organized, booking their flights well in advance with a travel agency and thereby getting special packages at very low rates. In August 2000, a group of about thirty persons took a flight for just $300 each, round-trip. During August, it is very common to see *Luz del Mundo* people who are arriving or members waiting for visitors at the Guadalajara airport. The faithful who take their vans or cars have to be in the United States legally in order to avoid problems at the border. They claim that they can drive from Houston to Guadalajara in less than eighteen hours, and there is a low incidence of car accidents among members, as they neither drink alcohol nor take illicit drugs. Driving their own cars allows them to take not only all the members of their usually large and/or extended families but also, if they have any room left, non–family members as well as small parcels from immigrants. Ministers and/or authorities of the church, who travel more frequently to Guadalajara than ordinary members, usually drive their own vehicles.

Social capital is a vital concept that allows us to analyze the benefits obtained as a result of family, church, or individual networks in the everyday activities of people. Bourdieu and Wacquant (1992:119) define social capital as "the sum of the resources, actual or virtual that accrue to an individual or a group by virtue of possessing a durable network of more or less institutionalized relationships of mutual acquaintance and recognition." To understand the manner in which transnationals from *Luz del Mundo* generate and transform social capital into specific advantages in their everyday lives, I use migrant networks as a unit of analysis. The concept *migrant networks* is used here as "sets of interpersonal ties that connect migrants, former migrants, and non-migrants in origin and destination areas through ties of kinship, friendship, and shared community origin" (Massey 1999:44).

In this case, I found that social networks are basically composed of kin and church members. It is difficult to separate these two institutions, as most people have social relationships mainly with those who are simultaneously relatives and co-members of the church. Most members I interviewed during my fieldwork were still attached to both their nuclear and their large extended families, often numbering about thirty adults plus a similar number of children. The religious community's bonds are maintained and reinforced by virtue of the endogamy practiced by the members. The church endorses endogamy implicitly and explicitly.[13] All the young members (female and male) interviewed in Houston told me that they would marry only someone within the church. This is highly likely, considering that most of their socialization time (excepting school and work) and entertainment activities are limited to church people. Nevertheless, their peers, playmates, or potential spouses can come from many parts of the world, thus reinforcing among members the belief in a common ancestry. Besides sharing a common ancestry and religion, they tend to live in the same neighborhood, especially in *Hermosa Provincia*. Even in Houston, despite some difficulty, family members also tend to live close to the church and to each other.

How do these family and church networks become social capital? Vital knowledge, information, and experience are shared and constantly transmitted between network members to ease their multiple everyday activities, such as traveling, getting jobs, education and housing, changing their legal status, sending remittances home, obtaining inexpensive health services, buying cars, and the like. For instance, as experienced transnationals, they know the best times and the easiest border-crossing spots. I was told many stories regarding the dangers, problems, and abuses that they have suffered on both sides of the U.S./Mexican border and how they were ultimately overcome. A young married woman explained to me how to arrange a bunch of dollar bills in advance to show at the U.S. border in case they are asked to do so. In many cases, when they have to stay in a border town such as Ciudad Juarez or El Paso, they seek out church members who offer them food and housing or assist them in getting in contact with the right people. A young member from Houston recounted a story that reflects how church networks help in a difficult situation. While living in San Diego, he was caught in the streets with no money on him: "The *migra* sent me back to Tijuana where I stayed the night with some members that I had met before. They fed me and I had a shower at their place. The next day I crossed the bridge and went back to San Diego with my uncle." In view of the wide and solid church networks existing in Houston, Guadalajara, and several other towns and cities in both countries, members can always find someone on whom to rely in case of problems, and, more important, they can always trust their co-members. Being a member functions as an identity card that ensures moral and material support in case of need. Border crossing is only one of the arenas in which church networks become social capital. In the following section, I present a case study of one family as an example of the benefits (social capital) that accrue from participation in this religious community network.

A Transnational Family

The Flores[14] extended family belongs to the Central congregation in Houston and to the *Hermosa Provincia* in Guadalajara. It is composed of twelve persons, seven of whom are new immigrants who were living in Houston at the time of my fieldwork: the parents, Jose and Madair; the eldest daughter, Beatriz; her husband, Amos; the second daughter, Marta, age twenty-six; and two grandchildren. Joel, an eighteen-year-old son, is also a new immigrant and was working in the state of Minnesota. The four children who remained in Guadalajara include Ruth (nineteen years old) and the three younger boys (seventeen, sixteen, and fourteen years old). The seven children belong to the fourth generation, and the grandchildren represent the fifth inside the church. In Houston, they rent a house that belongs to another member of the church located a few steps from the temple. Because of this location, I was able to visit them at their home almost every day, before or after the service. The location of the house is also very convenient for the family, as they, like most of the faithful, attend services at least once a day. Jose works for a small business packing rice; Madair occasionally works for an insurance company, clearing and cleaning houses or buildings that have had a fire. Amos works in the construction industry but sometimes takes videos and photos at celebrations, and Beatriz helps him on these occasions. Amos spent some time in Minnesota looking for a better and more steady job, but he came back to Houston, as he did not want to stay away from his family. Beatriz sells beauty products, cleans houses, and occasionally takes care of a small child. She is the only one who speaks English and is also a trained tailor but has not been able to find a job in this field in Houston. Beatriz's children are eleven and three years old. The eldest daughter goes to a public school in the area. Marta delivers flowers, and Joel lives mainly in the state of Minnesota, where he works in the construction industry. He shares a house with other male members of the church who work in the same field. In Guadala-jara, Rocio, the seventeen-year-old, works for a local branch of Kodak, and the three younger boys go to school and help their sister with the housework. Marta and her parents pay for most of the expenses of both households. They send money and phone Guadalajara at least once a week. Joel also sends money to his mother and helps with the expenses. Last summer in Houston, he bought his mother a new set of dining room furniture.

How did migration start among the Flores? Marta is a single woman aged twenty-six and the second child in the family. Before migrating to Houston, she had been in the United States twice. In 1986, she went to San Diego with her mother and other siblings to visit some relatives and stayed there for a couple of months. On this occasion, Marta did not work. The second time, she went to Los Angeles in 1991 because her mother's cousin invited her. This time she was em-ployed by a company that prepares packed lunches for airport workers. She liked working and making money and did that for a year. Her aunt in Los Angeles does not belong to the church, but Marta was able to attend a local congregation. "Part of the money I made then I sent it to my mum, but I spent most of it on myself. The last two months before I went back to Guadalajara [in August], I saved some money to buy things and for my trip. I went to Los Angeles because I knew it was convenient. I was going to have lodging and food and I could make some money." Her third trip to the United States was in 1996 when she arrived in Houston, where she has remained, although she travels to Guadalajara two or more times a year. Concerning her legal status in the United States, she said, "I could be con-sidered illegal because I do not have a work permit. I enter the country with a le-gal tourist visa and stay longer than what the visa says." However, Marta's aim is to arrange her papers so that she can stay legally in the United States.

In 1996, Marta went to Houston because her cousin Sara, who was already re-siding there, was pregnant and invited her to stay with her until the baby was born. A few months later, Sara introduced Marta to people who needed their houses cleaned, and later another friend from the church got Marta a job delivering flow-ers for a big company. While still living with her cousin, Marta's parents came for a short visit but stayed. It was then that they all moved to the house close to the temple. Marta's father had been made redundant in a factory in Guadalajara, but he still needed to support his children there. Through his relatives in the congre-gation, Jose found a job and decided to stay in Houston. Two years later, Marta's eldest sister, Beatriz, together with her own nuclear family, joined them. More or less at the same time, Joel also migrated to Houston and got a job as a mason. Of the seven siblings, only Marta is now living in Houston because Beatriz and her nuclear family returned to *Hermosa Provincia* in August 2000 while Joel has gone back to Minnesota.

In August 2000, all members of the Flores family in Houston traveled to Guadalajara to attend the *Santa Cena.* The parents, Beatriz, Amos, and the children took the church bus; Joel and Marta traveled by plane and stayed only four days (from August 12 to 15). On August 10, I visited the Flores family in *La Provincia.* *Hermana* Madair (the mother) was doing housework, just as she does in Houston. A small number of pilgrims were staying with the Flores. A few days after August 14, the parents left *Hermosa Provincia* and traveled by bus to Houston. Beatriz, her husband, and children stayed in Guadalajara because Amos wanted to apply to a government office to obtain credit for a house. He took a job selling car parts so that he could be officially registered as a worker in order to obtain the necessary credit. However, Beatriz and Amos said that they were not completely happy in Guadalajara because it is more difficult to survive in Mexico than in the United States. Amos traveled to Houston in March 2001 searching for a better-paying job but soon returned to Guadalajara, as he did not find anything attractive. As of June 2001, they were still in Guadalajara and had obtained the mortgage for their house. Their new home will be located very close to *Hermosa Provincia.* As soon as they get the house, they plan to rent it so that they can pay the mortgage and then remigrate to Houston. In *Hermosa Provincia,* Beatriz does volunteer work for the Elisa Foundation, a church organization devoted mainly to helping poor widows. For Mexican Independence Day (September 15–16), Beatriz and Amos spent many hours selling food on behalf of the foundation. In November 2000, Amos bought a hotdog cart from a church member, as Beatriz wanted to increase the family income. She sells hotdogs on a *Hermosa Provincia* street corner. Their lifestyle reflects the constant struggle that many people of their social class experience in Mexico. It also reflects Beatriz's and Amos's open minds concerning women's roles; they have a stable and egalitarian relationship.[15] Finally, it reflects a transnational orientation that seeks out the best economic opportunities available in Houston and Guadalajara.

In mid-November 2000, I went again to visit the Flores family in *Hermosa Provincia.* Madair and Jose had traveled from Houston to Guadalajara to spend a few days with their youngest son, Josue. It was Josue's birthday and church *presentation.* This is a rite of passage during which fourteen-year-old boys and girls commit themselves to the church. The parents present their child to the church and ask the community to help them in case the new, formally baptized member fails in his or her Christian life. *Hermana* Madair was very worried because she wanted to take her two youngest children to the United States with her, but she had recently been rejected in her applications for their visas. She is afraid to apply again because, if rejected a second time, they will have to wait for another year before reapplying. That November evening, Madair and I walked around the streets of *Hermosa Provincia* for hours. She introduced me to several of her sisters, nieces, nephews, in-laws, and many other members to whom she is related. They all live in the same place and belong to the same church. On Jose's side of the family, most of his siblings live in the United States, many in Houston. That is why Marta went to Houston in 1996. Sara, the daughter of one of Jose's brothers, has lived in Houston since the 1980s. Beatriz later informed me through e-mail that her mother's youngest brother and his family had been in Houston early in 2001 and intended to migrate as well.

The members of this family had previous migrant connections in Houston as well as in many places in California before their own migration. All of them found jobs and housing close to the temple, either through relatives or fellow church members. They send frequent remittances (money, clothes, and house appliances) through church members who travel to Guadalajara by bus or car. Any member who travels spreads the news and takes what he or she can carry. I did not find in this group the professional couriers analyzed by Mahler (1999) among Salvadoran immigrants. There is no doubt that in this case, geographic proximity and church solidarity among believers have prevented the need for this kind of service from arising. The Flores family illustrates the concrete ways by which *Luz del Mundo* members use kinship and church networks to provide the social capital that expedites their migration, settlement, economic empowerment, and sometimes remigration.

La Santa Cena

> If religious ceremonies have any importance at all, it is that *they set collectivities in motion;* groups come together to celebrate them.
>
> —DURKHEIM (1976:352; EMPHASIS ADDED)

Why are these Mexican migrants to Houston moved to attend the *Santa Cena* in Guadalajara? Here I concentrate on the members' experiences, meanings, and emotions in their most sacred place and time. In August 1999, like the pilgrims, I stayed in *La Provincia* for a week. Although I had an extraordinary time, I am sure that my experience would never be able to match the intense feelings enjoyed by the believers. Despite the fact that I am not a religious person, when I went back in August 2000 for the festivities, my heart was beating strongly. I felt the excitement of just "being there." The *Hermosa Provincia* is a small place with narrow streets. From August 8 to 14, it is transformed into a sacred place where religious services are held from 4:30 in the morning until 9:00 or 10:00 in the evening. During ritual time, *La Provincia* becomes even smaller as the streets turn into an extension of the temple. The temple can hold about 15,000 souls, but it is obviously not large enough to hold all the members during these days, so every single space outside the temple is overcrowded with children playing, eating, sleeping, resting, or crying and adults praying, listening, or talking with other members. Members have the feeling of being within a *community* in the strict sense of the word because everywhere in the area there are only members of the church, and their reason for being there helps strengthen their religious identity and separate them from the rest of the world.

The meanings that the ritual have for members are expressed and reinterpreted in diverse manners, but they all agree regarding its positive effect in their lives. A member explained to me, "In Guadalajara, during the August festivities there are more religious options than in Houston to select from and we can concentrate on learning more concerning doctrine. In Houston there are always more everyday distractions." Members are devoted to religious activities and define these days as extraordinary not only because they are far from their ordinary days of work, school, and routine back in Houston but also because they are able to be physically present at their most sacred place. Another member told me in Houston, "I am counting the days [to attend the *Santa Cena*]." A migrant believer, also from Houston, said, "It [the *Santa Cena*] means great joy for all of us, because we are here together from all over the world, and being together increases even more our emotion." In Turner's terms, these pilgrims are experiencing "a *liminal time*"[16] during the religious ritual, one "set apart from the ongoing business of quotidian life, when an interpretation is constructed to give the appearance of sense and order" (Turner 1982:75; italics added).

Within the framework of the main ritual, rites of passage are also performed that indicate changes in individuals' status, thereby adding meaning to the special time spent in *Hermosa Provincia*. August in Guadalajara is the appropriate time and place for seeing old friends and for meeting new people. Several members find their life partners during these days, precisely because most members of the family and friends are able to get together. For example, Silvia, a twenty-six-year-old woman who lives in Houston, met Virgil, an Anglo member of the church from El Paso, Texas, in February 1996 when they were both in Guadalajara. They met again in August of the same year at *Hermosa Provincia*. Finally, they got married the next year, in February 1997, in Guadalajara and went to live in Houston. When Silvia stayed in *La Provincia* at her parents' house, her little sister looked after her baby, so she was able to attend more religious services than in Houston. Silvia's case is only one among the similar stories that I was told at both research sites. After August 14, there were collective wedding ceremonies in the big temple. A high number of collective ceremonies seems to be common during the annual fiestas. The following paragraphs are a synthesis of my ethnographic notes from August 14, 1999 and 2000, in *Hermosa Provincia:*

> The morning of August 14, there was a thick atmosphere full of tension and high expectation. This day, instead of having the 4:30 A.M. prayers as on the previous

days of the week, the prayers were at 8:30. At midday there was a special service called "Time of Meditation and Preparation for the Supper." The streets appeared to be filled with even more people than usual. We could hardly walk around the temple, as believers were standing all around it. It was impossible to enter the temple, as it was packed with members on both sides, the women's and the men's. We were standing outside the temple, when all of a sudden a general lament started, and all the female members (we could only see women) got down on their knees and prayed. The crying was very intense and loud. For the first time, since we had arrived in *La Provincia*, we did not know how to observe and what to observe. We were unable to participate in the strict sense of the word. At the same time, the powerful collective crying was affecting us. We were physically very close to women who were entering into altered states, many of whom were experiencing glossolalia. The praying–lamenting lasted for ten or fifteen minutes.

Later on, the streets became deserted because members were getting ready for the ceremony. At 3:00 we were able to witness adults, youngsters, and little children all dressed up for the occasion. There were lines of people formed everywhere, and large and small groups were taking their places on all the terraces, front gardens, balconies, roofs, or any space that was left. The choirs from many places in Mexico and the United States were standing in lines waiting to get to their places in the temple. Each choir's attire was of a different color and style. Female dresses matched the color of their veils and the suits of the male singers.

Inside the temple, behind the altar, was the place for the U.S. choir, which was made up of 500 singers from many cities. Sitting below the U.S. choir were the members of the *Hermosa Provincia* choir, and in one of the mezzanines were the choirs from Zacapoaxtla, Puebla, and other states in Mexico. On the walls, flags of the thirty-two countries reached by the doctrine were hanging. In the middle of the altar was Samuel's big wooden chair with two lions, representing the leaders of the church, Aarón and Samuel, carved on the topsides. Surrounding the altar were huge plastic grapes and golden wheatears symbolizing the *Santa Cena.*

The actual Holy Supper ceremony lasted from 4:00 to 10:00 P.M. From four to six different ministers conducted the service while we were awaiting Samuel's arrival. Choirs from many Mexican states and from other countries sang hymns while individual testimonies were given.

At 6:00 P.M., a heavy silence filled the *Provincia.* All of a sudden thousands of followers stood up and waved white handkerchiefs to welcome Samuel. He entered the temple followed by most of the ministers and accompanied by the sound of six trumpets. All ministers, including Samuel, wore dark suits. From that moment on, Samuel headed the ceremony. First he anointed the new ministers, deacons, pastors, and bishops and informed the church of their new assignments. Following the anointments, Samuel blessed the bread and the wine. Inside the temple, the deacons split and placed the bread in golden trays and poured the wine into golden pitchers. The pastors took the trays and pitchers and went to administer the sacred bread and wine to the thousands of pilgrims gathered inside and outside the temple. Meanwhile, Samuel went to greet the youth concentrated at the

"Jezreel Field," and he ascended one terrace of the temple in order to see and to be seen by the crowds standing all over the place. The atmosphere in the streets surrounding the temple was pervaded with a collective, ecstatic religious devotion. I saw many women falling into a trance and many others just crying, loudly or silently. The people present were overjoyed with the ceremony. We saw a couple of young women who had collapsed in the temple being carried by two male members to the emergency center. Meanwhile, the remaining people were standing in perfect order.

Samuel announced the turn of the U.S. choir and asked them to sing in English, as God understands all languages. When all the people present had been given their bread and wine, Samuel had his at around 8:00. Just before 10:00, Samuel pronounced his last good-bye words to his followers. He thanked them for coming and said he hoped to meet them all again next year.

According to Durkheim, ritual and belief are the two categories of religious phenomena. While the latter refers to discourse and representation, the former "are particular modes of action" (Durkheim 1976:34). Assembled individuals are able to express their feelings "through actions in common." The *Santa Cena* constitutes the highest representation of a moral community in Durkheimian terms because it is able to provide the membership with a "collective conscience," in the emotional, cognitive, and normative meanings of the term. The ritual is an all-encompassing, integrative form that affects the thoughts, attitudes, and actions of thousands of believers throughout the world. It highlights the common origin of the members as the "chosen people" while at the same time renewing their faith and preserving the group's moral identity. Believers from multiple locations get together in Guadalajara to participate in a common sacred meal that revitalizes their bond. The act of consuming the sacred meal allows them to remake their kinship as parts of a body made of the same flesh and blood. Samuel constitutes the centerpiece of this ritual; the emotions aroused by him in the faithful do not parallel any others. The intense feelings produced by the presence of their living apostle are strengthened by the intimate relationships existing between people who are aware of sharing them. These feelings would not be the same if they were felt in isolation; it is the physical *community* and *communitas* that produces and reproduces a sacred, forceful energy, which in turn transforms religion into a powerful force, a source of dynamism.

Although a social drama such as the *Santa Cena* expresses harmony, joy, and sharing, it also demonstrates "where power and meaning lie and how they are distributed" (Turner 1982:78). Even though everyone feels and experiences equally the religious energy (*communitas*), there is a structured system that allocates participants so that each person is properly placed: women and children on one side, men on the other, youth in their own area, clerical hierarchy on a separate and upper floor, and Samuel, the highest figure of all, in his own special chair and pedestal. Choirs are also placed according to their status. The *Hermosa Provincia* choir sits closest to Samuel, and the U.S. choir sits just above the main altar. Both choirs sing every year in the main temple during the *Santa Cena.* There are several choirs (from many states in Mexico) who annually attend the ceremony but rarely have the privilege of singing in the main temple; these choirs are usually assigned to minor temples, such as *Bethel* or the *Aarón Joaquin.* Power, position, and privilege are reflected during the ceremony in many ways, yet simultaneously there is an overarching feeling of sameness and equality generated by the religious atmosphere that temporarily liberates individuals from their secular status and encourages the appearance of *communitas* among believers.

In my description of August 14, I have tried to reproduce the atmosphere of the place, filled with the excitement of the people. After six hours of listening, praying, and crying, believers are full of physical energy, which has a religious source personified in Samuel. Consequently, it is not only the symbolic meanings, the normative system, and the cognitive aspects of their faith that compel migrants to come every year to the *Santa Cena;* it is above all a series of complex feelings and emotions that fill them with sacred energy, something that they can obtain only from this religious ceremony. Rituals transform believers into stronger and freer persons who are "capable of doing more." As a Houston member stressed, "We come to the ceremony to regain our strength so we can go on with our life." At the same time, the annual ritual revitalizes the moral community, and the members renew their bonds of loyalty between themselves and with their spiritual leader. The members' solidarity is empowered, and their church networks become even stronger than before. Hence, each time migrant believers attend the ritual, it increases the likelihood that they will return to *Hermosa Provincia.*

Exploring the Category of Diaspora Migration

The present world is characterized by a more intense mobilization of people than ever before. Appadurai (1996), for instance, claims that a hundred million persons do not live in their places of origin. Recently, the term *diaspora* has acquired a broad meaning with some scholars (Clifford 1994; Helmreich 1992; Safran 1991; Shuval 2000; Tololyan 1991) applying it to a wide variety of migrating populations and including economic as well as political and religious motivations for the migration. According to Clifford (1994:310), the discourse of diaspora has recently become the voice of "displaced peoples who feel (maintain, revive, invent) a connection with a prior home," just as *Luz del Mundo* believers claim the right to return to a "mythical homeland," represented by *Hermosa Provincia. Luz del Mundo* migrants in the United States include people not only from Mexico but also from several other nations in Latin America and, more recently, persons from countries as far away as Russia. All of them are displaced people and represent minority groups in the United States. They share a history of dispersal and can be alienated as well from social and economic advantages in the receiving country. The *Luz del Mundo* church gives them the opportunity to construct an identity group that transcends national or regional identities; it provides its followers a discourse of a shared history, memory, longing, dreams, meaningful narratives, and a place to return, a place where everyone can feel at home.

Tololyan (1991:5) states, "Diasporas are exemplary communities of the transnational moment." He explains that people living in transnational situations tend to construct organizations or collectivities that go beyond the boundaries of nation-states. The notion of diaspora not only refers to the binary relationship between the community and their homeland but also includes "lateral relations among diaspora communities located in different sites within nation states and in different states" (Shuval 2000:44). This has led to the notion of "multiple centered diasporas" (Clifford 1994; Kearney 1995; Tololyan 1991), which we can observe among the multiple congregations of *Luz del Mundo* in Mexico, the United States, and elsewhere. The U.S. congregations are connected at multiple levels as well as with other congregations located in Mexico, El Salvador, Costa Rica, Colombia, and Spain. *Luz del Mundo* migrant believers are loyal to and identify not only with members in their sending country but also with co-members located in these other countries. With its utopian discourse, the *Luz del Mundo* religion succeeds in unifying dispersed populations and social minorities from diverse parts of the world into one religious community whose members see themselves as the "chosen people" who have been redeemed in modern times through their two apostles.

Diasporas often are the result of economic, political, religious, or racial oppression in both their country of origin and host nations. I have described earlier the minority church status of *Luz del Mundo* in Mexico. Immigrants in the United States do not experience religious discrimination as they do in Mexico, but they suffer racial discrimination and economic privation. The history of racial discrimination against Mexicans in the United States dates from the nineteenth century[17] and has continued to the present day. It is manifested, for example, in the substantial number of deaths at the U.S./Mexican border in recent years (Eschbach, Hagan, and Rodriguez 1999). Given this, a diaspora community offers a privileged social space that creates a sense of belonging to a welcoming and rewarding social entity. For people in diaspora situations, there is always a utopian land about which to dream in response to a present dystopia.

Although Mexican immigrant members feel a sense of attachment to their home country, it is mainly the "sacred land," or *Hermosa Provincia*, that draws them.

This can be seen through the close relations that Mexican members have with their counterparts from other countries, which are more important than ties to Mexican gentiles, who can be perceived as "foreigners." Communality of belief is considered more powerful than nationhood. Among the Salvadoran members whom I interviewed in Houston, all responded that they had no connections with people from their homeland unless they were members of the church. For both Mexican and Salvadoran members, nation-states do not seem to "be the most effective or legitimate units of collective organization." (Tololyan 1991:4). Today, global culture acts through electronic media transporting information and images across nations and allowing for frequent communication between congregations in one nation or many, thereby creating a transnational community of believers to whom nation-state is all but irrelevant. Unlike the rest of the Mexican population in the United States (native born and migrant), the members of this church have a strong, unified set of values and beliefs that are oriented toward a homeland myth, *Hermosa Provincia.* This is one of the major differences between diaspora migration and other types of migration (Shuval 2000).

Nevertheless, the church plays an important role in maintaining Mexican ethnicity or nationality. Spanish remains the ritual language used in congregations everywhere in the world, although in some places, when needed, the church is becoming more bilingual by adding English to its ritual practices. It is in Mexico that the headquarters are located, and the two great charismatic figures (Aarón and Samuel) are of Mexican origin, as are most of the followers throughout the world. However, within transnational environments, identities are not necessarily clear, fixed, or transparent; they are dynamic and able to transform themselves in unforeseeable ways (Hall 1997). A young member in Houston told me, "I consider myself a Mexican and represent Mexicans, but if I was more important I would represent my church, and if I was even more important I would then represent Hispanics." He does not want to give up any of the three identities and wants to speak from all. He resists and negotiates his difference and exclusion at the same time. That is the way in which members make and remake collective identities in diasporas—making claims to their sending country and appealing to their religion (but also to their receiving country) in apparently contradictory ways.

Conclusions

Because of geographic closeness, Mexican/U.S. migration, particularly from the western and northern regions, has been characterized by the tendency of migrants to return often to their home communities. In the case described in this chapter, religion constitutes the major motivation for return trips. This case shows what other sociologists have not shown in terms of transnationalism, namely, the central role played by a religious institution and, more specifically, a religious ritual, the *Santa Cena.* The institution coordinates the required activities for the ritual to take place, but it is individual believers throughout the world who decide whether to attend. Although for some their economic circumstances make it impossible to attend, the psychocognitive meanings of religion propel them "home." Within this religious community, members not only travel often but do so according to dates set by a liturgical calendar. Over the years, the time spent there becomes increasingly significant because "meaning arises in *memory*, in *cognition* of the past, and is concerned with negotiation about the 'fit' between past and present" (Turner 1982:75). Having eaten the sacred meal and experienced the high of intersubjective communality, individuals go back to their everyday lives. Attending the annual ceremony can be seen as that time and space where individual members construct and reconstruct the meaning of life here and hereafter and where they regain strength and the will for their everyday activities.

The collective identity provided by their "common ancestry," a shared ideology, a sense of dispersal, and a connection to a mythical home make transnationalism in this case a pattern of life that will continue among future generations. Both the church and the family ensure the transmission and reproduction of religious belief among youngsters. Through the wide networks that are constantly generated among member migrants, belonging to a community such as *Luz del Mundo* facilitates and reinforces not only the existence of transnational communities but also the process of migration itself. While co-members open pathways for new migrants by offering them shelter, food, jobs, and moral support, the church re-creates sacred spaces beyond nation-states by using modern information technology and by the reenactment of ceremonies performed by Samuel in diverse parts of the world.

Notes

1. Taken from my fieldwork notes of July 23, 2000.
2. The stable and constant connections that migrants maintain with their sending countries have been named by scholars "transnational migration circuits" (Rouse 1991), "transnational social fields" (Basch, Glick Schiller, and Szanton Blanc 1994; Mahler 1998), and "transnational communities" (Levitt 1998; Nagengast and Kearney 1990; Portes et al. 1999).
3. In 1996, the United States gross national product was six times higher than that of Mexico, and the difference in wages was equivalent to that as well (Roberts et al. 1999:240).
4. Between 1943 and 1946, the U.S. railroad program hired 130,000 Mexican workers (Morales 1982, quoted in Durand et al. 2001).
5. This questionnaire was designed by Sara Pozos (official of the church) and myself. The sample I use here takes into account only eighty-one questionnaires. The instrument

was used among young members of the church who attend study groups four or five days a week.

6. For example, it is well known that the majority of Mexican priests not only were born in this region but were also trained as clerics there. Guadalajara in Jalisco and Zamora in Michoacán have produced the highest number of priests not only for Mexico but also for other Latin American countries since colonial times.

7. Members and authorities of the church do not identify themselves as Pentecostals; however, because of its origin, development, ritual, and doctrine, I classify this church in this way. In contrast, they consider Pentecostal churches small groups divided among themselves. In Mexico and everywhere else, the *Luz del Mundo* members do identify themselves as evangelicals and Christians and define their religious system as "a well organized Church, or a unified *pueblo*" (people) in opposition to the fragmented Pentecostal "small groups."

8. To be in charge means being responsible for an age-group of members that ranges from 30 to 300 people. The members should be of the same sex as that of the person in charge. The group has prayer and doctrine studies three times a week for one hour or less (depending on the congregation), and the person in charge organizes the topic of doctrine to be discussed and also is aware of the absences or flaws of participants. In case of sickness, pregnancy, financial, or personal problems, the *encargada* or *encargado* will try to help the member unless it is something extremely serious, in which case she or he will call on the pastor of the congregation to discuss the issue. The *encargada* is a sort of spiritual guide for all members of the group she is taking care of. They must know the activities, jobs, and possibilities of the people in their groups to be able to advise, support, or even admonish when necessary.

9. *Bethel* is a neighborhood near *Hermosa Provincia* with a big temple that has become the second most important place for the *Luz del Mundo* church in Guadalajara.

10. During the intensive fieldwork done in *Hermosa Provincia* from August 8 to 14, 1999, I was accompanied by a young female anthropologist, Celia Magaña García, who played her role as research assistant beyond expectations. Her presence meant to me not only professional but, more important, emotional and moral support.

11. Every year, ministers distribute the work among a group of different members, as it is tough work and starts very early in the morning and ends late in the evening. Each congregation has a list of those members who cannot afford their food expenses that it sends to the people in charge in Guadalajara who issue tickets so that each day these members can eat three meals free.

12. The last choice, according to the members, is very comfortable because the bus leaves from the temples in Houston and arrives exactly in *La Provincia* or *Bethel* in Guadalajara. It is also a very agreeable way to travel because it is not a commercial trip, so they have their own brethren as company.

13. This was demonstrated by the following statement given by a minister during a service in *Hermosa Provincia:* "Do not give away your children to the gentiles." Members have internalized the idea.

14. Family names and first names have been changed to maintain individuals' anonymity.

15. On various occasions, I saw Amos preparing lunch or supper for everyone. He seems to be a modern man, able to cook, look after his children, and at the same time be the main provider. Beatriz considers herself a lucky woman with a man such as Amos. She is a very free woman compared to many of her social class in Mexico.

16. According to Turner (1969, 1982), liminality means being out of time, or out of secular status, at the margin of social life.

17. After the U.S./Mexico war in 1848, European immigrants defined themselves as whites "in opposition to persons of Mexican, Chinese, and Japanese descent." White Europeans, in claiming their own American identity, described the other populations as "biologically incapable of culture and civilization" (Glick Schiller 1999:105).

References

Alarcón, Rafael. 1999. "La integración de los ingenieros y científicos mexicanos en Sillicon Valley." In *Fronteras Fragmentadas*, edited by Gail Mummert. Zamora, Michoacán: El Colegio de Michoacán, CIDEM.

Alvarez, Robert R. 1995. "The Mexican-U.S. Border: The Making of an Anthropology of Borderlands." *Annual Review of Anthropology* 24:447–70.

Anderson, Benedict. 1993. *Comunidades Imaginadas*. Mexico City: Fondo de Cultura Economica.

Appadurai, Arjun. 1996. *Modernity at Large, Cultural Dimensions of Globalization*. Minneapolis: University of Minnesota Press.

Basch, Linda, Nina Glick Schiller, and Cristina Szanton Blanc, eds. 1994. *Nations Unbound: Transnational Projects, Postcolonial Predicaments, and Deterritorialized Nation-States*. Amsterdam: Gordon and Breach.

Bourdieu, Peirre, and Loic Wacquant. 1992. *An Invitation to Reflexive Sociology*. Chicago: University of Chicago Press.

Clifford, James. 1994. "Diasporas." *Cultural Anthropology* 9:302–38.

De la Torre Castellanos, Renée. 1995. *Los hijos de la luz: Discurso identidad y poder en La Luz del Mundo*. Guadalajara: ITESO, CIESAS, Universidad de Guadalajara.

Durand, Jorge. 1996. *El Norte es como el mar: Entrevistas a Trabajadores Migrantes en Estados Unidos*. Guadalajara: Universidad de Guadalajara.

Durand, Jorge, Douglas S. Massey, and Rene M. Zenteno. 2001. "Mexican Immigration to the United States: Continuities and Change." *Latin American Research Review* 36:107–27.

Durkheim, Émile. [1915] 1976. *The Elementary Form of the Religious Life*. London: Allen & Unwin.

Eschbach, Karl, Jacqueline Hagan, and Nestor Rodriguez. 1999. "Death at the Border." *International Migration Review* 33, no. 2:430–54.

Fortuny-Loret De Mola, Patricia. 1995. "On the Road to Damascus: Pentecostals, Mormons and Jehovah's Witnesses in Mexico." Ph.D. diss., University College, London.

Gamio, Manuel. 1930. *Mexican Migration to the United States*. Chicago: University of Chicago Press.

Gelbard, Alene H., and Marion Carter. 1997. "Mexican Immigration and the U.S. Population." In *At the Crossroads: Mexican Migration and U.S. Policy*, edited by Frank Bean, Rodolfo O. de la Garza, Bryan R. Roberts, and Sidney Weintraub. Lanham, MD: Rowman & Littlefield.

Glick Schiller, Nina. 1999. "Transmigrants and Nation-States: Something Old and Something New in the U.S. Immigrant Experience." In *The Handbook of International Migration: The American Experience*, edited by Charles Hirschman, Philip Kasinitz, and Josh DeWind. New York: Russell Sage Foundation.

Goffman, Erving. 1988. *Internados: Ensayos sobre la situación social de los enfermos mentales*. Buenos Aires: Amorrortu Editores.

Hall, Stuart. 1997. "Old and New Identities, Old and New Ethnicities." In *Culture, Globalization and the World-System: Contemporary Conditions for the Representation of Identity*, edited by Anthony D. King. Minneapolis: University of Minnesota Press.

Helmreich, Stefan. 1992. "Kinship, Nation, and Paul Gilroy's Concept of Diaspora." *Diaspora* 2:243–49.

Hervieu-Léger, Danièle. 1997. "Faces of Catholic Transnationalism: In and Beyond France." In *Transnational Religion: Fading States*, edited by Suzanne Rudolph and James Piscatori. Boulder, CO: Westview.

Kearney, Michael. 1986. "From the Invisible Hand to Visible Feet: Anthropological Studies of Migration and Development." *Annual Review of Anthropology* 15:331–61.

———. 1991. "Borders and Boundaries of State and Self at the End of Empire." *Journal of Historical Sociology* 4:52–74.

———. 1995. "The Local and The Global: The Anthropology of Globalization and Transnationalism." *Annual Review of Anthropology* 24:547–65.

Levitt, Peggy. 1998. "Social Remittances: Migration Driven Local-Level Forms of Cultural Diffusion." *International Migration Review* 32: 926–48.

Lomnitz-Adler, Claudio. 1992. "Concepts for the Study of Regional Culture." In *Mexico's Regions: Comparative History and Development*, edited by Eric Van Young. San Diego: Center for U.S.-Mexican Studies.

Mahler, Sarah J. 1998. "Theoretical and Empirical Contributions toward a Research Agenda for Transnationalism." In *Transnationalism from Below*, edited by Michael Peter Smith and Luis Eduardo Guarnizo. New Brunswick, NJ: Transaction.

———. 1999. "La industria salvadoreña de remesas." In *Fronteras Fragmentadas*, edited by Gail Mummert. Zamora, Michoacán: El Colegio de Michoacán, CIDEM.

Massey, Douglas S. 1999. "Why Does Immigration Occur? A Theoretical Synthesis." In *The Handbook of International Migration: The American Experience*, edited by Charles Hirschman, Philip Kasinitz, and Josh DeWind. New York: Russell Sage Foundation.

Morales, Patricia. 1982. *Indocumentados Mexicanos*. Mexico City: Editorial Grijalbo.

Nagengast, Carol, and Michael Kearney. 1990. "Mixed Ethnicity: Social Identity, Political Consciousness, and Political Activism." *Latin American Research Review* 25:61–91.

Portes, Alejandro, Luis Guarnizo, Luis Eduardo, and Patricia Landolt. 1999. "The Study of Transnationalism: Pitfalls and Promise of an Emergent Research Field." *Ethnic and Racial Studies* 22:217–37.

Roberts, Bryan R., Reanne Frank, and Fernando Lozano-Ascencio. 1999. "Transnational Migrant Communities and Mexican Migration to the U.S." *Ethnic and Racial Studies* 22:238–66.

Rodriguez, Nestor. 2000. "Hispanic and Asian Immigration Waves in Houston." In *Religion and the New Immigrants*, edited by Helen R. Ebaugh and Janet S. Chafetz. Walnut Creek, CA: AltaMira.

Rouse, Roger. 1991. "Mexican Migration and the Social Space of Postmodernism." *Diaspora* I (spring):8–23.

Safran, William. 1991. "Diasporas in Modern Societies: Myths of Homeland and Return." *Diaspora* I (spring):83–99.

Shuval, Judith T. 2000. "Diaspora Migration: Definitional Ambiguities and a Theoretical Paradigm." *International Migration* 38:41–57.

Sikkink, Kathrin. 1993. "Human Rights, Principled Issue-Networks, and Sovereignty in Latin America." *International Organization* 47:411–41.

Smith, Michael Peter, and Luis Eduardo Guarnizo. 1998. *Transnationalism from Below.* New Brunswick, NJ: Transaction.

Taylor, Paul Schuster. [1928] 1970. *Mexican Labor in the United States.* Vols. I and 2. New York: Arno Press.

Tololyan, Khachig. 1991. "The Nation-State and Its Others: In Lieu of a Preface." *Diaspora* I (spring):3–7.

Turner, Victor. 1969. *The Ritual Process. Structure and Antistructure.* New York: Aldine.

———. 1982. *From Ritual to Theatre: The Human Seriousness of Play.* New York: PAJ Publications.

U.S. Bureau of the Census. 1997. *Statistical Abstracts of the United States: 1997.* Washington, DC: U.S. Government Printing Office.

Forty Years of Religion across Borders   3
Twilight of a Transnational Field?

DAVID A. COOK

A s my family and I board a flight from Houston to Newark, we run into
Esteban and Mary Gaston, full-time "workers" at the *Iglesia Cristiana
Evangélica Compasión y Amor* (hereafter ICE), an immigrant Latino congregation where I did participant observation over a two-year period. We are all on
our way to Mendoza, Argentina, via Santiago de Chile. It is not surprising that we
should run into each other given that similar events motivate our travel. Esteban
is the featured speaker at the national conference of denominational leaders in
Mendoza, and I am on my way to attend the same event as part of a project on
"transnational religion." My purpose in traveling is partly to study the role of people like Esteban and Mary, who build and maintain "transnational social fields"
(Glick Schiller 1999:97) in their travels between Houston, Mendoza, and other
cities. Fortuitously, I am able to join the Gastons on one of the many journeys
that spin a web between Houston and Mendoza. In this chapter, I explore how and
why a specific transnational social field emerges, including the role of people such
as the Gastons in this process.

A growing number of social scientists speak of transnationalism as a dis-
tinctly contemporary economic, political, and cultural phenomenon in which
people and institutions in nations of origin and settlement are linked together
in complex ways (Basch, Glick Schiller, and Szanton Blanc 1994). In the United
States, much of the literature on transnationalism is prompted by the ties of
new (post-1965) immigrants to their countries of origin. Scholars interested in
things transnational conceptualize the phenomenon or its implications in a variety of ways: as a new political/cultural form that undermines the nation-state
as it is currently known (Levitt 1998a:76; Soysal 1994) and deterritorializes
civic membership (Basch et al. 1994; Cohen 1997:173; Glick Schiller, Basch,

and Szanton Blanc 1992), as a dimension of a long-term process of global capitalist penetration (Portes, Guarnizo, and Pandolt 1999:227), and as a migration perspective that tries to escape from the "tyranny of the national" (Noirel,
cited in Gabaccia 1999:1115). In the United States, transnational "communities" are said to provide an alternative path to assimilation and a potential site
of resistance to dominant structures (Portes et al. 1999:228; Roberts, Frank,
and Lozano-Ascencio 1999).

As a cultural system and basis of social organization, religion has recently become prominent in discussions of transnationalism. Peggy Levitt's work (1998a,
1998b), for example, has been most prominent in examining various cases of
cross-national religion. She argues not only in support of macro-level claims
(e.g., the impact of transnationalism on the nature of nation-state membership)
but also for the importance of transnational religious ties in understanding everyday immigrant religious life (Levitt 1998a; Levitt, Maira, and Purohit 1997).
The argument is really one about religious globalization or, more specifically, the
way in which changes in the world order affect religion at a local level. Levitt's
work is important in that it highlights the potential importance of religious institutions for sustaining social relations and political institutions across national
borders. She also contributes to our analytical tool kit the notion of "social remittances," a concept that focuses scholarly attention on the "ideas, practices, and
social capital that flow from receiving to sending-country communities"
(Levitt 1998a:76, 1998b).

While sympathetic to Levitt's endeavor, one may nonetheless question the
sense in which the ties, public spheres, collectivities, and relationships are
"transnational." Is the adjective meant to underscore the simultaneous involvement
of immigrants in the affairs of sending and receiving countries? Is it meant primarily to emphasize a sense of "consciously belonging to a group that [spans two
settings]" (Levitt 1998b:929)? Is it meant to call analytical attention to social
spaces where the exclusive claims of nationhood are contested and negotiated and
alternative axes of identification and organization are developed? Does *transnational*
refer to all of this? The answer is not entirely clear. Analytically, it seems worthwhile to distinguish how *transnational* is being used in specific contexts; otherwise,
it is difficult to assess claims made in this and other work on "transnational" phenomena. For example, Levitt (1998a:87) claims that "contemporary global connections are likely to lead to more permanent homeland religious influences [rel-
ative to ones in the past], albeit constantly evolving ones." Here the sense seems to
be one of involvements in two or more countries. Does this necessarily imply
transnational identifications? It is entirely possible that while the former persist or
evolve, identifications develop in a more locally grounded context. I will pick up
on this point later in this chapter.

In an effort to push the underlying explanation of transnational phenomena further, I suggest a relational definition of the term *field* that specifies how and why specific social actors generate and maintain fields. By transnational social field, I mean a set of historical relations between actors that cross—but nevertheless are constrained and enabled by—geopolitical borders between nation-states. Referring to relations as *historical* means that one takes time and place seriously in examining how they come to be and how they change (Tilly 1994:3). Speaking of a *field* underscores the quality of relations between actors. The relational configuration between actors on different sides of borders is endowed with a specific "gravity" imposed on objects and agents that enter it (Bourdieu and Wacquant 1992:17). As new actors enter the field or change their positions, the configuration of power and the quality of relationships change. Hence, it is a space of competition in which actors vie to establish monopoly over, in the case related here, authority and status in the religious field. I make no claims that nationhood as an institutional configuration or nationness as a quality of relations between people who think of themselves in national categories change as a result (although they may). Rather, I explore the actual mechanisms of field formation and change under specific circumstances. Their embeddedness in larger fields is a matter for further empirical work.

In what follows, I limit the scope of transnationalism to occupations and activities that require for their implementation regular and sustained social contacts over time across national borders (Portes et al. 1999:219). The point of departure is the history and activities of individuals who comprise the networks that make transnational enterprises possible. The focus is primarily sociocultural rather than economic and political.

The data presented in this chapter tell a story of how and why a relational web spanning several cities in four countries came to be and changed over a forty-year period. The process (i.e., the "how") by which a transnational religious field emerged may be thought of as twofold. First is the typical chain migration process by which a pioneer facilitates the migration of relatives and friends who, in turn, do the same for other friends and relatives. As the migrant community matures, its institutions and organizations become more prominent. In the case at hand, the church becomes the central institution in the lives of Argentine migrants in Houston. Second, and not surprisingly, the church offers a field where religious authority and social status become linked and the object of competitive relations. Migrants in Houston view the "world" as the stage on which their evangelistic endeavors can be played out to fulfill and perhaps exceed the goals of their religious predecessors.

Why do social actors in a religious migrant network engage in constructing a transnational social field? On a broad historical level, the "transnational agents" described in this chapter are following the vision of late nineteenth- and early twentieth-century religious missionaries from western Europe and the United States to Argentina. That vision, one with an elective affinity to capitalist expansion, was to go out into the world and spread the Christian gospel. While there is a discursive similarity between the old wave of English-speaking missionaries to Argentina and the new cadre of Latin American convert missionaries described here, the latter find themselves in a world of rapid and accessible communications that enhances their ability to "span" the world. They do this by building and maintaining a social field with actors in the United States, Spain, Honduras, and Argentina.

Why do these particular people engage in activities across national borders? From the actors' perspective (both ordinary members and others who became leaders and missionaries), engaging in activities beyond geopolitical borders is part of responding to the divine call to spread the gospel. Heeding the call implies considerable personal and family sacrifice (e.g., loss of income, home, and family network). At the same time, sacrifices made for the sake of following a divine call elicit the admiration and respect of congregation members. Those who go to the mission field merit considerable social status among ordinary members. This explanation should not be construed as questioning the personal motivation of transnational leaders. My contention is that, given the religious frame of reference briefly outlined previously, it is understandable that the actors described here choose the transnational religious sphere as an alternative career path and status attainment venue. Midlevel service-sector jobs in the United States, no matter how profitable, do not offer the level of status and/or meaning to which these people aspired. It is not surprising that most church leaders who remained in the United States when others left for the mission field work in middle-class occupations (accounting, engineering, and technology). While becoming a missionary represents significant financial downward mobility (at least initially), it also offers a career path with potentially high-status yields.

Few studies of transnational phenomena consider local-level data over a period as long as the one considered here. Even fewer give full attention to sociocultural, particularly religious, phenomena. Nor do they emphasize the distinctive role of and logic deployed by cultural agents in a religious field. Finally, recent work has not clearly shown the mechanisms by which transnational ties involve change in the sending and receiving communities. By studying the evolution of this religious field over a forty-year period, I show the actual mechanisms by which receiving communities influence sending communities and vice versa.

Data, Methods, and Context

The data discussed in this chapter came from several ethnographic methods (participant observation, informal interviews, and semistructured intensive interviews) that I employed during the RENIR I and II projects. I observed the activities of a Protestant congregation in Houston, Texas (ICE), composed primarily of Argentines (50 percent) but with a considerable representation of Mexican (16 percent), Central American (14 percent), other South American (10 percent), and Caribbean immigrants (8 percent). I interviewed members, leaders, and converts, including first- and second-generation representatives in each category. I spent about thirty months as a participant observer of this congregation, during which time I conducted intensive interviews with fifteen converts, twenty first- and second-generation leaders, and eight second-generation members. In addition, I informally interviewed more than 50 church members in a variety of contexts, and I gathered socioeconomic data on 270.

It became clear during RENIR I that Argentine migrants maintain significant ties to their community and congregations of origin. Therefore, in RENIR II, I have focused on transnational ties between the ICE in Houston and congregations in Mendoza and neighboring Luján, Argentina. I spent the summer of 1999 in Argentina observing these congregations and interviewing church leaders and members. I spoke to thirty-two people in formal interviews and more than eighty people in less formal contexts. I also spent a considerable amount of time observing and participating in congregational life during the two-month period and was able to attend the annual meeting of all Argentine Brethren leaders. In June–July 2000, I followed up with additional questions to leaders and members in Houston and attended services and weekday activities at the newly completed Family Ministries Center.[1]

Changing Field Configuration

In examining how the transnational religious field changed over time, I consider two intertwined dimensions of religious transformation: structural (who is part of the social network and what are the symbolic boundaries between subgroups) and cultural (what resources flow in what directions and with what effect). I find that this particular transnational religious field is best understood by studying changing resource flows between Houston and other network congregations. Over the past forty years, the social field in which actors from Houston, Mendoza, and Luján interact has changed in terms of who is involved, the relative positioning of actors, the resources exchanged, and the frequency of interactions. In broad strokes, during the early stage of settlement in the United States, economic resources flowed primarily from Houston to Mendoza and Luján, while cultural resources followed a reverse route. Subsequently, economic flows to the South continued, but the flow of cultural resources became more reciprocal, after which cultural resources began to follow a North-to-South route. Recently, financial transfers from Houston to Argentina have all but disappeared (or shifted to other regions), while cultural flows from the North have become more hegemonic. The following paragraphs weave together the stories of key actors in the field-building and maintenance endeavor. A brief history of the Brethren in Argentina and Mendoza provides an important frame for these stories.

The Brethren in Mendoza, Argentina

The Plymouth Brethren movement emerged in 1829 to "unite all true believers in a biblical fellowship, reacting against institutionalism and ecclesiology" (Douglas 1970:117). The founders were a group of young men from Trinity College, Dublin, who sought to promote worship and fellowship across denominational barriers. They advocated a straightforward reading of the Bible that emphasized the grassroots, anti-institutional perspective of the church in New Testament times (Bruce 1993). The movement was a reaction to Methodism and a highly structured ecclesiastical apparatus in Great Britain (Lang 1955; Wilson 1967). Initially, the movement was ecumenical in scope and included Anglicans, Presbyterians, and Methodists. It spread rapidly throughout England, continental Europe, and then to the New World, where it continued to develop according to regional factors.

The Plymouth Brethren arrived in Argentina just as the phenomenal immigration flow from Europe got under way in the late nineteenth and early twentieth centuries.[2] In contrast to the ethnic Protestant denominations that emerged with the great migratory wave to Argentina, the Plymouth Brethren did not identify with a specific immigrant enclave and made significant efforts to recruit "Argentines" of various national origins. Along with other evangelical denominations, the Brethren were responsible for much of the increase in the Argentine Protestant population (Enns 1971; Martin 1990; Monti 1969). Beginning in 1882, Brethren lay missionaries traveled throughout Argentina, employed by British railroads, banks, and other commercial ventures. Lay[3] and professional missionaries alike were, in historically complex ways, influential agents of Northern cultural hegemony (cf. Comaroff and Comaroff 1991:7ff.).

The Brethren came to the province of Mendoza in the early 1920s and were relatively successful among the working class and those aspiring to the middle class. Jaime Russell, an English missionary, started a small group in the provincial capital (also called Mendoza) that became the first Brethren congregation in the area. Members of the Mendoza congregation eventually founded a church in nearby Luján de Cuyo. Brethren congregations in Mendoza and Luján were composed primarily of Italian and Spanish migrants and their descendants (although there were also immigrants from Holland, Czechoslovakia, and France) as well as Creoles. The first members of the Brethren congregations in Mendoza and Luján were generally craftsmen, farmers, or vineyard workers; only a handful were professionals. However, the next generation was expected to attend school and pursue a traditional profession (medicine, accounting, or engineering). Although some pursued higher education at local public universities, many moved from the vineyard to newly built oil refineries. Not content with the long-term prospects offered by either of these alternatives in a context of declining economic possibilities, others migrated to Buenos Aires or abroad. Many had already made the geographically less distant move from the small town of Luján to the city of Mendoza. Socioeconomically, Mendoza became a more affluent congregation than Luján, where even today many members are part of the working poor.

Emergence and Consolidation of the ICE in Houston (1958–72)

In the mid-1950s, dissatisfied with the opportunities available in Argentina, some of the church youth in Mendoza and Luján decided to migrate to the United States. Gabriel, the first youth to migrate to Houston (via Buenos Aires), investigated work possibilities extensively at the local American Cultural Institute. He also talked about his plans with the American missionary, who was serving as pastor to the Mendoza congregation. Gabriel traveled to the United States in 1957 with the American missionary's son, Alex Clifford. After a failed attempt at finding work in Miami, he followed Alex to Houston. Alex's relatives offered Gabriel two weeks' worth of hospitality and then helped him find room and board at the local YMCA.

Gabriel quickly found work as a waiter at a local continental restaurant and advanced to a managerial position. He was able to offer siblings, relatives, and friends migrating from Argentina work on arrival. As more people from Mendoza and Luján arrived and found employment (in the restaurant industry or in other parts of the rapidly expanding service sector), the options for subsequent migrants multiplied. The initial cohort had at least a high school education, and some had technical and/or university training. According to several informants, service-sector employers preferred Argentines both to other Latin American nationalities and to African Americans for supervisory jobs.

The exodus of capable young men and women, as aging leaders in Mendoza still refer to this process, was deeply felt by the congregations in Luján and Mendoza. This is not surprising when one considers that most Brethren congregations are financially self-supporting and lay led. Not only did membership drop precipitously (four large family groups left in a three-year period), the cohort of emerging young leaders was almost totally depleted. Further, the departure of a large contingent for the United States happened at a time of infrastructural expansion: Both Mendoza and Luján were engaged in building bigger facilities. At least one new ministry in an outlying neighborhood was affected by the departure of young leaders. Younger leaders and the numerical growth of both congregations eventually filled the vacuum left by emigrants to the United States.

As more Argentines arrived in Houston, they began to hold religious services in the facilities of an American Brethren congregation (1959–62). Although the native Brethren apparently did not object to meeting with the Argentine contingent, according to informants on both sides, each had a different style and language of worship that made it difficult to worship together. At this point, the Argentines organized their worship and ministry to replicate the Mendoza and Luján practices as closely as possible. "In the first years," recalls one female participant, "this was an almost exclusively Argentine club." Theologically, the group was very dependent on Mendoza. For example, even as late as the early 1970s, the pastor of the Mendoza congregation sent recorded sermons to which Houston members listened during Sunday worship service. Visiting preachers from Argentina were received with considerable deference. The general orientation during the early phase of the Houston congregation's life was to replicate the way things were done in Argentina.

The group continued to grow and arranged to meet in the garage of another English-speaking Brethren congregation (1963–67). By 1967, it had grown significantly through migration and evangelizing efforts, and the leaders decided to purchase a house to use as a meeting place. During this time, two highly respected lay preachers from Buenos Aires visited Houston and encouraged the new congregation to start an evangelistic radio ministry and to think about ways to evangelize beyond the Argentine population. The radio ministry was successful in recruiting other Latin Americans, many of whom are still members. A prison ministry and a crisis hot line in Spanish were added to the congregation's ministerial repertoire, partly because of the visiting preachers' inspiration. Houston leaders remember these projects as a turning point in the congregation's ministerial vision. One woman, who was gone for a three-year period during this time, recalls that on returning she "found the church totally changed. They had started a radio program at a secular Mexican station and at the end of each program Bibles would be offered" and then delivered by a church member. It was no longer an "exclusively Argentine club." The possibility of reaching a more inclusively defined Spanish-speaking audience became an increasingly influential frame of reference for the church. Accounts by members and leaders suggest the emergence of a tension in the congregation's discourse between the universalistic cast of the gospel and the strong kinship ties among Argentine members, a tension that was to grow in the following decades.[4]

As the members of the congregation became more established, they sent financial remittances to their relatives and also designated gifts for the ministry in Mendoza. Don Pedro, who became pastor of the Mendoza congregation in the early 1960s, views financial remittances to church members as an indirect contribution to the church. On the one hand, financial remittances meant that the church would not have to support members in need, as it might otherwise be obligated to do. On the other hand, members' giving increased as a result of funds received from relatives in the United States. Further, Don Pedro received gifts designated for him personally, as the following field note excerpt illustrates:

> [Don Pedro] relates an experience where he was personally affected by an offering sent from Houston. As a Brethren missionary he had no guaranteed income but received "offerings" every month. He had been wanting to make a missionary trip to the Patagonia where he had ministered in the past. One day he was very ill. . . . A Christmas card arrived [from Gabriel Gaston in Houston]. When Don Pedro opened it, he found a $100 bill. . . . He was very impressed by this. He knew it had to be for a specific purpose since in the past he had also received money like this to meet a specific need. . . . He prayed about what to do with this money. He asked his wife for a little piece of paper where he had come up with an itinerary and budget for his missionary trip to Patagonia. . . . When he looked at his budget it came out to $98. He then called his brother-in-law and they set out on their trip. . . . When he returned . . . a month later he had $25 left over. This was one of many experiences where God used someone from the US to allow them to carry out a ministry here in Argentina.

Don Pedro also received equipment that would help his ministry (e.g., a reel-to-reel recorder used to record sermons and take them to the sick or send them to the United States). However, direct congregation-to-congregation contributions were and remain rare.

In 1969, the ICE in Houston purchased a church facility from an English-speaking Brethren congregation that was moving to the suburbs. It was considerably larger than the small house where the congregation had been meeting, but it too was soon full to capacity. Migration from Argentina and various recruitment ministries continued. By the early 1970s, attendance averaged between 180 and 200 on Sundays. From this point forward, the ICE continued to expand its ministries, particularly in other countries.

The Missionary Phase (1973–93)

The increase in church membership coincided with and was fueled by a vision of missionary expansion. In the early 1970s, the leaders and members increasingly shared a sense that they were to take the gospel message to the ends of the earth. For example, a church missionary recalls being motivated

> to go to Spain by Juan Gerardi, a traveling evangelist from Barcelona who visited Houston in the early 70s. Gerardi knew of the Houston congregation through

contacts in Argentina. Esteban felt that because Spain had no knowledge of the Scriptures and the gospel, he should go there. After praying about this for some time and talking to the church elders, he and his wife decided to go to Spain. (Field notes)

Three families were "commissioned" as missionaries.[5] One went to Honduras, one to Spain, and a third to a rural village in Mendoza. In addition, three other families who were active in the Houston congregation returned to Argentina for work reasons, became active lay leaders there, and maintained ties to Houston. Several of the families that left during this time were charter members of the ICE and very active in church ministries. However, the level of participation was such that several strong leaders remained in Houston. Those who left and those who stayed shared strong bonds of friendship and family that were important to future mission projects. The adults in each of the missionary families, as well as several ICE members who returned to Argentina, were to act as carriers of ministerial, ritual, and theological innovation. In the following sections, I give a detailed account of one missionary couple and briefly discuss two others as well as lay leaders who became liaisons between Houston and other congregations. I focus on camp ministries as an illustration of a ministerial model developed in Houston, used in Spain and Mendoza, and "reengineered" for an urban context in Houston.

THE GASTONS. Who are the cultural agents and engineers of the transnational social field that came to encompass actors in the United States, Argentina, Spain, and Honduras? My travel companions on the trip from Houston to Argentina are among their number. Mary Gaston is the Argentine-born daughter of American Brethren missionaries. She had some tertiary education and experience in business administration before she immigrated to Houston. In the Mendoza congregation, Mary had been very active in lay ministries among poor children. In the United States, she worked at home raising four children and was an active leader among the church's women. She and her husband, Esteban, are charter members of the Houston congregation. Before emigrating, Esteban was a youth leader of the Mendoza congregation and by his late twenties an elder at the ICE in Houston. He is a graduate of a prestigious preparatory school in Mendoza but did not attend college. In Houston, he worked as an installer for a successful interior design firm. Even by current standards, the Gastons were financially well off. Yet there was a disjuncture between the relatively high status accorded leaders at the ICE and the status of a manual services worker. In the religious sphere, congregation members ascribed to Esteban and other church leaders a degree of status not readily available in the workplace (cf. Warner and Wittner 1998:25). In this sense, the religious sphere, particularly the transnational social field, became an alternative status attainment venue.

In 1973, the Gastons left Houston to become missionaries in Spain, where they spent eight years. Once there, they founded a Brethren church and helped develop a camp/retreat ministry still in operation. Esteban gained a reputation among Brethren in Spain, the United States, and Argentina as a charismatic speaker and an effective organizational leader. While in Spain, he was invited to Argentina and Houston for religious conferences. Not all was smooth sailing, however. The Gastons struggled to make it financially on a meager and unpredictable missionary salary. Both Esteban and Mary became ill during their time in Spain and struggled with the aftereffects for many years. The Gaston children struggled in the very rigid educational system of Franco's Spain.

The Gastons' links to evangelicals in Spain were to have a long-lasting impact on Mendoza and Houston. For example, the Gastons became friends with Mariano Gonzalez-Navarro, a computer systems consultant and well-known Spanish Brethren theologian. They introduced him to leaders in Houston and Mendoza who then regularly invited him to speak at conferences and special lecture series. Gonzalez-Navarro recruited a young leader from Mendoza who now pastors a church in northwestern Spain. Another young Argentine leader spent time in Spain ministering in various congregations, and two others are being recruited to work with churches in that country, all through contacts with Gonzalez-Navarro.

In 1982, the Gastons moved to Mendoza, where they served as missionaries for a brief period before settling in Luján. They ministered there until 1993. In addition to pastoral duties in Luján, Esteban and Mary were charged by several congregations in the greater Mendoza area with starting a camp/retreat center. During an interview and subsequent visit to the *Parque Evangélico Fuente de Vida* (Fountain of Life Evangelical Park), Esteban explained that his vision was originally to develop something along the lines of the retreat center in Spain. In turn, the model for that camp was loosely based on what Esteban learned from his experiences at Brethren camp facilities in west Texas, where he served as a church retreat director and, along with several others, had spiritually consequential experiences such as feeling "a call" to become a missionary or a leader in the church. On a more mundane level, Esteban knew the administrative inner workings of a retreat center through his service on the camp board.

Thus, the park in Mendoza drew on experiences garnered in the United States and Spain. It would have lodgings for large and small groups; a multipurpose building for meetings and indoor sports activities; soccer fields; tennis, volleyball, and basketball courts; as well as swimming pools, gazebos, and other amenities. The land not used for park activities would be cultivated and used to sustain the project. How to accomplish this in the midst of severe economic instability proved to be a challenge. Esteban met it by drawing on his connections in the United States and Spain. In fact, the park was built primarily with donations from two or three wealthy Houstonians who funded the project primarily because Esteban asked. Esteban also negotiated a legal status for the park independent of any one particular congregation, and this facilitated the solicitation of funds overseas. In addition, Esteban served as chairman of the nonprofit foundation board that administered Brethren schools and properties in the province of Mendoza. In fact, he reorganized the nonprofit church association very much along the lines of the 401 (b) he had known in Houston. In the process, control of church assets shifted from the Brethren denominational board in Buenos Aires to Mendoza. Esteban's status on this national board, where he also served as a member, made this transfer of organizational power relatively uneventful.

In 1993, Mary and Esteban returned to Houston with an offer to oversee the development of a new family ministries center. Leaders of the Houston congregation, now close to 300 members, wanted to build a complex that incorporated features of a camp or retreat center with those of a multipurpose community center. The Gastons were involved in the purchase of a fifteen-acre plot in a growing Houston suburb and in the design and implementation of the project. They concluded the first phase of the project in September 1999 but are still involved in its ongoing operation. For anyone familiar with the retreat center in Mendoza, the conceptual similarities are striking, yet the urban location and array of services to be offered at the complex sets the Family Ministries Center (FMC) apart as a distinctive adaptation to local circumstances.

During the past eight years, the Gastons have continued their involvement in the administration of the retreat center in Argentina. The official administrator, Esteban's former project foreman, calls weekly from Argentina to consult about park matters. He also visits Houston on a regular basis to assist Esteban in the arduous building project. During visits to Mendoza (generally twice a year), the Gastons spend considerable time ministering in Luján and attending to park matters.

THE SABBATINIS. Shortly after the Gastons moved to Spain, Houston sent a second missionary couple to Argentina. Evelyn and Gabriel Sabbatini have spent most of the past twenty-five years in the province of Entre Ríos, in northeastern Argentina, where they minister to a Brethren congregation of German immigrants. Before leaving Houston, their socioeconomic profile was very similar to that of the Gastons. In Houston, Evelyn worked at home raising three children and was an active leader in the women's group. Gabriel was a very successful salesperson at a high-end decorating supplies firm. He had among the highest incomes in the congregation before he "heard the call to the mission field." Like the Gastons, the Sabbatinis were also oriented to the church community as a source of social recognition. As they became well known in Brethren circles in Argentina, they gained considerable status both there and in Houston.

The Sabbatinis started a camp/retreat center in a rural area of Entre Ríos much like the one the Gastons had developed in Spain. In fact, they visited the Gastons in Spain at least twice and were also familiar with the retreat center in west Texas. They eventually moved to the retreat center and developed a self-sustaining project through the sale of agricultural products and organic fruits, jams, and so on, something that the park in Mendoza has not been able to achieve.

In the mid-1970s, the Sabbatinis, along with the Gastons, attended a religious conference in Germany where they made contacts with German evangelical organizations that later funded significant portions of the project in Entre Ríos. The participation of German immigrants in the Entre Ríos Brethren congregation had been attractive to these organizations. The camp/retreat center also received funds from Houston. The Sabbatinis traveled to Houston on a regular basis, particularly after their children returned to the United States for college. Their daughters married two cousins from Córdoba, another Argentine province, who are now worship leaders.

The Sabbatinis played a key role in adding new actors to the religious network emerging between the United States and Argentina. Their contacts with Brethren churches in nearby Santa Fe initiated a relationship between these congregations and the ICE that persists to this day. For example, Rodolfo Donati, a lay preacher from Santa Fe, visited the ICE at least once a year over the last decade. A missionary from his congregation who works with street children regularly approaches ICE members for funding. Other acquaintances from Santa Fe congregations visit Houston regularly and are a source of renewed Argentine influence in the congregation.

In the early 1990s, the Sabbatinis spent two years in Houston working with a church-planting ministry and in fact founded a congregation composed primarily of Central American members. They recently returned to Houston, where their children now live. They continue to be involved in the administration of the camp facility in Entre Ríos and maintain contact with Brethren in various Argentine provinces. The Sabbatinis also collaborate with the FMC and perform pastoral duties at the ICE.

THE LOPEZES. A third missionary couple went to Honduras at about the same time the Gastons and the Sabbatinis left for Spain and Argentina. Both Fernando and Lucia were employed in the oil and gas industry in Houston and were very comfortable financially. Like the Gastons and the Sabbatinis, the Lopez family started a camp/retreat center in Honduras. In addition, because of the significant medical needs in the semirural region where they settled, the Lopezes established a community medical center. They have become highly respected in Honduras and frequently travel to Houston for visits and to participate in church conferences and retreats. Church members travel to Honduras and serve on short-term projects. One elderly woman spends several months at a time helping the Lopezes in Honduras. While this part of the Houston network has not been very influential in Argentina, it recently benefited from the Houston–Argentina link. After Hurricane Mitch devastated Honduras in 1998, the Lopezes funneled almost $30,000 in direct aid to victims. As word of the catastrophe spread from congregation to congregation over the Internet, funds were sent from all over the United States, Spain, and Argentina to Houston. An elder in the ICE opened a special account and in turn transferred the funds to the Lopezes in Honduras. The Houston congregation also coordinated shipment of a large container with vital supplies for hurricane victims. All this happened before other nonprofit organizations in Houston were able to figure out how to get aid to Honduras. Through this event, the Houston ICE gained considerable visibility among Brethren congregations elsewhere in the United States, Europe, and Argentina.

LAY FAMILIES FROM HOUSTON. During my visit to Argentina, it became clear that it was not only missionaries who contributed to the emergence and maintenance of a transnational religious field but also several lay families that returned to Argentina in the mid-1970s (about three couples and their families). As it happens, these couples were close friends with the Sabbatinis and the Gastons. While they were active in supporting the camp ministry, they also initiated several ministries that were innovations in the Argentine context. For example, Nidia and Fernando, two native *Mendocinos*, recalled the success of home Bible studies started in Mendoza by one of these couples in 1977. Hosts to one of these gatherings, Nidia and Fernando recounted how surprising it was to find themselves discussing spiritual matters with neighbors, many of whom they had known superficially for many years. The church in Mendoza started to grow as people from these neighborhood groups began coming to Sunday services as well as in response to several other innovations introduced by the couples from Houston. In addition to developing a fifty-member choir with "serious rehearsals" and auditions, one migrant returnee started a Sunday school for adults and a weekend Bible school. Several youth who had drifted from the church in the tempestuous 1970s returned to engage in serious theological discussions. While Nidia and Fernando tell this as a story of the church's own returning to minister in Argentina, it is clear that these innovations, which are common practices in Houston, constitute a clear case of Northern influence on Argentine congregations. These couples also renewed friendships and social ties at a time when the congregations in Houston and Argentina were slowly drifting apart. Their influence continues to be felt as they travel on a regular basis between Mendoza and Houston.

The Gastons, Sabbatinis, and other families were frequently mentioned in interviews as influential leaders in Mendoza and Luján. Camp ministries, home

Bible studies, and liturgical innovation are some of the topics that arose often during interviews. I have focused primarily on the camp ministry because it is relatively easy to trace the origin of this ministerial model and its adaptations by actors in the different locations of the transnational social field examined here. While the foregoing account privileges the role of specific individuals, one should keep in mind that, for the most part, they were acting in an organizational capacity. An *organization* encompasses historically specific, well-bounded clusters of social relationships in which people in one position have the right to commit collective resources across boundaries (Roy and Parker-Gwin 1999; Tilly 1998). The Gastons, Sabbatinis, and others were in Mendoza, Luján, and Spain with the support of, and in keeping with the evangelistic philosophy of, the Houston congregation. Simply put, they acted with a mandate from the Houston congregation: They were elders or acknowledged lay leaders in Houston and/or commissioned as missionaries (which involved financial and organizational support). Argentine denominational leaders also recognized them as leaders. Thus, they were able to mobilize resources (financial and symbolic) across borders and affect the congregations of Houston, Mendoza, Luján, and elsewhere (e.g., the creation of multifunctional retreat centers in Mendoza, Entre Ríos, and most recently Houston). Their links to Houston, along with its range of weak and strong network connections in Spain and elsewhere in Europe and the United States, significantly affected Brethren congregations in Argentina. They continue to act as carriers of ideas and practices between congregations, demonstrating that this process is at least somewhat reciprocal. In sum, a small number of Houston leaders have had a significant impact on ministerial practices and network extension in Mendoza, Luján, and Houston. They are the clearest example of organizational links and influences between nodes in a changing transnational web of Brethren organizations.

Houston as the Established Core of the Network (1994–2001)

The Houston ICE gained considerable recognition in Brethren circles because of the Family Ministries Center. As the project became a reality and visitors perceived it as a success, Houston's position as an important player in a transnational religious field became consolidated. If in the early 1970s the ICE was viewed as an energetic and (possibly overly) ambitious congregation, the ties established between Honduras, Argentina, Spain, and the United States, as well as the success of the projects undertaken by its representatives, confirmed to people in the know that this was a trendsetting congregation. Indeed, four of the main speakers at the 1999 national leadership conference for Brethren in Argentina (with the theme "Evangelization for the Twenty-First Century") were from the ICE, including the keynote speaker. In a workshop presented by a Houston missionary and a lay leader, Argentine church leaders asked many questions about the sorts of ministe-rial strategies that these two leaders saw as most important for the twenty-first century. It was clear in these exchanges that Argentine leaders were very interested in and deferred to the opinions of the speakers because of the Houston congre-gation's success in various ministries and its key role in binding together believers in the several countries.

Transnational Social Fields and the Children of Immigrants

To recapitulate briefly, as migrant networks between Mendoza and Houston be-came established and as migrants in Houston acted on their global evangelistic vi-sion, a religious field encompassing several countries emerged. Actors and their rel-ative importance in the field changed. At one time, religious actors from Mendoza were relatively more influential in the religious field. Over time, however, religious actors from the North gained greater ascendancy, and they looked to the more or-ganizationally sophisticated actors in the South for interaction (e.g., leaders in Buenos Aires). Houston's transnational actors also developed important ties with religious organizations in Europe, particularly Spain. The previous account shows that the religious field spanning Houston and other cities is largely the product of efforts by a small number of people (even if a broader range of field participants were impacted by their activities). What happens when these key players are no longer active? Will this field continue to exist once its mostly first-generation par-ticipants become inactive? As the burgeoning literature on the children of post-1965 immigrants shows,[6] the answer to these questions depends largely on their role in transnational social fields.

Participant observation of and interviews with children of immigrants at the ICE underscore the precariousness of the religious field described previously. Given a limited institutionalization of transnational ties, the very existence of a transna-tional social field depends on the participation of the children of immigrants. Pre-liminary findings in a new exploration of immigrants' children at the ICE point in the direction of different experiences among the misleadingly titled "second gener-ation." However, even when taking into account age and differential experiences in terms of the community's maturity in the U.S. context, one is left with a very dis-tinct impression that, insofar as its future depends on the children of immigrants, the religious field described is close to its demise or that, at best, the ties that sus-tain it may survive but serve some other purpose (e.g., to facilitate future migration). The experiences of Terry, Dylan, and Pablo illustrate the possibilities and challenges to the persistence of the transnational social field examined earlier in this chapter.

Terry grew up in the ICE as the youngest of three children. Her parents are founding members of the congregation. Her early childhood friends were mostly from church. However, as she became older, Terry developed friendships and relationships with children from school and later from her dance troupe. In Terry's estimation, an important difference between her experiences and those of her siblings is that she was allowed much more frequent interaction with people outside the church (whom she often conflates with "Americans"). She attributes this to her independent personality and rebellious streak. She cites an example of bringing home an American boyfriend whom she knew her parents would not like (he wore earrings and did not attend church) and recalls her siblings' astonishment when she confronted her parents. Becky, her older sister, confirms that she could not get away with confronting her parents like Terry. Traveling on a trip to Guatemala with her then fiancé and now husband was another action that Terry's siblings would never have been allowed to carry out.

Distinguishing herself from her parents and siblings as an independent, self-sufficient American woman, Terry nevertheless identifies much more strongly than her siblings as "Hispanic," an identification she associates with her parents' "Argentineness" and as a "nonwhite" category. Although she has been to Argentina only once, as a toddler, she feels very drawn to exploring these ties. Visits by two of her cousins during her sister's wedding prompted her to foster family connections. She now maintains almost daily contact with them by e-mail. She also tracked down the e-mail address of a cousin who lives in Buenos Aires with whom she corresponds regularly. They view family pictures on their respective web pages.

Interestingly, religious ties are missing from this account. Terry attends the ICE about once a month. She feels somewhat alienated from her parents and relatives because they hassle her about her dancing profession. As a performer of Latin American folkloric dances, she feels that this is a way to connect herself and the teenagers in her troupe to a common heritage. Terry is aware of missionaries who worked in Argentina, Spain, and elsewhere, but she does not know the details of their connections in various countries, and these do not seem very relevant to her life. Were the ICE to continue its focus on local activities while transnational ties became frayed or severed, she would not feel at all affected. The opportunity to teach Latin American folklore to youngsters at church is what matters to her. Thus, while symbolic ethnicity is important to Terry, the maintenance of organizational ties to Argentina is a pursuit very distant from her everyday experiences and desires.

Dylan, on the other hand, has a much greater appreciation of current ties with religious organizations outside the United States. His father is the main leader who remained in Houston during the missionary phase outlined earlier and the main link to North American Brethren churches and organizations. Dylan is being groomed to lead the youth and, someday, the congregation. He also had an experience very distinct from that of his four older siblings. He attributes this to coming of age in the 1990s rather than in the 1980s. Growing up in the 1980s meant that his siblings' lives revolved largely around ethnic community activities. In the 1990s, Dylan was much more attuned to American society and had many ties outside the Latino community. Church has been central to his life experience. He even relearned Spanish so that he could be a more effective church leader. During the summer of 2000, Dylan visited a large church in Buenos Aires that has an urban as well as rural ministry, especially for poor children. In Argentina, he met a young woman whom he began dating. One would expect Dylan to be the perfect candidate to foster existing ties with religious organizations in Latin America and Europe. Indeed, he is the only person of his generation to return to Argentina for an internship. Nevertheless, he believes that the Family Ministries Center will be the focus of his ministry. His frame of reference is clearly in the United States. He is now in his second year of premedical studies and does not even consider the possibility of living in Argentina or elsewhere (although he continues to date an Argentine woman).

Pablo, the oldest child of immigrants I interviewed, would appear to be a more likely candidate to succeed in the maintenance of religious transnational ties. He came to the United States at age four. His father was one of the main leaders who remained at the ICE while others left as overseas missionaries. In the early 1980s, Pablo, his father, and several others left the ICE and founded a splinter charismatic group called *Aguas Vivientes* (Living Waters). The initial core group was largely Argentine but self-consciously sought to incorporate people of other Latin American origins. The group grew tremendously and by the early 1990s had a Sunday attendance of 500 to 700. Pablo became the senior pastor, and in 1994 the church purchased the facilities of a television station. Since the mid-1980s, Pablo, his father, and a cousin have traveled to Argentina, Colombia, Chile, and Venezuela on a regular basis. They established several churches, including one in Mendoza, as an extension of the U.S. ministry. Pablo's church also became affiliated with a North American charismatic denomination that saw these transnational ties as an indicator of Living Waters' potential to minister to Latin Americans living in the United States. As these congregations became self-sustaining, Pablo traveled less frequently and was less involved in transnational religious activities, although his father continues to travel for speaking engagements. Pablo's interest turned increasingly to the life of his congregation in Houston and professional opportunities in the religious market. He is currently writing a book about ministerial possibilities among Hispanics. His children, although very involved in church activities, would never consider going to Argentina other than for brief visits.

These three examples illustrate the array of experiences and the potential for maintaining a transnational religious field. Terry, generally representative of many younger children of immigrants, is focused on the ICE to the extent that it can bolster her sense of symbolic ethnicity. Her contemporary, Dylan, is much more involved in ICE organizational activities and has a relatively comprehensive knowledge of ties with religious organizations in other countries although little interest in actively pursuing them. Pablo, closer in his experiences to Terry's and Dylan's older siblings, has been an actual participant in a transnational religious field but has withdrawn his attention from it. Whatever the significance of their differential experiences, and despite differences in perceived potential as transnational religious actors, none of these children of immigrants seems inclined to participate in the sort of religious field described earlier. I conclude that its days are numbered.

Under what circumstances might one expect a different outcome? The field might persist if other actors became more proactive in maintaining ties. This will likely be the case if religious actors find a mutually beneficial point of exchange, for example, if Argentine congregations are able to offer religious workers that match Houston's needs. Given the low participation by immigrants' children as church leaders, projects such as the Family Ministries Center may drive up the demand for religious workers from elsewhere. Uninterrupted migration streams from Argentina and other Latin American countries may drive this demand even further. In the course of three months in 2000, five people from different parts of Argentina appeared on the doorsteps of the Sabbatinis and Gastons in Houston looking for help in settling. These people's children were about the same age as the children of some second-generation members. This means that third-generation children are being exposed to newly arrived migrants with strong connections to Argentina. If this new migration coincides with an increasing valuation of symbolic ethnicity by current children of immigrants, transnational religious ties may be fostered. Thus, the strength of future migration streams likely will play a major role in determining whether transnational ties are maintained in the future.

From a more explicitly organizational perspective, ties that contribute to the maintenance of a transnational space may come into play if they are perceived to provide some sort of advantage in the local or global ethnic and/or religious market. For example, to be perceived by American-based denominational organizations as a trendsetting congregation with strong ties to Latin America and innovative ministries among Hispanics may put the ICE at a competitive advantage in terms of available resources for programs. Indeed, the ICE and the Family Ministries Center have already started to reap the benefits of such a position. Likewise, when the religious marketplace is thought to include the entire Spanish-speaking world, strong relations to Latin America and Spain are likely to be fostered and maintained much more instrumentally than they have been thus far. However, this would be the case only if strong relations with Latin America were associated with an ability to minister in the U.S. ethnoreligious market.

In brief, contrary to Glick Schiller's (1999:96) hunch that transnational social fields may persist beyond the first generation, I conclude that their durability requires a possible but as yet unrealized change in circumstances. Further, one can envision other scenarios that would limit the persistence of transnational social fields, at least in the more restricted sense used in this chapter. For example, migration policies could change and migration streams could be interrupted.[7]

Conclusions

How and why did the transnational religious field with actors in Spain, Honduras, the United States, and Argentina come to be and change over the past four decades? Building on the migration network spanning Mendoza and Houston, certain actors became key leaders, first at the local level and then in the transnational field they helped generate. With time, Argentine immigrants in Houston came to exert considerable influence in this field. Why did these particular actors engage in a transnational social field? Inspired by evangelical discourse about spreading the gospel to all nations and at considerable personal cost, religious actors found an alternative career path and status attainment venue, first at the local and then at the transnational level. They generated a field within which they and the ICE congregation came to have considerable weight. However, they also bore the responsibility of maintaining this field. As key transnational players with ties in Houston became less active and returned to Houston, the very existence of the field has come to seem precarious. New generations at the ICE have not seemed interested in maintaining this field. Other venues of status attainment are available to them in the U.S. context to which they are primarily oriented. While portions of this field may survive (e.g., the field encompassing religious organizations in Spain and Argentina), it is likely that it will not persist in its current configuration. Simply put, as some of the players sit out of the religious game, no substitutes step in to keep the ball in play.

What can a case study tell us about transnational social fields more generally? Emigh (1997:657) notes that "generalizability may not be the best use of single case studies. Instead, the role of negative cases in developing the content of theory, not the range of its applicability, may be more important." In this sense, the data presented suggest the need to further conceptualize the conditions affecting the durability of transnational fields. Focusing on the individual careers of organizational actors suggests a logic for understanding when transnational social fields are durable. Insofar as no social capital is at stake in a given field, one would expect that it will not persist. To the extent that children of immigrants no longer need these fields for the same purposes, they will fade or evolve into something very different. Children of immigrants can gain a sense of affiliation with their parents' homeland, if they so desire, without maintaining the sorts of intensive ties found in transnational social fields. They can buy Argentine music in the United States, view the daily news on the Internet, correspond with friends and relatives, and buy ethnic foods without participating in such a field. This also suggests that while time- and space-compressing technologies may have qualitatively affected the experiences of newcomers relative to those of an older generation of migrants, that alone does not ensure the durability of transnational social fields. My findings recommend caution in making claims about the persistence of transnational social fields. A relatively short life span does not imply that a social phenomenon is unworthy of scholarly attention. Indeed, it may weigh on the future of immigrants in very consequential ways. I suggest merely that we consider the historical contingency of transnational phenomena (cf. Al-Ali, Black, and Koser 2001).

Notes

1. In previous work (Cook 2000), I recorded that the ICE purchased fifteen acres of land and began construction of a multifunctional church and community service complex. The first phase of the project was completed in September 1999.

2. According to Skidmore and Smith (1992), the demographic impact of this immigration was the greatest experienced by any country in the Western Hemisphere. Net immigration between 1857 and 1930 was about 3.5 million, and 60 percent of the total increase in population during this period could be attributed to immigration (Rock 1987). About 80 percent of the immigrants to Argentina came from Mediterranean countries; half were Italians, a quarter Spaniards, and the others Ottomans, Russians, French, Germans, and Portuguese. The causes of migration to Argentina were complex (Moya 1998, 2001) but included economic incentives and deliberate government recruitment in Europe. Early immigrants achieved swift social mobility. Immigrants after 1870 remained mostly proletarian (Recchini de Lattes and Lattes 1974; Rock 1987).

3. A significant proportion of Brethren leaders are lay rather than professional clergy. The only significant difference between professional clergy and the laity is a formal recognition by the congregation as an *obrero* (worker). The person may or may not have specialized theological education and may or may not receive a steady salary. The Brethren believe that God provides for his workers on a day-to-day basis. The lay preachers mentioned here paid their own way and combined ministry with business trips. It is no coincidence that many of the Brethren's most popular conference speakers are fairly affluent businessmen and executives.

4. Elsewhere (Cook 2001), I explore how these immigrants from Argentina recognized that their social classificatory "in-betweenness" placed them in an advantaged position from which to capture a portion of the emerging "Hispanic" religious market.

5. This is Brethren-speak for the official recognition of missionary status. "Commissioning" means that the congregation assumes the responsibility of providing financial and

spiritual support for the family (although no fixed amount of financial support is guaranteed).

6. To name just some of the many important contributions: Foner (2000), Portes and Rumbaut (1996, 2001), Portes and Zhou (1993), Waldinger and Perlmann (1997), and Waters (1999). Ebaugh and Chafetz (2000) document the place of children of immigrants in religious communities.

7. This chapter makes only oblique reference to broader macrostructural factors that shaped the development of this transnational religious network. State migration policy is one such factor. The Harts-Cellar Act of 1965 and the 1991 U.S.-Argentina Agreement (by which Argentines could enter the United States without a visa) had a significant impact on the evolution of the transnational social field described here. Missionary leaders were able to enter Spain, Honduras, and Argentina because of the passports they held (generally dual Argentine–U.S. nationality). Thus, a final factor shaping the future of this transnational religious field will be whether the nation-states spanned by it decide to impose restrictive policies. The hard realities of state migration policies and their role in circumscribing the movement of people from the periphery to the core (see Zolberg 1999) is one dimension that seems neglected in some portrayals of transnational phenomena.

References

Al-Ali, Nadje, Richard Black, and Khalid Koser. 2001. "The Limits to 'Transnationalism': Bosnian and Eritrean Refugees in Europe as Emerging Transnational Communities." *Ethnic and Racial Studies* 24:578–600.

Basch, Linda, Nina Glick Schiller, and Cristina Szanton Blanc. 1994. *Nations Unbound: Transnational Projects, Postcolonial Predicaments and Deterritorialized Nation-States.* Langhorne, PA: Gordon and Breach.

Bourdieu, Pierre, and Loïc Wacquant. 1992. *An Invitation to Reflexive Sociology.* Chicago: University of Chicago Press.

Bruce, F. F. 1993. *In Retrospect: Remembrance of Things Past.* Posthumous ed. Grand Rapids, MI: Baker Book House.

Cohen, Robin. 1997. *Global Diasporas: An Introduction.* Seattle: University of Washington Press.

Comaroff, Jean, and John Comaroff. 1991. *Of Revelation and Revolution: Christianity, Colonialism and Consciousness in South Africa.* Chicago: University of Chicago Press.

Cook, David. 2000. "Iglesia Cristiana Evangélica: Arriving in the Pipeline." In *Religion and the New Immigrants: Continuities and Adaptations in Immigrant Congregations,* edited by Helen Rose Ebaugh and Janet Saltzman Chafetz. Walnut Creek, CA: AltaMira.

———. 2001. "Shared Memories as Cultural Resources in a Religious Immigrant Congregation." Paper presented at the annual meeting of the American Sociological Association, Los Angeles, August.

Douglas, Mary. 1970. *Natural Symbols: Explorations in Cosmology.* New York: Pantheon.

Ebaugh, Helen R., and Janet Saltzman Chafetz. 2000. *Religion and the New Immigrants: Continuities and Adaptations in Immigrant Congregations.* Walnut Creek, CA: AltaMira.

Emigh, Rebecca J. 1997. "The Power of Negative Thinking: The Use of Negative Case Methodology in the Development of Sociological Theory." *Theory and Society* 26:649–84.

Enns, Arno W. 1971. *Man, Milieu and Mission in Argentina.* Grand Rapids, MI: Eerdmans.

Foner, Nancy. 2000. *From Ellis Island to JFK: New York's Two Great Waves of Immigration.* New York: Russell Sage Foundation.

Gabaccia, Donna. 1999. "Is Everywhere Nowhere? Nomads, Nations, and the Immigrant Paradigm of United States History." *Journal of American History* 86(December):1115–34.

Glick Schiller, Nina. 1999. "Transmigrants and Nation-States: Something Old and Something New in the U.S. Immigrant Experience." In *The Handbook of International Migration: The American Experience,* edited by Charles Hirschman, Philip Kasinitz, and Josh DeWind. New York: Russell Sage Foundation.

Glick Schiller, Nina, Linda Basch, and Cristina Szanton Blanc, eds. 1992. *Towards a Transnational Perspective on Migration: Race, Class, Ethnicity and Nationalism Reconsidered.* New York: New York Academy of Sciences.

Lang, G. H. 1955. *The Local Assembly: Some Essential Differences between Open and Exclusive Brethren Considered Scripturally and Historically.* Belfast: Raven.

Levitt, Peggy. 1998a. "Local-Level Global Religion: The Case of U.S.-Dominican Migration." *Journal for the Scientific Study of Religion* 37:74–89.

———. 1998b. "Social Remittances: Migration Driven Local-Level Forms of Cultural Diffusion." *International Migration Review* 32:926–48.

Levitt, Peggy, Sunaina Maira, and Teena Purohit. 1997. "From Gujarat, India, to Lowell, Massachusetts: Localized Transnational Hinduism." Paper presented at the Association for the Sociology of Religion, Toronto, August.

Martin, David. 1990. *Tongues of Fire: The Explosion of Protestantism in Latin America.* Oxford: Basil Blackwell.

Monti, Daniel. 1969. *Presencia del Protestantismo en el Río de la Plata Durante el Siglo XIX.* Buenos Aires: Editorial La Aurora.

Moya, Jose C. 1998. *Cousins and Strangers: Spanish Immigrants in Buenos Aires, 1850–1930.* Berkeley: University of California Press.

———. 2001. "Spanish Emigration to Cuba and Argentina." In *Immigration in Latin America,* edited by Samuel Baily. Wilmington, DE: Scholarly Resources.

Portes, Alejandro, Luis E. Guarnizo, and Patricia Landolt. 1999. "The Study of Transnationalism: Pitfalls and Promise of an Emergent Research Field." *Ethnic and Racial Studies* 22:217–37.

Portes, Alejandro, and Min Zhou. 1993. "The New Second Generation: Segmented Assimilation and Its Variants." *Annals of the American Academy (AAPSS)* 530(November):74–96.

Portes, Alejandro, and Rubén Rumbaut. 1996. *Immigrant America: A Portrait.* 2nd ed. Berkeley: University of California Press.

———. 2001. *Legacies: The Story of the Immigrant Second Generation.* Berkeley: University of California Press; New York: Russell Sage Foundation.

Recchini de Lattes, and Zulma y Alfredo Lattes. 1974. *La Población Argentina.* Paris: CICRED.

Roberts, Bryan, Reanne Frank, and Fernando Lozano-Ascencio. 1999. "Transnational Migrant Communities and Mexican Migration to the U.S." *Ethnic and Racial Studies* 22:238–66.

Rock, David. 1987. *Argentina, 1516–1982: From Spanish Colonization to Alfonsín.* Berkeley: University of California Press.

Roy, William G., and Rachel Parker-Gwin. 1999. "How Many Logics of Collective Action?" *Theory in Society* 28:203.

Skidmore, Thomas E., and Peter H. Smith. 1992. *Modern Latin America.* 3rd ed. New York: Oxford University Press.

Soysal, Yasemin N. 1994. *Limits of Citizenship: Migrants and Postnational Membership in Europe.* Chicago: University of Chicago Press.

Tilly, Charles. 1994. *The Weight of the Past on North American Immigration.* Toronto: University of Toronto, Centre for Urban and Community Studies.

———. 1998. *Durable Inequality.* Berkeley: University of California Press.

Waldinger, Roger, and Joel Perlmann. 1997. "Second Generation Decline? Children of Immigrants, Past and Present—A Reconsideration." *International Migration Review* 31:893–923.

Warner, R. Stephen, and Judith G. Wittner, eds. 1998. *Gatherings in Diaspora: Religious Communities and the New Immigration.* Philadelphia: Temple University Press.

Waters, Mary C. 1999. *Black Identities: West Indian Immigrant Dreams and American Realities.* New York: Russell Sage Foundation.

Wilson, Bryan R., ed. 1967. *Patterns of Sectarianism.* London: Heinemann.

Zolberg, Aristide R. 1999. "Matters of State: Theorizing Immigration Policy." In *The Handbook of International Migration: The American Experience,* edited by Charles Hirschman, Philip Kasinitz, and Josh DeWind. New York: Russell Sage Foundation.

Religion and the Process of Migration   4
A Case Study of a Maya Transnational Community

JACQUELINE MARIA HAGAN

espite the diversity and prominence of religious beliefs and practices among immigrants in the contemporary United States, scholars of both immigration and religious studies have only recently begun to explore the role of religion in the migration process. Prominent among this emergent body of literature are a number of case studies that carefully document the functions of the church in immigrant settlement and in the formation of ethnic communities (e.g., Ebaugh and Chafetz 2000; Hurh and Kim 1990; Leonard 1992; Lin 1996; Min 1992; Mullins 1988; Numrich 1996; Warner and Wittner 1998; Waugh 1994). Less well researched is the role of religion in other aspects of the migration process, especially the resources it provides to prospective migrants planning the journey north and the organizational conduit it provides in the development of transnational activities between families and communities in sending and receiving areas (Levitt 2001; studies in this volume).

In this chapter, I attempt to address these various issues by tracing the substantial role played by religion in the migration process of one transnational community. Specifically, I examine (1) the way that spiritual resources provided by religion empower prospective migrants with the will to endure the arduous journey, (2) the network infrastructure religion provides to recent immigrant arrivals, and (3) the transnational fields it helps build between families and communities in sending and receiving areas via resources flowing through migrant- and community-based social networks. The analysis is based on fieldwork among a transnational Maya community that encompasses one municipality in the department of Totonicapan in the western highlands of Guatemala and several neighborhoods of new immigrant settlement in Houston, Texas.

The Research Process

The data in this chapter were collected during two phases of fieldwork among the Maya in Houston and their home community in the Guatemalan highlands. The first phase was conducted in Houston in the late 1980s and early 1990s and produced an ethnography of the development of a Maya immigrant community in Houston (Hagan 1994). In this early research, I lived for several years among the Maya, traveling back and forth from Houston to Guatemala. I followed the development of the Houston Maya community, tracing the role of migrant-based social networks in the successful settlement histories of both pioneer and later migrants. During this early phase of fieldwork, which focused largely on the development of the Maya community social structure, I restricted my examination of religion to the role of the Maya evangelical church in Houston in the settlement of new migrants in the area (Hagan 1994).

The second stage of the field research was done ten years later, in the spring of 2000, when I reentered the community to focus explicitly on the role that religion plays in the migration process of the Maya. I spent two months conducting observations in Maya churches in Houston and then returned to Guatemala, along with a returning migrant and two of my students, for one month of fieldwork in the San Pedro area. During this aspect of the fieldwork, we focused on the development of transnational religious ties on both the organizational and the household level. While in the home community, the four-member research team attended daily services and meetings at three evangelical churches whose members include many congregants who have family in Houston, some of whom were also members of these churches prior to migration. The team also interviewed six evangelical pastors in the area, members from each church, leaders and members of church committees, migrant family members, and a number of return migrants who returned for the *Fiesta Titular*, the annual patron saint's festival. Thus, much of what follows in this chapter goes beyond my direct observations to reflect the stories and experiences recounted by members of the San Pedro transnational migrant community.

The Home Community in Religious and Economic Context

This study focuses on the relationship between migratory and religious activities among members of a largely evangelical Maya community, which stretches from one *municipio* (township, but administratively more like a U.S. county) in the western highlands of Guatemala to several neighborhoods in Houston. The home community, to which I refer with the pseudonym San Pedro, is situated at an elevation of 6,300 feet in the Sierra Madre Mountains in the department of Totonicapan, which is often cited as the birthplace of Protestantism in the Guatemalan highlands (Garrard-Burnett 1998).

The *municipio* of San Pedro includes the town center of San Pedro, seven *cantons* (hamlets), and three *aldeas* (smaller rural farming settlements). According to the most recent census of the area, the *municipio* is home to approximately 28,000 persons, of whom roughly 6,000 live in the town of San Pedro and the remainder in surrounding *cantons* and *aldeas* (Municipal Unidad Tecnica 1999). More than 80 percent of the *municipio*'s residents are of *indigena*, or Maya, origin. Its people speak a local variety of the K'iche' language, although most of the youth also speak Spanish. The majority of the older inhabitants own their own *milpas* (corn plots) and supplement the income from these with remittances from Houston or with artisanal production that they sell in local handicraft stores and in daily markets linked to the highlands' rotating market system. The primary artisanal occupations of San Pedro's residents are weaving and tailoring. As educational levels of youth in the area increase, however, a growing number are entering the urban labor market and assuming professional jobs as teachers, accountants, bank tellers, and the like.

The town center of San Pedro houses two historical Catholic churches, twenty-three evangelical churches, and another dozen or so evangelical ministries housed in the homes of independent ministers. A large majority of the evangelical churches and ministries are Pentecostal and were constructed after 1970, when non-Guatemalan missions and churches were increasingly rejected and the appeal of nationalist churches mushroomed (Garrard-Burnett 1998:116). A small number of the evangelical churches originally established by American missionaries but now under Guatemalan pastorship have been around for decades, but most are recent. Many of these contemporary constructions are spin-offs of existing churches established by native members who wished to begin their own ministry or Guatemalan *indigena* church. It is not uncommon, therefore, to find as many as five or six Church of God or Prince of Peace churches in the *municipio*, each distinguished only by a number following its generic name.

Scholars of religious transformation in Guatemala provide several explanations for the surge in Protestantism in Totonicapan and the western highlands more generally in recent decades. Chief among these is the disruptive effect of state militarization on Maya identity and community in the 1980s (Garrard-Burnett 1998; Green 1999). For example, the repressive campaign by the Guatemalan military against the Catholic Church in the late 1970s and early 1980s, which included among other atrocities the random murder of priests and congregants alike throughout the highlands, sent scores of Catholics fleeing to evangelical meetings (Garrard-Burnett 1998; Green 1999; Stoll and Garrard-Burnett 1993; Wilson 1995). This massive conversion was especially strong and rapid in Totonicapan, where the number of Protestant churches more than tripled in the early 1980s, reaching 270 by the mid-1980s (Garrard-Burnett 1998).

Several additional factors have drawn Guatemalans in general and the Maya specifically to Pentecostal churches. For one, the emotional and spontaneous form of worship in Pentecostal services, especially the practice of speaking in tongues, is especially attractive to the Maya, as these practices resonate with their traditional religious practices. Moreover, to many of the rural poor, the lively and spontaneous Pentecostal services offer free entertainment with which no other local institutions can compete (Garrard-Burnett 1998).

The economic context for understanding the migration from San Pedro to Houston can be traced to the late 1970s, when political conflict in the western highlands, especially the government's counterinsurgency campaigns, constrained the ability of many Maya to participate in the regional marketing system. This, along with increased inflation in the area, forced many households in San Pedro to seek other sources of income, one of which is wage labor in Houston. The costs of migration were high for the pioneers, but over time the development of migrant social networks in Houston lowered the risks for future flows, as new migrants relied increasingly on these networks to cover the financial burden of migration and to assist in initial settlement (Hagan 1994, 1998). When I investigated the Maya settlement process in Houston in the late 1980s, the size of the community had already mushroomed to about 2,000. I now estimate that it surpasses 3,000. Since their initial arrival in the late 1970s, the Totonicapan Maya have developed strong community organizations, including several soccer teams and at least three ethnic evangelical churches that have mission counterparts in the home community. The Maya community in Houston has also maintained strong social ties with the home community, including substantial contact and interaction with kin and friends in the home *municipio.* This occurs through a variety of means, including letters, telephones calls, couriers, and the like. All these means serve to circulate material and nonmaterial resources for ethnic cultural reproduction among the migrant households in Houston and their households of origin in San Pedro. Like an increasing number of immigrant communities in the United States, the first generation of many migrant families from San Pedro have become transnational in their behavior.

The Emergent Role of the Evangelical Church in Preparing for Migration

Migration from San Pedro has become self-perpetuating through the successful operation of migrant social networks and a well-established community structure to accommodate new arrivals (Hagan 1994; Rodriguez 1987). Most prospective migrants now face escalating financial costs and dangerous risks in their attempts to gain entry into the United States. The cost of securing a *coyote* to traverse two heavily guarded international borders, for example, has more than tripled in the past decade, reaching now as high as $4,000 per migrant. To pay the *coyote*, the families of prospective migrants often put up their home as collateral. Moreover, the long trek from the highlands of Guatemala to Houston is a difficult and dangerous one, including thousands of miles of open land with treacherous terrain and often poor weather conditions. Death during the voyage due to environmental hazards is not uncommon; indeed, it has increased in recent years (Eschbach et al. 1999). Consequently, news of migrant deaths is regularly published in local Guatemalan newspapers. In this context of increased costs and dangers, prospective migrants from San Pedro now find themselves turning to evangelical churches to help them prepare spiritually for the arduous journey.

To assist them in their preparations, pastors are contacted, and their advice and prayer in the matter of migration are requested. At these initial meetings, migrants are advised to pray and are challenged about the motivations behind the journey. They are also urged to contemplate the necessity of migration and to think about the potential ramifications for family left behind.

Migrants also seek divine counsel through formal religious services, but, especially and most important, they attend *ayunos*, fasting and informal prayer services, followed by extensive prophesizing. In the Guatemalan highlands, *ayunos* are held in the homes of independent pastors or on designated Maya sacred grounds. In traditional Maya religion, the most sacred grounds for worship are cornfields and mountaintops, which were home to many Maya shrines (Green 1999; Tedlock 1992). Contemporary evangelical pastors who lead *ayunos* have adopted these same locations. Like the shamans of traditional Maya religion, evangelical pastors leading *ayunos* are believed to have the power to hear the will of God for other people, and attendees have steadfast faith in the predictions and prophecies spoken by the pastors, regardless of outcome.

In Totonicapan, the most celebrated *ayuno* for migration counseling is held each Wednesday morning on a mountaintop about ten miles from the town center of San Pedro. It is also the location for monthly vigils, which can last up to forty-eight hours and draw as many as 200 persons from a variety of churches and communities. Every second month, followers make the long trek to attend *ayunos completos*, which can last up to several days and draw as many as 400 persons from nearby villages as well as faraway cities, such as Guatemala City. On the Wednesday morning we attended an *ayuno*, several dozen people showed up to hear the minister. The service began with an *oracion* (conversation with God), followed by *Alabanzas con Dios* (a time of praise and worship during which the spirit of God is experienced by the attendees). The pastor then spoke to the group through God. With Bible in hand, he spoke in tongues, then translated into K'iche'. The form of worship at *ayunos* holds special appeal to the Maya, in that speaking in *lengua* (tongues and then translated into K'iche' rather than Spanish) had historically been central in their traditional religious practices, with glossolalia replacing indigenous prayer that reflected contact with the divine (Garrard-Burnett 1998).

We were unable to communicate directly with the largely K'iche'-speaking attendees during the *ayuno*, but we did have the opportunity to interview the presiding pastor. The pastor, an elderly Maya man and resident of an adjacent province, told us that although attendees seek counseling on a variety of matters, including health and family issues, an increasing number come for migration counseling. For example, one of the attendees on that particular morning, a woman from a nearby village, had come to pray for her son, from whom she had not heard since his departure some weeks earlier. Another attendee, the father of a young migrant, came to pray for his continued success in the United States. According to this pastor, migration counseling has become more central to the *ayunos* because the security of the migrant is increasingly in question. Another pastor of an independent ministry told us that "because the investment is so high, the risk so much, and crossing the borders implies uncertainty, the majority of those in our community who make this voyage are focused on seeking divine intervention in their undertaking." Moreover, for some, the pastor's prophecies at *ayunos* constitute the final decision. Following the *ayuno*, the presiding pastor told us, "Lots of young people attend months in advance of contemplating a journey north. When God tells me that the journey will be a safe one, they proceed with their plans. If God tells me their journey will not be a safe one, they postpone or cancel their migration plans."

In sum, for many of the Evangelical Maya in the western highlands of Guatemala, the decision to migrate, although driven by economic considerations, can ultimately be based on the advice or premonitions of evangelical pastors. Additionally, the prayer support provided by the *ayunos*, vigils, and spiritual retreats appears to help prospective migrants feel more comfortable in whatever decision they make.

Even after a decision to migrate to the United States has been made with the consent of the pastor, the involvement and influence of the church continues. As preparations for the journey are made, migrants continue to look to the church for support and guidance. Religious activities, such as attendance of *ayunos*, conferring with pastors, and individual prayer, continue if not heighten. Further, the migrant's family becomes increasingly involved in these religious activities as they also seek counsel with the pastor and church. As travel documents are prepared and money is secured, migrants look to religious leaders to pray for their success and to interpret the will of God in the way arrangements fall together. At an *ayuno* in the home of a minister in a small farming settlement outside the town center, the pastor, an older Maya woman, told us that she had been visited the day before by thirty-five migrants en route to the United States. On a table were displayed bundles that contained the traveling clothes of ten potential migrants who were attending the *ayuno* that day. The migrants brought the clothes they would be wearing on their journey north to be blessed by God through the attending minister. The ten migrants had already received the consent of the evangelical church to make the voyage but had come for additional prayer and guidance to prepare for their journey. I spoke at length with these young men and was really taken back with how little they knew about the potential dangers that lay ahead despite the fact that their kin and friends had made the journey before them. These young men were placing total trust in the *coyote* and the will of God. For this reason, I was told, pastors often meet the *coyote* whom a migrant has secured to determine whether he is honest.

Thus, at any time during the preparation for the journey, the church has the spiritual power to withdraw its consent and advise against the trip. If the migrant's pastor feels that travel arrangements are not falling into place as expected or if the emotional hardship for the family is perceived as being greater than the potential economic benefits of migration, the pastor will reverse his decision and advise the migrant to postpone or cancel the trip. If, on the other hand, the travel arrangements come together easily, one pastor told us, "this is indicative of the will of God that the journey be prosperous."

Once the migrant has embarked on the journey north, dependence on the church for counsel and guidance often continues. The trip from San Pedro to Houston can take up to several weeks, and throughout this period the migrant's family and pastor are on call. During the journey, the migrant's family continues to conduct prayer meetings at home and attend, in some cases, several *ayunos* a week in addition to formal church services. At both the *ayunos* we attended, there were parents of migrants who had not heard from their children in some time. Fearing an unsafe arrival or perilous journey, the parents brought pictures or personal items of the children, and the minister and attendees prayed over them. In one case, a father had not heard from his son in several months. Not knowing whether he had arrived safely in the United States, he asked the pastor to ask God whether his son and companions were lost. To the observable relief of the weeping father, the pastor informed him that they had not yet arrived in the United States but were safe in Mexico.

Perhaps most surprising to me was the crucial role the pastor assumes if a migrant is apprehended during his or her journey north. In this event, the pastor serves as a spiritual guide but also helps in more practical matters if possible. The pastor may try to reach the migrant's kin in the United States or solicit outside help from someone such as myself who may have contacts with the legal system to help the detained migrant. For example, shortly after my return from Guatemala, I received a telephone call from Sarah, a young Guatemalan undocumented migrant, who was calling me from Mission, Texas. She and her young daughter had recently been apprehended by police in an apartment she shared with other migrants in Ohio and had been deported by the Immigration and Naturalization Service to Reynosa, Mexico. She and her daughter succeeded in reentering the United States by swimming the Rio Grande and were now staying with a family in Mission. She had attempted several times to make the trip to Houston, where she has an aunt and uncle. Both times they were stopped short by border patrol checkpoints. She was stuck in Mission. She could not go home because she could not face her parents without money, as they had put up their home as collateral against the *coyote's* fee to cover the voyage north. She could not proceed further because of a lack of funds and beefed-up enforcement around Mission. What did she do? She called her pastor in Guatemala, who in turn gave Sarah my number in Houston.

Less than an hour after hanging up the phone with Sarah, I received a call from Pastor Sapon, who ministers to Sarah's family, along with a hundred or so other families in San Pedro. We spoke at length about Sarah's predicament. He also told me about another young migrant from the village, Armando, who had spent the last two months in detention in Laredo. The young man had called the pastor for counsel, and they had prayed together on the phone. The pastor called me and asked whether I could locate a lawyer to visit Armando in detention to find out what was going on in his case. He went on to tell me that he had spent most of the last few days with Sarah's and Armando's families, counseling with and praying for them. Both children were the subject of much prayer at the daily *ayunos* and at more formal prayer services. Pastor Sapon then talked about the increasing dangers and costs of migrating north. He feared for his congregation, who, he said, had no other choice at this point but to put their fate in the hands of God.

What became apparent to me from these telephone conversations and my observations and conversations with the Maya and their ministers in Guatemala was that there are many instances in the migration process when religion, in the form of prayers, pastors' aid, and comfort, and formal religious institutions and practices are drawn on by journeying migrants. Two other pastors with whom I spoke also told me of episodes in which they had prayed at length over the phone with apprehended migrants. Following the phone calls, the pastors had then counseled the family at length. On rare occasions, such as a failed trip, the pastor will lend some economic support to the destitute family, which in some cases has put their home up as collateral for the costly *coyote* fee and now faces its loss as repayment.

Migrants also spoke of receiving money or shelter from priests and pastors in Mexico while en route to the United States. The dangers associated with U.S.–Mexico border crossing have also drawn the attention of churches along the U.S.–Mexico border. For example, a Tucson-based coalition of eleven churches, Humane Borders, installed along 200 miles of desert as many as 800 water stations containing jugs of water, food, and clothing. Some persons willing to help migrants display bumper stickers with a North Star logo that shows water pouring from the Big Dipper, indicating to migrants that a person is willing to give aid.

Once migrants are successful in reaching their U.S. destination, they maintain contact with their pastors in Guatemala, either directly or indirectly through family. News of a safe arrival takes several forms. Sometimes calls are made directly to the pastor. In many cases, however, successful migrants send back pictures of themselves to their families to document their safe and successful arrival. These pictures are then brought by families to the *ayunos*, and the congregation continues to pray for their success and well-being. The pictures are numerous, attesting to the ongoing interaction between the home religious community and the migrant, even as he or she is forging a new life in the United States. Indeed, at one of the churches we visited in San Pedro, the pastor asked his congregants to request pictures of their recently arrived family members in the United States so that the congregation could post them on one of the interior church walls.

In addition to keeping the pastor and religious community updated on one's progress in the United States, migrants and their families may continue to turn to the pastor for counseling. The family especially seeks counseling if the migration has adverse effects on the migrant's family situation. Several of the pastors gave accounts of wives of migrants who sought counseling after they learned that their husbands were involved or cohabiting with other women in the United States. In one dramatic case, the pastor presiding over a vigil told his ministry that the spouses of three of the attending women were in trouble. According to observers of the incident, at that moment three women stepped forward and told all present that their husbands were involved with other women in the United States. The pastor asked the women to come forward and receive the spirit of God. All present cried in prayer. According to this pastor, the primary goal of the church in times of family hardship such as this is to keep the well-being of the family at the center of the spouse's focus.

The Role of the Ethnic Church in Immigrant Settlement

The first organizational structure that most Maya migrants of a Protestant faith in San Pedro encounter in their new life in Houston is the ethnic evangelical church, of which there are three in Houston. Each of these churches has an established mission counterpart in the home township, although no formal institutional linkages have been developed between the home and receiving churches. As in Guatemala, the Maya congregants in Houston bear the financial costs of maintaining community churches. The church members pay to rent the church building, for utilities, and for other operational costs of the church. Several times a year, women prepare tamales to raise funds for the churches. The pastors of two of the Houston evangelical churches are Guatemalan and are from the province in which San Pedro is located. A Mexican American leads the remaining evangelical church. The church members are overwhelmingly Maya and come from several highland municipalities, although the majority are from San Pedro.

Although no formal programs have been developed to ease the settlement of new migrants, the evangelical churches, along with other community organizations, such as the soccer league, perform a series of important functions for newcomers to Houston.

Because the churches provide for regular interaction between newcomers and more established residents through multiple religious services each week, newcomers are quickly linked to various Maya social networks that assist them in finding housing, jobs, and so on. The churches are so important in the initial settlement process that many newcomers convert to the Protestant faith soon after their arrival.

The churches also function to reproduce Maya culture and evangelical religious practices in the United States. Except for the noticeable absence of *ayunos,* the number and type of religious activities organized by the Maya evangelical church in Houston closely resemble those held in the churches in the home community, including Sunday worship service, weekly Bible classes, women's and men's group meetings, youth group meetings, and celebrations of major life cycle events (e.g., birthdays and marriages) that often are held in the churches. The committee structure of the church is also similar to that found in the home community, with members serving on maintenance committees, construction committees, band committees, and so on. Indeed, except for the urban environment outside the churches, there is little to distinguish them from their Guatemalan counterparts. Members would agree, however, that they are less involved in religious activities in Houston than they were in Guatemala, reflecting their busy work schedules and the long distances between their homes and their churches. Although they try to make up for this by holding prayer services in their homes, they cannot re-create the collective involvement that they enjoyed in the home community.

Membership in one of the Houston evangelical churches does not preclude continued involvement with a church and pastor back home. Migrants continue to communicate with their pastor in Guatemala and transmit updates to the religious community there through letters and the remittances of goods and monies sent home via co-ethnic couriers. This relationship becomes most salient in the final stage of the migration process—the maturation of the migrant community structure.

The Development of Transnational Community Relations

As is the case with an increasing number of other Latino migrant communities, the newcomers from San Pedro have developed substantial transnational community relations. Although a few migrants have little or no contact with the community back home, most maintain substantial contact with kin and friends in the town of San Pedro and the surrounding farming settlements of the *municipio*. These exchanges operate through a variety of means, including letters, telephone calls, audio- and videocassettes, couriers, and trips home. All these mechanisms serve to circulate resources (money, materials, information, and so on) used for ethnic cultural reproduction among the migrant households in Houston and their counterparts in the home *municipio* (Rodriguez and Hagan 2000).

During the initial stages of migrant settlement in Houston in the late 1970s and early to mid-1980s, the pioneer migrants from San Pedro relied almost exclusively on letters and telephones to communicate with family and friends back home. In Guatemala, friends and family of migrants traveled to Quetzaltenengao, a sizable city located about ten miles from San Pedro, to call Houston from the offices of GUATEL, the Guatemalan national telephone company, because no long-distance telephone service existed in the community. By the mid-1990s, however, private international courier and telephone companies (e.g., *Rapido Express* and *Envois Urgentes*) established businesses in San Pedro, facilitating a more efficient and direct means of communication between the two communities. Video recorders also became a popular means to share events between the two communities. For example, it was not uncommon for migrants returning to visit Guatemala to film community events (e.g., birthdays, festivals, religious processions, and soccer games) that would then be watched by migrants back in Houston. Similarly, kin and families in Guatemala received videocassettes of community activities and events in Houston.

By the mid-1990s, many of the pioneer migrants had obtained legal status through the 1986 legalization program. Armed with legal residency, most petitioned to bring family to the United States, and many family members arrived in Houston during the mid- to late 1990s. When interviewed in the summer of 2000, the mayor of San Pedro estimated that by that time at least 15 percent of the approximately 6,000 households in the municipality of San Pedro had family members in Houston.

Most migrants with legal status in the United States, Catholic and Protestant alike, make the yearly visit to the home community to celebrate the *fiesta* of the patron saint, which is held in July. Many make the trip home several times a year. Some of the migrants have invested in homes and businesses in Guatemala. Others spend a couple of years in wage labor in Houston working in low-skilled jobs, return to San Pedro to farm their *milpas*, build new homes or initiate a family enterprise, and then return again to Houston to earn more money, only to travel home again.

Three men, originally from San Pedro and holders of either temporary visas or green cards, have established a thriving courier service between Houston and San Pedro. They play an especially important role in keeping cultural and economic resources circulating between the migrants in Houston and their families back home. Although individual couriers increasingly face competition from private international courier companies that have, in recent years, penetrated the Guatemalan highland communities, they still do a handsome business. Over the years, I have interviewed two of the three couriers in their homes in Houston and in San Pedro. The most recent round of interviews was conducted in the summer of 2000, when I was doing fieldwork in San Pedro. They reported that in most months they deliver to families in San Pedro as much as $500,000 in remittances (cash, money orders, and household goods) from Houston migrant families. In a typical month, the couriers purchase one or two vehicles in Houston, usually an old school bus and/or used Toyota truck, and load it with goods that they have collected from families in Houston. The fee paid to the couriers can be as little as $5 or as much as $100, depending on the amount of goods being transported. During the three-day trek to Guatemala, the couriers face the danger of bandits as they cross two borders transporting cash and household and personal items worth tens of thousands of dollars. Once in Guatemala, the couriers deliver their goods and sell their vehicles on the open market. When they return by air or bus to Houston, they bring to migrant families many traditional cultural goods, such as clothing and foodstuffs, that cannot be purchased in the United States.

How Migrant Networks and Community Organizations Reproduce Religion

These well-established social networks linking Houston and San Pedro that operate at the personal level of individuals and families and at the organizational level of ethnic organizations (such as courier systems, soccer leagues, and churches) also serve over time to reproduce religious practices and activities between the two communities.

Migrants and nonmigrants alike began, in the late 1980s and early 1990s, to increasingly distribute the celebration of family life cycle and community events across churches in both Guatemala and Houston. For example, migrants (and sometimes their pastors) in Houston will collect funds from other migrants and then reach out to churches in the home community to organize *quinzeneras* for nonmigrant family members, or funerals for the bodies of deceased migrants sent home for burial. Similarly, weddings celebrated in Houston are increasingly accompanied by visits from kin, friends, and *padrinos* (godparents) from back home who are able to secure visas for the trip. During these occasions, ideas are exchanged; in some cases, the traditional religious rituals are reproduced, and in others they are transformed. In a recent wedding celebration in Houston, for example, family members of the groom from San Pedro were able to secure tourist visas to attend their son's wedding. Prior to the wedding, the bride's parents decided to host a shower for the bride, a ritual quite foreign to the wedding and marriage practices of Maya in rural Guatemala. The shower drew about seventy members from the community, including men, children, and the elderly as well as women. Shortly after the presents were opened and the food was served, the guests formed several circles and began to pray and provide individual testimony, practices very reminiscent of religious services in the home community. In this situation, the presence of family members from home transformed an innovative secular event, a wedding shower, into a somewhat traditional religious event.

Over time, religious resources flow in both directions. For example, in the 1980s and early 1990s, two pastors migrated from the San Pedro area to establish evangelical churches in the Houston area to service the growing Maya community. Conversely, on several occasions non-Maya pastors from Houston have accompanied migrants returning to the home community to celebrate an event, such as a wedding or the blessing of a newly constructed home. Sustained pastor-to-pastor or church-to-church relations, however, have never been established between the two communities. I suspect there is some degree of competition between Houston and San Pedro pastors because they are forced to compete for a share of the meager funds available to their parishioners for contribution to a religious purpose. An interview with a pastor at *Iglesia de Dios* Church in San Pedro confirmed my suspicions. He told me that he had met one of the Houston pastors at a joint blessing of a migrant home in San Pedro. He went on to say that he suspected that neither had reached out to forge relations between their respective churches because it was so difficult "to contemplate forging these types of relations when one is just trying to keep his church going."

In recent years, family, friends, and church committees in San Pedro have begun to reach out to their Houston family and friends for funds to maintain their churches back home. While in San Pedro, we spent considerable time interviewing members and observing services in three evangelical churches in each of which a substantial number of the members had family and friends in Houston. Interviews with pastors, committee members, and parishioners in two of the smaller and more impoverished churches spoke of the enormous financial contributions family and friends in Houston had made to their churches. The techniques developed by members of the two churches to recruit financial help from the Houston community varied, but in both cases the members themselves and their families, not the churches, organized the remittance drives.

The first case involved a split in membership in a church in San Pedro. Half the members wanted a new pastor, while the other half wanted to retain the same one. The current pastor and his remaining flock were eventually forced out of the church and temporarily set up services in the pastor's home. News of these events was relayed to migrants in Houston and other U.S. cities in early 1997, and a group of eighty migrants organized a fund-raising campaign to help the old pastor and his remaining congregation. It took the group a little over two years to purchase the land and construct a new church. According to the pastor of this church, 79 percent of the Q135,000 ($20,000) it cost to buy the land for the new church came directly from migrants. Most of the money was sent via Western Union directly to members of the construction committee of the church. The cost of the construction of the church itself was nearly twice the cost of the land, almost Q245,000 ($35,000). We were told that 35 percent of the cost for the building was sent directly by migrants, while another 60 percent was provided by the families of migrants. Thus, the combined direct and indirect migrant contribution totaled 95 percent of the cost of the new church structure. The father of a migrant and member of the church also told us that when his son last visited Guatemala, he donated Q15,000 ($2,000) to cover the cost of purchasing chairs and windows to be installed in time for the church's inauguration.

Another case involves a small church located in one of the farming settlements just outside the town center. The members number about 200, and most are destitute. Their goal is to construct a home above the church for their pastor. In this case, it was the members of the Church Construction Committee who developed the strategy for securing funds from migrants in Houston. They began by writing to the pastors of the Maya churches in Houston but were unsuccessful. As they explained, "They have their own needs, so we weren't expecting much." They then approached two members of the church in Guatemala who are also two of the three community couriers. On their next trip, the couriers separately visited the various Guatemalan evangelical churches in Houston soliciting funds. They were not successful in soliciting funds from the pastors but managed to secure donations from individual members. They also requested funds from families who were using their services to send goods back home. They were modestly successful. On their first trip, which was in the spring of 1999, they collected about Q3,000 ($400). Although the amounts collected during each trip are modest, the pot for the pastor's home is growing. The couriers continue their fund-raising activities and anticipate that the pastor's home will be completed during the next year. Again, the important message here is that the members of the church in Guatemala and their families in Houston drive the remittances. As one of the members of a church committee in San Pedro told us, "Pastors come and go, sometimes as often as every two years. We do not. We can't depend on their strategies but must depend on our own. This is our church."

Conclusion and Discussion

Most migration theories that seek to explain why the decision to migrate is made in the first place rely on some combination of economic variables operating at different levels of analysis to predict migration. Migration theories also argue that the conditions that trigger international migration are quite different from those that sustain it. The persistence of international movements is explained largely by the development of new conditions during the course of migration, such as migrants' personal networks that reduce the cost of migration for others in the home community (Hagan 1998; Massey et al. 1987) or the development of institutions that come to support transnational movement.

By relying on economic considerations in driving the decision to migrate and social explanations for sustaining the process, theories on international migration have overlooked the cultural context of migration. More specifically, within this context they have not addressed the role of religion in the migration process, especially the spiritual resources it provides for some immigrant populations in the decision to migrate, and the psychological effects of this on migrants' commitment to see it through, to endure the hardships of the migration. The data presented in this chapter suggest the importance of religion at all stages of the migration and settlement experience. Churches in communities of origin are well aware of the spiritual needs of prospective migrants and their families and cater to them; so too, migrants who cross international borders without papers may use local religious leaders and practices for guidance and protection in their often perilous journey. Studies of present-day Ghanaian Pentecostalism also find that prospective migrants often turn to the healing and deliverance rituals of prayer camps in Ghana for spiritual counsel and protection during their travel (Van Dijik 1997). Similarly, an analysis of Mexican *retablos* (small votive paintings expressing thanks that are left at religious shrines) produced by U.S.-bound Mexican migrants show that migrants often pray and give thanks to the saints of the Catholic Church for a successful journey (Durand and Massey 1995).

Once migrants successfully arrive in the United States, the role of religion in the migration process continues. In addition to maintaining contact with churches and pastors in the community of origin via letters and pictures, recent arrivals begin to rely on churches and pastors in receiving communities for counsel and settlement assistance. As is the case with recent arrivals in many immigrant communities, the Maya ethnic churches provide the organizational setting for regular interaction between newcomers and more established residents. As such, newcomer Maya are quickly linked into migrant personal networks that assist them in finding housing and jobs, thus easing the overall initial settlement process.

As the length of settlement in the United States increases, the more established migrants in the community may acquire the financial and legal resources to return to the home community and eventually travel between the United States and the home community on a regular basis. As the migration patterns of the community become transnational in nature, leading to more established relations between the two communities, some migrants employ these relations to establish entrepreneurial activities. Couriers increasingly cart goods back and forth, and in some cases remittances sent home via these couriers become an important resource to sustain impoverished institutions back home, including community-based churches.

What is clear from the case study of the Maya is that the well-established social network structure spanning Houston and Guatemala provides a foundation through which social and cultural resources, including religious ones, flow between the two communities. It is unlikely that the reproduction of religious practices and institutions in either community would occur in the absence of migrant-based transnational social networks.

My findings dealing with the role of religion in different stages of the migration process are based on one case study of an evangelical group of undocumented Maya who face a difficult and often perilous trip north. Other research on other undocumented immigrant groups of various national origins and religions needs to be done to see whether my findings are more generalizable. For example, are my findings a function of an extremely difficult and dangerous crossing? That is, do migrants make more use of, or rely more strongly on, religion when they feel little control over the situation or when the risks are extremely high? Or perhaps my findings are unique to members of evangelical churches or to the Maya themselves. Again, it would be fruitful to examine how evangelical Mexicans and other evangelical migrant groups use religion in the migration process. These are but a few of the research questions that need to be addressed if we are to understand the role of religion in the migration process. To address these questions, we are currently interviewing a sample of 300 Latino migrants who vary by religion, national origin, gender, and legal status. The ethnosurvey we are conducting asks about the role of religion in the entirety of the migration process, from the decision to migrate to the flow of religious resources between mature immigrant communities and their community of origin.

References

Durand, Jorge, and Douglas S. Massey. 1995. *Miracles on the Border: Retablos of Mexican Migrants to the United States.* Tucson: University of Arizona Press.

Ebaugh, Helen Rose, and Janet Saltzman Chafetz. 2000. *Religion and the New Immigrants: Continuities and Adaptations in Immigrant Congregations.* Walnut Creek, CA: AltaMira.

Eschbach, Karl, Jacqueline Hagan, Nestor Rodriguez, Ruben Hernandez-Leon, and Stan Bailey. 1999. "Death at the Border." *International Migration Review* 33:430–54.

Garrard-Burnett, Virginia. 1998. *Protestantism in Guatemala: Living in the New Jerusalem.* Austin: University of Texas Press.

Green, Linda. 1999. *Fear as a Way of Life: Mayan Widows in Rural Guatemala.* New York: Columbia University Press.

Hagan, Jacqueline Maria. 1994. *Deciding to Be Legal: A Maya Community in Houston.* Philadelphia: Temple University Press.

———. 1998. "Social Networks, Gender and Immigrant Incorporation: Opportunity and Constraint." *American Sociological Review* 63:55–67.

Hurh, Won Moo, and Kwang Chung Kim. 1990. "Religious Participation of Korean Immigrants in the United States." *Journal for the Scientific Study of Religion* 29:19–34.

Leonard, Karen. 1992. *Making Ethnic Choices: California's Punjabi Mexican-Americans.* Philadelphia: Temple University Press.

Levitt, Peggy. 2001. *The Transnational Villagers.* Berkeley: University of California Press.

Lin, Irene. 1996. "Journey to the Far West: Chinese Buddhism in America." *Amerasia Journal* 22:106–32.

Massey, Douglas S., Rafael Alarcon, Jorge Durand, and Humberto Gonzalez. 1987. *Return to Aztlan: The Social Process of International Migration from Western Mexico.* Berkeley: University of California Press.

Min, Pyong Gap. 1992. "The Structure and Social Functions of Korean Immigrant Churches in the United States." *International Migration Review* 26:1370–94.

Mullins, Mark R. 1988. "The Organizational Dilemmas of Ethnic Churches: A Case Study of Japanese Buddhism in Canada." *Sociological Analysis* 49:217–33.

Municipal Unidad Tecnica. 1999. *Diagnostico Integral Del Municipio San Cristobal, Totonicapan.* Municipalidad de San Cristobal Totonicapan.

Numrich, Paul David. 1996. *Old Wisdom in the New World: Americanization in Two Immigrant Theravada Buddhist Temples.* Knoxville: University of Tennessee Press.

Rodriguez, Nestor. 1987. "Undocumented Central Americans in Houston: Diverse Populations." *International Migration Review* 21:4–25.

Rodriguez, Nestor, and Jacqueline Hagan. 2000. "Maya Urban Villagers in Houston: The Formation of a Migrant Community from San Cristobal Totonicapan." In *The Maya Diaspora: Guatemalan Roots, New American Lives,* edited by James Loucky and Marilyn Moors. Philadelphia: Temple University Press.

Stoll, David, and Virginia Garrard-Burnett, eds. 1993. *Rethinking Protestantism in Latin America.* Philadelphia: Temple University Press.

Tedlock, Barbara. 1992. *Time and the Highland Maya.* Albuquerque: University of New Mexico Press.

Van Dijik, Rijk A. 1997. "From Camp to Emcompassment: Discourses on Transsubjectivity in the Ghanaian Pentecostal Diaspora." *Journal of Religion in Africa* 27:135–59.

Warner, R. Stephen, and Judith G. Wittner, eds. 1998. *Gatherings in Diaspora: Religious Communities and the New Immigration.* Philadelphia: Temple University Press.

Waugh, Earle H. 1994. "Reducing the Distance: A Muslim Congregation in the Canadian North." In *American Congregations,* vol. I, edited by James P. Wind and James W. Lewis. Chicago: University of Chicago Press.

Wilson, Richard. 1995. *Maya Resurgence in Guatemala Q'eqchi's Experiences.* Norman: University of Oklahoma Press.

Catholicism and Transnational Networks   5
Three Cases from the
Monterrey–Houston Connection

EFRÉN SANDOVAL (TRANSLATED BY YLIANA IRUEGAS)

The Catholic Church, one of the most international institutions in the world, serves as an intermediary for the creation of transnational networks between immigrant Catholics and their sending communities, although often unintentionally. Catholic immigrants and their relatives in the home country use parish and other church groups, as well as Catholic customs and values, to maintain connections between their communities. In this chapter, I describe how, mostly through families and neighbors, the Catholic religion contributes to the creation and maintenance of transnational ties linking Monterrey, Mexico, and Houston, Texas. There are no formal ties between parishes in Houston and Monterrey. Some nuns, priests, and seminarians from Monterrey spend time, often a number of years, in parishes north of the border, including in Houston. On occasion, a few Houston priests have visited parishes in Monterrey. However, little of this cross-border activity by religious personnel is institutionalized, which is why I focus on grassroots transnational networks composed of laypersons.

Houston has become "an important destination for *regiomontano* [Monterrey-born] migrants . . . [since] the mid-1970s, when the city became a global center for the oil extraction and oil technology industries" (Hernandez-Leon 2000). Three factors contribute to the attraction Houston has for migrants from Monterrey:

> Firstly, the tremendous economic growth that this city underwent during the 1970s boom years. Secondly, the fact that many *regiomontano* migrants were able to transfer their industrial manufacturing skills and experience to the Houston labor market. Thirdly, the development of networks that connect not only kin but also neighborhoods and workplaces between the two cities. (Hernandez-Leon 2000:175)

The arrival of large numbers of *regiomontano* industrial workers during the early 1970s paved the way for Houston to become the principal destination of future *regiomontano* migrants, as Hernandez-Leon, quoting Massey, explains:

> Once a few migrants from a community become established in a particular occu-
> pational-industrial niche, they acquire the ability to obtain jobs for friends, rela-
> tives, and other townspeople. Over time, therefore, migration from particular
> communities tends to focus not only on specific destinations but also on partic-
> ular niches in the U.S. occupational-industrial structure. (Hernandez-Leon
> 2000:176)

Through networks of social and economic relations, migrant and nonmigrant households in Houston and Monterrey have developed a "binational and interurban field of social action: the Monterrey-Houston connection":

> This includes not only the activities and transactions oriented toward labor mi-
> gration but also the interactions and exchanges that individuals and families un-
> dertake with purposes such as social and cultural reproduction. Viewed from this
> perspective, the Monterrey-Houston connection is a social field where many dif-
> ferent things take place: cultural consumption, binational child-rearing strategies,
> reciprocity and solidarity, redefinition of gender and family roles, formation of
> small-business ventures and movement of material and cultural remittances. The
> notion of a Monterrey-Houston connection suggests that an increasingly complex
> web of ties organized at the grassroots level links these two cities. (Hernandez-
> Leon 2000:177)

Monterrey is the third-largest city and most important financial center in Mexico. Historically, its growth has been related to industrial development. It is also one of the main centers of Catholicism in Mexico. Monterrey has long been recognized by the rest of the country for the strength of its Catholic values, including family, faith, order, and obedience, as well as for its entrepreneurial values of progress and hard work. Catholic discourse pervades Monterrey's mass media, schools and universities, families, economic enterprises, and even government declarations; the opinion of the Catholic hierarchy about public issues is important. It is also important that the average person conform to Catholic customs as expressed through the sacraments, attendance at Sunday mass, and respect paid to sacred images. The *regiomontano*'s identity cannot be understood without taking Catholicism into account, nor can the Monterrey–Houston connection. Catholicism is an important aspect of the grassroots connection between Monterrey and Houston despite the absence of institutional links between parishes in the two cities. Rather, kin and neighbor networks are the principal structures through which individuals build transnational relations, using Catholicism as a link.

The remainder of this chapter is organized into three parts. In the first, I briefly review literature that connects transnationalism and network analysis in order to present a theoretical orientation with which to analyze the data presented later. In the next section, I describe my fieldwork and present data obtained from it. Here I demonstrate how Catholics in the two cities use their customs and beliefs in order to build and maintain transnational networks, how participation in Catholic parish groups influences these networks, and how transnational neighbor and kin networks have an economic impact on a Monterrey parish. Finally, I present my conclusions.

Theoretical Background

Most individuals who migrate from one country to another do not have the support of the state or any other formal institution during the migration and subsequent settlement processes. They typically build networks composed mostly of kin and neighbors to garner support in their host community while at the same time extending these networks outward toward their sending communities, thereby increasing transnational links. In this way, people create new transnational communities, practices, and spaces apart from those of the institutions through which social remittances (including ideas, behaviors, and identities) and social capital flow (Levitt 1998:927).

A network is a "specific type of relation linking a defined set of persons, objects or events," called *actors* or *nodes*, that "posses some attribute(s) that identify them as members of the same equivalence class for purposes of determining the network of relations among them" (Knoke and Kuklinski 1991:174). Networks have the additional property that "the characteristics of these linkages as a whole may be used to interpret the social behavior of the persons involved" (Mitchell 1969:2). Social networks are created by individuals through their capacity "to appropriate, reproduce, and, potentially, to innovate upon received cultural categories and conditions of action in accordance with their personal and collective ideals, interests, and commitments" (Emirbayer and Goodwin 1994:1442–43). Mitchell (1969) lists a set of morphological and interactional variables that can be used to describe network linkages, including (1) anchorage, an initial starting point, like a person or group; (2) reachability, the degree to which a person's behavior influences and is influenced by network relationships; (3) density, the degree to which network members know each other; (4) range, the number of direct ties existing within a network; (5) content, the meanings that persons in a network attribute to their relationships; (6) directedness, the level of exchange reciprocity among network members; (7) intensity, the degree to which individuals are prepared to honor obligations and feel free to exercise the rights implied by their network participation; and (8) frequency, the number of contacts among network members.

Networks can, of course, span political, social and geographic borders, thus becoming transnational. In Rodriguez's words, "Transnational communities carry out functions of social reproduction across international boundaries as if these boundaries did not exist" (1999:34). Transnational networks not only contribute to the migration, settlement, and adaptation of migrants to the new society but also allow individuals to continue being members of kin, neighbor, and other kinds of social networks in the community of origin. Transnationalism exists at three levels of relations: (1) networks of social relations between individuals, (2) networks that link their communities in the sending and receiving nations, and (3) broader institutionalized linking structures (Portes, Guarnizo, and Landolt 1999:220). Transnationalism can also be conceptualized as emanating from "below" or from "above," from grassroots impulses or elite action (Popkin 1998:269). In order to study the Monterrey–Houston connection and the role of Catholicism in the formation, development, and modification of kin and neighbor transnational networks, I will emphasize the process of transnationalism from below.

Kin and Neighbor Transitional Networks and Their Relationship to Catholicism

Research Methods

The data in this chapter are the product of fieldwork conducted in neighborhoods and parishes in Houston and Monterrey during September 2000 in Houston and October and November in Monterrey. In Texas, I interviewed Catholic immigrants from Monterrey whom I began identifying at the Immaculate Heart of Mary Parish (IHM) during two brief visits in January and May 2000. This parish is located in Magnolia, the original and still most important Mexican neighborhood (*barrio*) in Houston. Although I had originally intended to restrict my attention in Houston to this one parish, I was led to other groups and parishes because of family and friendship networks that spilled out of IHM to include others. I will focus on the networks that I began to trace through two IHM parish groups, the Catholic Family Movement and the parish youth group. In Houston, I interviewed two priests and nine lay immigrants (five males and four females). In addition, I participated in an IHM youth group meeting and attended four Sunday masses there and one at Pius X Parish. I witnessed the rehearsal of a religious play in Christ the King Parish with the youth group, where I also interviewed a *regiomontana* nun.

In Monterrey, I conducted thirteen interviews and two field visits to observe daily life in the *La Fama* neighborhood. I interviewed two nuns who belong to congregations that have links with Texas and three priests who have visited the United States. The rest of the interviews were with relatives of people whom I had already interviewed in Houston and with people who have relatives living there. I concentrate on the case of *La Fama* because of my interest in examining how the migrant tradition of this neighborhood impacts a *regiomontano* parish.

The purpose of the interviews and observations was to locate whatever transnational relationships exist between the cities of Houston and Monterrey that involve and affect Catholicism, including the exchange of religious artifacts and practices and the impact of monetary remittances from Houston on parishes and religious practices in Monterrey.

Overview of Findings

Certain findings reappear repeatedly from the interviews with priests, nuns, and laypersons. Catholic participation in parish groups increases on arrival in the United States as a way to become integrated into the community, begin new relationships, and interact with people who speak the same language—in short, as people say, as a way to get "a family here in Houston." Belonging to a social network structured around the parish also provides a means of support in times of need. For relatives in Monterrey, migrant participation in parish groups in Houston assumes symbolic importance and affects the communication, social contacts, and goods exchanged between migrants and their kin in Mexico as well as religious practices and behavior in both places. In what follows, I describe in detail three case studies of the Houston–Monterrey connection that exemplify these general findings. The first depicts a transnational kin network centered on a married immigrant couple that is very active in church groups. The second centers on the experiences of one young man from Monterrey who lives in Houston and is also actively involved in church life. In the third case, a migrant tradition in a *regiomontano* neighborhood, which impacts a parish in Monterrey through transnational kin and neighbor networks, is described. Before turning to these three cases, I briefly describe the Houston parish that serves as the center of the transnational networks under examination.

The Houston Parish

The IHM, one of the first parishes developed for Mexicans living in Houston, is located in Magnolia, the first Mexican *barrio* to develop in Houston. The IHM serves 2,300 families, nearly all Hispanic, according to the 2000 Directory of the Galveston-Houston Diocese. According to Father John (parochial vicar of IHM), people participate in many ways, the most basic of which is attending Sunday mass. At the other extreme are people such as Juana and Joaquin Herrera, leaders of the Christian Family Movement, who attend meetings almost daily. They will comprise the focus of the first case study.

The IHM is configured into more than twenty groups. Those that have been at the parish the longest, known as the "old societies," are, according to Father John, "formed by the elderly, who chat about things they have in common and pray, but do not contribute very much more." There is also a group of adolescents and one of young adults. The adolescents, who speak English during their meetings, were all born in the United States. The somewhat larger group of young adults almost always speak in Spanish, and most were born in Mexico. The second case study focuses on Guillermo, a leader in this group. Both boys and girls participate in the Altar Boys Group, composed of about thirty children and an adult leader. The parish has four choirs, three of which sing in Spanish and one in English. In addition, the parish offers numerous classes where Christian values, responsibility, and self-esteem are taught. About twenty people comprise a group responsible for the socially and financially important Festival of Jamaica, which takes place in early October and generates, according to Father John, "the largest amount of money for the parish" while also serving "to unite the parish." Another parish group, the *Caballeros de Colón*, promotes fraternity among men and supports the pastoral work of the parish. Also important to pastoral work are thirty catechists who teach catechism lessons in English and Spanish as well as a committee of five people who talk with the parents and godparents of those about to be baptized. The Altar Society is responsible for cleaning and decorating the altar and is composed of four or five women. The IHM has thirty Eucharistic ministers who administer communion, thirty-five readers, and a program of twenty or more members that prepares adults for the sacraments of initiation (e.g., baptism, communion, and confirmation). Finally, the Bible study groups at the parish attract about forty people. In general, women participate more than men, although according to Father John, "there is not much difference; here we have more men participating than in other Mexican parishes." In short, there are a wide variety of groups and activities available to involve members in parish life.

Case Study 1: The Herreras

The Christian Family Movement (CFM) is a worldwide Catholic movement whose object is to promote Catholic family morality. Each week, groups of three to six couples meet to study a Catholic book or to discuss family problems. Only after CFM members have devoted three years to the organization are they able to assume a leadership position. The CFM is organized along national, regional, and diocesan lines, and each diocese contains several zones.

The Herreras (Juana, from Monterrey, and Joaquin, from Nueva Rosita, Coahuila) are coordinators for zone 2 of the nine Houston CFM zones and, therefore, are responsible for staying informed about thirty-two marriage groups spread among several Houston parishes. Each of these groups has from three to six families, and therefore the Herreras coordinate 105 families out of nearly 600 who participate throughout Houston. As a result, the Herreras know a lot of couples, at IHM parish and beyond. Through CFM, they have built several social networks in Houston and now anchor transnational kin networks as well. Because of their leadership roles in CFM, they wield substantial influence with members of these diverse networks.

Juana arrived in Houston from Monterrey in 1976 at age sixteen. Before leaving Monterrey, she had graduated as a nurse and worked in a public hospital as a nurse's assistant. She went to Houston to join her mother and four sisters, who had previously migrated there (Juana has five sisters and one brother). Her mother had come to the United States for the first time when Juana and her sisters were little. "Two of my brothers and sisters were born here, but everyone returned to Mexico to grow up," she told me. When her brothers and sisters were adolescents, they decided to go the United States to look for work and were eventually able to arrange for their mother to return to Houston. Subsequently, the rest of the family migrated north, the last being Juana and her father. Juana says that while she was still in Monterrey, her mother sent her letters from Houston preaching the necessity of attending mass, but Juana never participated in any parish groups. She explains that "here [in Houston], everything is different; here you feel isolated," which is one of the reasons Juana began to go to church.

Juana's first job in Houston was in a refrigeration parts factory, a job she acquired through a sister who also worked there. Afterward, thanks to another sister, she took a job in a company that makes air conditioners and subsequently one as a nurse's assistant in a Houston hospital followed by a job in a nursery. Within two years after her arrival in Houston, she had married Joaquin, and with the birth of her first child, she left the labor force. When her son was a bit older, she worked as a housekeeper for five years, after which she and her husband began the business that they have owned for thirteen years, transporting schoolchildren.

Juana used her kin network to acquire her first jobs in Houston, and, with her marriage to Joaquin, she gained another social network, his family. Her marriage occurred despite the fact that her family opposed it because Joaquin was a man with alcohol problems and "macho behavior." As a result, they had a civil ceremony, and Joaquin's mother and two sisters were the only family members who attended from Mexico. The Herreras' first child was baptized in Nueva Rosita (Joaquin's home community) "because our roots are in Mexico." Joaquin's parents decided the date of the baptism and who the child's godparents would be. They paid all the baptism expenses (the child's clothes, the food. and church fees), while Juana's family paid for travel to Mexico. The Herreras' second child was baptized in Houston. One of Juana's sisters and her husband went to Mexico, where "they bought the outfit, the Christ and the bracelet for the child, and the gifts." In Mexican Catholic baptisms, it is traditional to give the guests a souvenir, usually a religious figure or picture, a prayer, or verse. In the case of Juana's second child, those were also brought from Mexico to Houston by Juana's sister. The Herreras' third child was again baptized in Nueva Rosita because Joaquin's sister was to be godmother. The Herreras and their child's godparents made all the arrangements for the baptism by phone, and while Juana and Joaquin attended prebaptism talks in Houston, the godparents did likewise in Nueva Rosita. The godparents took responsibility for arranging the religious ceremony, but the Herreras brought the food and beverages for the meal from Houston. Joaquin's sister paid for the religious ceremony "because it is expected that the godparents pay for everything and the child's parents provide the food."

In short, the Herrera couple created a transnational network around the religious and social ceremonies connected to baptism, the content of which included economic support flowing in both directions as well as shared religious beliefs, practices, and customs. At the same time, the Herreras began to build a new network in Houston that would impact the old transnational kin network, changing its content and extending it to Monterrey.

The Herreras joined CFM when, "by accident," they wandered into a meeting shortly before they were married. Later, they received telephone calls inviting them to other meetings, and they joined after getting married. Joaquin commented that at first he did not like it: "I had a very macho attitude and wouldn't speak." He stopped participating, but because of two events, Joaquin changed his mind. He was in prison and, after being released, had an accident with a school bus: "I thought that I had to change and that God was in some way punishing me for having left the Movement, and it is for that reason that I don't even want to leave because it seems to me that something [bad] would happen to me."

Little by little, the Herreras developed social relationships both in CFM and in their neighborhood. Eventually, they assumed positions of leadership in CFM. Despite the fact that they have no relationship with any CFM group in Mexico, their participation in it has influenced kin in both Nueva Rosita and Monterrey. They have tried to change the religious practices of family members with invitations, by phone, to "get closer to God." In addition, during their visits to see relatives in Mexico and the visits their relatives make to Houston, they have tried to involve them in CFM. As CFM coordinators, their importance transcends the border and has become a model for family members in Mexico: "It's like the people there become aware of what you do here and send or bring us pictures and other religious things." Juana's mother-in-law, for example, has on many occasions given them religious pictures. Now, Juana collects prints to give to her mother-in-law when she visits Houston, or she sends them with someone who is traveling to Nueva Rosita. In fact, when I interviewed Juana and Joaquin, she showed me the envelope in which she keeps the prints. There were more than thirty images of saints and virgins, which she gets at flea markets or from CFM members who know that she collects them. Her mother-in-law arranges the prints, decorates them, cuts them out, and gives them to prisoners when she visits them with her prayer group, even though such images are easily found everywhere in Mexico.

Another example of the Herreras' influence on the religious practices of their relatives in Mexico concerns Joaquin's sister in Nueva Rosita, who is not in the habit of going to mass. When she visited them in Houston,

> She stayed at our house and we chatted about the Christian Family Movement and I showed her the books from the Movement. While she didn't say anything, my mother called me afterwards and told us that my sister has started going to mass, and now she is even involved in a religious group in Nueva Rosita.

In addition, Joaquin has a sister who lives in Houston, and, thanks to their invitation, she has been a CFM member for four years. The same thing is happening with Joaquin's cousin, who is involved in CFM in another zone. Juana has a nephew in Monterrey who lived with them for a year and a half while studying English in Houston. The Herreras are also godparents to this nephew's son. They say that their nephew is proud that his aunt and uncle belong to CFM, "and when we go to Monterrey, he introduces us to his friends and tells them what we do in the CFM in Houston." When they speak with him every two or three weeks, they encourage him to join a religious group or the CFM in Monterrey. Juana says that her sister and nephew now attend mass thanks to her invitations, although they are not members of CFM in Monterrey.

The meanings that the members of the Herrera couple's CFM and kinship networks attribute to their relationships (i.e., network contents) include religiosity along with the importance of kin and friends. This couple serves as an anchorage for two kin networks that are infused with Catholicism because of the Herreras' role in a third network, CFM. The primary direction of influence (reachability) flows outward from the Herrera couple to kin in Mexico and other relatives in the United States who, through visits in both countries and phone calls, are encouraged to increase their religious participation and assume new religious ideas, values, and practices. These constitute "social remittances." There is also a two-way flow of material remittances in religious images and other articles between kin in Mexico and Houston. The Herrera case suggests that network phenomena change over the life cycle. When the Herreras first arrived in Houston, they used a kin network based in Mexico for their child's baptism. Later, as they became increasingly involved in CFM, they became part of a durable Catholic network that functions to enhance both transnational networks and the adaptation process to the host society.

Case Study 2: Guillermo

Guillermo is a thirty-year-old member of the IHM youth group who immigrated to Houston in 1994, after his brother, who had immigrated twelve years earlier, invited him and their father to come to Houston to help him remodel his house. The youngest of six children, Guillermo's other four siblings remain in Mexico. He had completed high school but was unemployed when he decided to accept his brother's invitation. When he went to Houston, he planned to work for a year; now he does not want to return to Monterrey because he lacks the "capital" he thinks necessary to support himself there. Guillermo's brother provided him with an initial place to stay, but he now lives with a friend from Monterrey.

Guillermo's family in Monterrey is close. His siblings visit or telephone their mother every day, and he sends money to her, mostly by way of the friend with whom he lives and who goes to Monterrey every three or four weeks. His mother, in turn, has sent some religious artifacts, but mostly she sends him family photos and videos of Guillermo's new nephews and his cousins' weddings as well as clothes.

Guillermo joined the Young Adult Group at IHM two and a half years ago. He went because a friend from his English class invited him, and he stayed because "everyone was friendly." Participation in the Young Adult Group changed Guillermo's daily activities, and he experienced a radical change in personality. He has ceased spending his leisure time consuming beer with his friends from work and spending most of his money on alcohol. Even communication with his mother in Monterrey and his brother in Houston has changed. He no longer feels so lonely, so he no longer calls his mother every week (he now calls her every three weeks), and he almost never calls his brother, who now calls him:

> Now, I have more things to do. Before, I'd arrive home, shower, turn on the television and open a beer. Now I get there, take a nap, shower and come to planning group meetings or to the parish. Before my passion was soccer and I switched it for Christ. This is a testimonial that I share with young people when I give my talks. I tell them that it is fine that we play sports, but we should give some time to Christ. Soccer was my passion, but I changed.

The fact that Guillermo stopped calling his mother every week means a decrease in the frequency of communication but not in its intensity. He maintains a special kind of communication with her because of his delight in playing the gui-tar. Guillermo is now one of the leaders of the Young Adults Group of IHM, where he plays the guitar. The story behind this guitar illustrates how remittances symbolize linkages between family members and how individuals can infuse re-mittances with special importance. Guillermo learned to play the guitar in Mon-terrey, but he gave his away to his best friend before moving to Houston. After he had lived in Houston for a year, one of his brothers in Monterrey sent a guitar to him with a friend. On its arrival, Guillermo called his mother in Monterrey and sang "*Las Mañanitas*" to her. "My mother was very moved," he says. The following year, Guillermo made a tape with his mother's favorite songs, and on May 10, the Mexican Mother's Day, he had her listen to some of the songs by telephone. The guitar, which Guillermo uses to inspire the group of young adults at IHM, is a gift that his brother gave him after he found out that Guillermo participated in the group. Therefore, although his participation in a religious group has not pro-voked any of his siblings in Monterrey to change their religious practices or com-mitments, they still support his commitment, ironically in the form of a material "remittance"—a guitar—that flowed from Mexico to the United States.

In addition to serving as coordinator of the Young Adult Group at IHM, Guillermo is also a member of the Meeting Group for Youth Promotion (GYP), an international Catholic youth organization begun by a Spanish priest. The Houston chapter is comprised of a board of directors and different committees that are responsible for organizing get-togethers for young adults from different parishes. Guillermo is a member of an organizing committee and sometimes gives talks at chapter get-togethers. The GYP in Houston has a Local Correspondence Union that communicates with other groups in the United States and an Inter-national Correspondence Union that communicates by e-mail with groups from other countries. This group has international meetings, and in 1999 the world meeting was held in Houston. His activities at GYP and the Young Adult Group at IHM are the principal things Guillermo does with his free time.

Guillermo is an undocumented immigrant, and therefore he will not cross the border because he fears that he will not be able to return. It is for that reason that he has returned only once to Monterrey since he migrated to Houston, on the oc-casion of his father's serious illness and subsequent death. "I took a good amount of money to help with the expenses associated with his sickness and burial. This money helped a lot and I felt good in Monterrey." Members of both the IHM Young Adults Group and the Meeting Group for Youth Promotion were aware of the reason for his trip, and they responded with support and aid:

> The young people from both groups sent me money to Monterrey. They told me,
> "We know you will need it." They asked me how I sent money to Monterrey, so I

told them it was through Adame's bus. During the month I was in Monterrey, I received maybe fifteen telephone calls. My girlfriend and Irma from IHM called me, and some of the members of both groups. . . . While there, I sent an e-mail to the office of the Meeting group. In it I advised them to value their parents, to kiss them, to call them in Mexico.

Irma, the young secretary of IHM, played a central role in collecting money for Guillermo. Before he left Houston to travel to Monterrey, Guillermo went to Father John to tell him that he would be out of the city and could not attend the youth group meetings. Afterward, Guillermo talked with Irma, and she asked him for his telephone number in Monterrey. Irma called Guillermo two days after he left to find out how his father was doing and then shared the news with the youth group members. She gave them the number at Guillermo's family's house so that "whoever wanted could call him." During one of the telephone conversations, Guillermo asked Irma to organize a prayer night, to which Irma and Father John invited the members of both the Young Adult Group and GYP. The prayer night involved saying a rosary "asking for Guillermo's father's health." Twenty people attended that gathering, which took place at IHM. After Guillermo's father's death, there was another prayer night attended by forty people. On both nights, Irma asked for "a monetary donation" and had done the same thing during the meeting of GYP when she told them the reason for Guillermo's trip. She was able to collect a total of $600. When Guillermo returned to Houston, he attended a young adults' meeting where he received "a very large envelope with a letter on which each person had written a message of support." They also gave him a video filmed during the second prayer night.

In order to return to Houston worry free, Guillermo renewed his passport as well as his driver's license. A cousin, who is an accountant, obtained the necessary paperwork for Guillermo to show U.S. customs that he was employed in Monterrey and visiting Houston for only a few days. Obviously, Guillermo did not work while he was in Monterrey, but thanks to his cousin he could "prove" that he was employed there. Guillermo returned to Houston without difficulty and is planning to stay until he can collect more money. Even so, he is very vague when he speaks about returning to Monterrey. I asked Guillermo how he envisioned his future, and he answered that he saw himself married and active in GYP or other groups, "just like the Herreras." I think that his commitment to Catholic organizations in Houston has become his main reason for staying.

In the context of his family crisis, Guillermo used his family network in his home city and his overlapping Catholic networks from the host city. Guillermo's ego-centered network is not very dense in the sense that many of its members do not know each other because not all who are part of the Young Adult Group at

IHM know those involved in GYP, and members of these groups do not know Guillermo's relatives in Monterrey. In addition, membership turnover in the Young Adult Group is very high, and, while Guillermo knows most because he is a leader, many do not know one another. However, the reachability of these networks for Guillermo is considerable because of his central roles in each. The normal network content of the Catholic groups centers around sharing religious beliefs, values, practices, and rituals as well as friendship. However, in a crisis, the content was expanded to incorporate economic support as well.

Case Study 3: La Fama

The case of the La Fama neighborhood illustrates how, even in the absence of institutional linkages, Catholic parishes can be affected by transnational networks at the grassroots level. La Fama, a barrio in Santa Catarina, which is one of eight municipalities that together comprise Monterrey, is the most important center of regiomontano migration to Houston. This working-class neighborhood was founded in the early twentieth century around a textile factory (Cortés 1996:13). During my fieldwork there, I focused on the impact of transnational kin and neighbor networks on the local Catholic parish, San Vincente de Paul (SVP). However, I was disappointed when members of two parish groups and the SVP priest (Father Miguel) told me that they did not know of anyone who had relatives in the United States. Father Miguel went on to say that "migration to the United States is not common around here. Here, what is common, is for people to migrate to other states in the Republic [of Mexico]." I asked whether it was common at his parish to find dollar bills in the alms, and Father Miguel laughed and answered, "Not at all; in addition, I don't know anything about anyone sending money from the United States to help the parish." Father Miguel was incorrect in saying that migration to the United States is not common from that parish, but it seems he was correct when he said that no one sends money from the United States to help the parish, a phenomenon apparently more likely to occur in rural parishes. However, the fact that no one sends money directly designated for parish support does not mean that monetary remittances do not make their way from Houston to the parish. They do so via family and neighbor networks that link the parish and Houston. How this occurs is the subject of this case study.

At a meeting of the Damas Vicentinas, a parish women's group, I found Doña Marcela, a seventy-year-old woman who has four children (two women and two men) living in Houston. Her two oldest have lived in Houston for more than twenty-five years and are U.S. citizens. The youngest ones do not have papers permitting them to work legally in the United States, which is why they do not visit Doña Marcela often, so she travels to Houston every two or three months.

When Doña Marcela is in Houston, her children take her to Saint Jerome Parish for Sunday mass. One of her sons and his wife are Eucharist ministers at that church, who give communion and also lead talks. In addition, each Tuesday while in Houston, one of her sons takes her to Saint Jerome for the healing mass, similar to the one she normally attends at SVP in Monterrey. During her visits to Houston, her children give her money, which is her only source of income. She uses some of it to buy prayer books at Saint Vincent de Paul Church back in Monterrey, which she then gives to one of her daughters. She attends mass every day at SVP and always leaves "two or three pesos" (twenty or thirty cents) in the collection basket. She also participates in the organization of the San Jose festival and the celebration of the *Medalla Milagrosa*. For each of these events, she buys two tickets that cost fifteen pesos each ($1.50). Because of her participation in organizing these celebrations, Doña Marcela contributes an additional twenty pesos to the organization ($2). It is through her involvement with the church in Monterrey that remittance dollars from Houston find their way into the parish. In addition, when her older children visit Monterrey every December, they attend Sunday mass and "give some money like everyone else." Father Miguel said it is very rare to find dollars among the donations collected during the masses, but Doña Marcela never leaves dollars. Father Miguel is mistaken if he believes that the absence of dollars means that people at his parish do not migrate to the United States and that their remittances are not part of his parish's income.

In addition to attending the *Damas Vicentinas* meeting at Saint Vincent de Paul, I felt it was important to find other types of contact that did not involve people who participate in parish groups. I took advantage of Ruben Hernandez-Leon's visit to Monterrey to gain an introduction to Beto, a twenty-year-old, recently returned migrant who had lived in Houston for several years with his three brothers. Two of the brothers are in the United States illegally and have not returned to Monterrey for over a year. The one who lives in Houston legally, Francisco, visits Monterrey more or less regularly. In Houston, Francisco lives with his wife, who was a neighbor in *La Fama*. Beto's mother, Doña Flor, and Francisco's wife's mother, Doña Adriana, are old friends. Beto's three brothers send their mother money from Houston. She also receives money from her husband's pension fund (she is a widow) and, until she gave it up a month earlier at the request of her children, the profits from a small convenience store.

Neither Beto nor his mother participate in parish groups, in part because, until recently, she spent the whole day attending her store. According to Beto, "Sometimes, these women get together to pray and such but my mother only goes to the church on Sundays when she attends mass. Sometimes, I go with her." However, Beto's brothers maintain some special ties with their neighborhood that affect the parish's income. Beto has five nieces and nephews in Houston. Two were born in Houston, one of whom was baptized at the parish in *La Fama*. "My brother Francisco wanted him to be baptized here, and he paid the church" (a fee equivalent to $97). Two of Beto's nephews died in Monterrey:

> One died right after he was born; he suffocated. My brother had come with his children and wife specifically to baptize the child, but he died. A year later, he sent money so that they would say a mass for this child at the church. One of my brother Francisco's small children also died before he went to the United States for the first time. Since then, each year, he sends money for a mass for the boy and we take flowers to the cemetery.

It appears that an important reason to maintain links with the parish in the sending community is the religious commemoration of deceased members of the family. It is Catholic custom to ask for a mass each year for the *difuntos*, a practice that constitutes one motive to send money from Houston to the SVP parish in Monterrey.

In Houston, Francisco takes Doña Flor to the church of Saint Jerome when she visits because that is where he and his wife participate in a parish group. Beto comments about the religious participation of Francisco's wife:

> Here [in Monterrey], she didn't go so regularly to church. It seems to me that she started participating there [in Houston] because she felt guilty for having gone and left her mother here. Also, it could be because there, people miss the environment here, and so go to a church to speak Spanish and meet people from here.

In addition, Beto knows that Francisco's wife participates in a parish group, the *carismáticos*, and sends religious cassettes to her mother, Doña Adriana, in Monterrey. Through Beto, I was able to interview Doña Adriana, a seventy-year-old woman who has two daughters living in Houston, one of whom is Francisco's wife. Doña Adriana lives in *La Fama*. Although she is not in the habit of exchanging religious objects with her daughter, "she [did] send me a cassette with some songs from Saint Jerome because I heard those songs there, once when I went. Then, I told her to get me a cassette and she sent it to me." According to Doña Adriana, her daughters do not send money to her in Monterrey but take advantage of her visits to Houston to give her small amounts of money, mostly to cover the cost of the trip. Like Doña Flor and Doña Marcela, Doña Adriana goes to Saint Jerome parish when visiting Houston: "I see women there and later I see them here," she comments.

During one of my visits to *La Fama*, I was conversing with Beto and Tato, a friend of Beto's who has also immigrated to Houston. After a while, another friend of theirs arrived in a pickup with Texas license plates. Beto told me that he is the brother of another friend who lives in Houston. During the ensuing conversation, I found out that this man had come to Monterrey to organize a *quinceniera* (formal religious ceremony marking a girl's fifteenth birthday) for his daughter, who also lives in Houston. "I came to take care of things for the *quinceniera* , the church and the food. I just came to organize that and then I'm heading to Houston." The man in the pickup invited them to the *quinceniera* and then added, "I'm not giving you a [written] invitation because you are like family." The man further explained that as soon as his children finished the school year, he would return to Monterrey with the whole family to continue preparing for this event. Beto explained that the reason people come back to Monterrey to celebrate *quinceniera* and other kinds of rituals is that "here, we all go, we all know each other and go [to the party], and also here the people can do the party even in the street; there [in Houston] people must be in special halls."

The relationship between Doña Flor and Doña Adriana, the marriage between their children, the accidental meeting of a man who traveled from Houston to Monterrey to organize a *quinceniera*, the nature of this man's invitation to Beto and Tato, and even the fact that I could not interview two other women, friends of Doña Flor and Doña Adriana, because they were in Houston at the time together led me to consider the importance of the kin and neighbor ties between *La Fama* and Houston. These networks are conduits for constantly flowing financial remittances that reach the parish as alms and as payment for a mass, baptism, *quinceniera*, or wedding, albeit already changed into pesos.

Conclusion

In this chapter, I have shown how Catholic customs, rituals, and beliefs are woven into the grassroots links that help to maintain the broader Monterrey–Houston connection. Parish participation in Houston is used as a strategy to "get a family" in their new community, to meet people who share the same values and beliefs and who speak the same language. Several consequences flow from such participation, including the development of new networks in the host society, through which they can exchange favors, economic, and social support. These new networks also affect the kind of relations immigrants maintain with Monterrey. I used three case studies to illustrate the diversity of network ties that link religious life in the two cities, the Herreras, Guillermo, and *La Fama barrio* in Monterrey.

The Herreras are a well-known couple in the Magnolia neighborhood of Houston who serve as a connecting node between three networks, one composed of Catholic organization members in Houston and two composed of kin, most of whom live in two cities in Mexico. Over time, transnational influence shifted from returning to Mexico for religious rituals to influencing the Catholic practices of kin in Mexico. This case demonstrates the symbolic importance that individuals who integrate transnational networks may attach to religious participation and how Catholic values, commitments, and objects can constitute forms of transnational remittance.

Guillermo's case demonstrates how participation in Catholic organizations helps an individual create a support network that is able to reach across the border to provide spiritual, social, and economic support in a moment of crisis. The parish youth group, along with another Catholic group in Houston, organized a collection and religious ritual events around an event taking place on the other side of the border in Monterrey. In this way, the two groups responded to the transnational context of one of their members despite the lack of organizational ties linking Houston and Monterrey parishes. Guillermo's case also shows how the development of new networks in the host society can simultaneously reduce the frequency of communication with the sending community yet maintain the intensity level of transnational linkages.

The case of *La Fama* shows how Catholic customs and the social importance of kin and neighbor networks are the primary ways by which economic remittances from Houston arrive at the parish in Monterrey. Dense ties of family and friendship encourage immigrants to return to Monterrey for important life cycle rituals and to remit money for memorial services there. In addition, remittances to family members often end up on the collection plates of churches in Mexico, albeit in the form of pesos.

In the cases discussed in this chapter, the Catholic Church, as an institution, does not directly generate transnational linkages despite the fact that it is an international institution. Religious ties across borders are constituted at the grassroots level via family and neighborhood networks, as these are mediated by the Catholic commitments of their members. Immigrants frequently turn to the Church in Houston to ease the settlement process. There, they develop both a deeper commitment to their faith and one or more networks composed of religiously oriented fellow immigrants. They remit both their new religious commitments and their dollars to families in Monterrey and to family members who visit Houston. In turn, parish life in Monterrey is affected to the extent that the family members become more religious and/or contribute money as alms or payment for ritual events.

References

Cortés García, Jesús. 1996. "Santa Catarina en los Albores del Siglo XX." In *Santa Catarina: Un Acercamiento a su Historia*, edited by J. Cortés García, F. Supúlveda García, H. S. Garza, M. Cuellar, and J. R. Tamez. Monterrey: Presidencia Municipal de Santa Catarina.

Emirbayer, Mustafa, and Jeff Goodwin. 1994. "Network Analysis, Culture, and the Problem of Agency." *American Journal of Sociology* 99:1411–54.

Hernandez-Leon, Ruben. 2000. "Urban Origin Migration from Mexico to the United States: The Case of the Monterrey Area." Ph.D. diss., State University of New York at Binghamton.

Knoke, David, and James H. Kuklinski. 1991. "Network Analysis: Basic Concepts." In *Markets, Hierarchies and Networks: The Coordination of Social Life*, edited by G. Thompson, J. Frances, R. Levacic, and J. Mitchell. London: Sage.

Levitt, Peggy. 1998. "Social Remittances: Migration Driven Local-Level Forms of Cultural Diffusion." *International Migration Review* 32:926–48.

Mitchell, J. Clyde. 1969. *Social Networks in Urban Situations: Analysis of Personal Relationships in Central African Towns.* Manchester: Manchester University Press.

Popkin, Eric. 1998. "Guatemalan Mayan Migration to Los Angeles: Constructing Transnational Linkages in the Context of the Settlement Process." *Ethnic and Racial Studies* 22:267–89.

Portes, Alejandro, Luis Guarnizo, and Patricia Landolt. 1999. "The Study of Transnationalism: Pitfalls and Promise of an Emergent Research Field." *Ethnic and Racial Studies* 22:217–37.

Rodriguez, Nestor. 1999. "The Battle for the Border: Notes on Autonomous Migration, Transnational Communities and the State." In *Immigration: A Civil Rights Issue for the Americas*, edited by S. Jonas and S. D. Thomas. Wilmington, DE: Scholarly Resources.

The Evolution of   6
Remittances from Family to Faith
The Vietnamese Case

THAO HA

As Vietnamese refugees settled into life in the United States, they did not forget the family and friends they left behind. Once those in America found that there were surviving relatives in Vietnam, they began to send aid. It is estimated that Vietnamese Americans currently send home $700 million a year to fund needy relatives and friends. The number of *Viet Kieu* (overseas Vietnamese) visiting Vietnam increased from 160,000 in 1993 to 300,000 in 1997 (Pike 1998). Through their remittances, the Vietnamese have developed what Faist (2000) describes as a transnational kinship group. This type of transnational social space is exemplified by the remittances of family members from country of immigration to that of emigration and is part of the larger phenomenon of transnationalism. Levitt (1998) focuses specifically on transnational religious connections between the local level of personal networks and the institutional level of religious organizations. Like Levitt, in this chapter, I document the ways in which micro-level family networks evolve into transnational ties established on the organizational level of religious institutions among Vietnamese Catholics and Buddhists. The Houston data show that the Vietnamese have formed transnational communities in different ways over time, with religious institutions providing one of the newest pathways for remittances.

Data are derived from interviews with members of two religious communities in Houston—a Vietnamese Buddhist temple and a Vietnamese Catholic church—as well as with community and religious leaders. Interview questions focused on the respondents' participation in and knowledge about remittances to Vietnam, both material and social (e.g., interpersonal networks for jobs, housing, and so on). The sample included forty-four persons of Vietnamese descent, ranging from sixteen to sixty-three years of age. Among the females, there are ten Buddhists and fifteen Catholics; among the males, there are eleven Buddhists and eight Catholics. Of the twenty-five females, seven are students, thirteen are employed in various fields, four are housewives, and one is retired. The nineteen males include five students, twelve employed in various fields, and one retired person. All but two members of the sample are able to speak some English. Thirty-five of the respondents were foreign born, and among the foreign born more than half arrived in the United States at least ten years ago. In addition to those affiliated with the church and temple, I also interviewed several Vietnamese business owners and members of Vietnamese organizations who are knowledgeable about the issue of remittances among the Vietnamese in Houston.

Evolving Immigrant—Home Country Ties in the Early Years: Family Connections

In 1970, there is no census record of any Vietnamese in Houston (U.S. Bureau of the Census 1972), but by the 1980 census, 9,481 Vietnamese were counted (U.S. Bureau of the Census 1983), a number that more than tripled to 31,000 in 1990 (U.S. Bureau of the Census 1993). By 1997, the American Community Survey (U.S. Bureau of the Census 1999) counted 60,489 Vietnamese in Harris County (which contains the city of Houston). Vietnamese community leaders estimate that by 2010, there will be well over 100,000 Vietnamese Americans living in the Houston metropolitan area.

An overwhelming majority of Vietnamese immigrants send money and gifts to Vietnam in astonishing amounts and at intense frequency. Between 1975 and 1984, Vietnamese in America were unable to send money home to relatives and friends because the Vietnamese government did not allow its citizens to receive it. They were allowed to send merchandise, and therefore a growing need developed for a service center that Vietnamese Americans could use to send gifts abroad, a need that expanded as the local Vietnamese population grew. In 1981, Vietnamese businesses known as *dich vus* (service centers) began to emerge. The first one was located in downtown Houston in the Vietnamese business district. Vietnamese Americans could buy goods from the selection at the *dich vus* or bring merchandise purchased elsewhere to ship overseas. The owner of AF *Dich Vu* describes how the process worked:

> Our customers would buy items from us or bring in items bought somewhere else. We boxed the merchandise and then sent the package through Air France shipping services. The French airline flew into Vietnam, and the packages were taken to a government post at the airport. Government officials notified family members that they had a package waiting for them. It would usually take anywhere from one to two weeks for the families in Vietnam to receive their packages from the date of shipment.

The delay often was lengthened further because, if the items were worth $100 or more, recipients had to pay a tax of roughly $30 in order to receive them on time; otherwise, they had to wait several days, even weeks, after arrival. Families in Vietnam commonly complained about this practice in letters to families and friends in Houston. Complaints about lost or stolen items were also made. A forty-two-year-old computer engineer describes how difficult it was for his mother to get her medicine from him twenty years ago:

> My mom was sick, and my family members wrote that it was because she had so little to eat. I sent medicine to make her better and vitamins to give her enough nourishment. I got a letter from her over a month after I sent it. She told me the government was holding the package until she could pay the tax on it. Finally, they gave her the goods, after making her wait over two weeks. They must have realized that she really didn't have the money to pay for the supposed tax on the package.

Nevertheless, sending goods was the only way immigrants could help family and friends in Vietnam. Respondents reported sending items to Vietnam at least every two or three months, including electronics (cameras, radios, and walkmans), vitamins, textiles, small toys, watches and clocks, candles, lighters, and any other items that they felt their families might need. Soon, service centers to handle these gifts were popping up all over Houston.

By the mid-1980s, the Vietnamese government permitted its citizens to receive money, and the *dich vu* became a type of Western Union. Their fee was usually $15 to $20 per $100 remitted. All respondents either sent money back on a monthly basis or knew someone in their immediate family who was doing so at least every two or three months. The money was paid at the *dich vu*, which then faxed the information to the post in Vietnam. The post in Vietnam contacted the receiving family, who would come to the post to receive the money. This took only a few days, and there was no merchandise to be lost or stolen. Soon, monetary remittances took the place of merchandise.

During this time period, Vietnamese Americans from the first wave had been in the United States for nearly a decade and were becoming financially established. In 1980, only 112 Vietnamese households in Houston reported an income of more than $50,000 per year, but by 1990, 734 households reported the same (U.S. Bureau of the Census 1983, 1993). During the initial phase of resettlement and adaptation, spanning five to ten years, Vietnamese American families moved close to each other or were brought together through family reunification (Haines 1989). This resulted in a loosely structured community that enabled the pooling and sharing of resources, a necessary collective survival strategy. Resource pooling has been a response other economically disadvantaged communities have also used, such as the Chinese (Glenn 1996). Each individual was impoverished and distressed, but a cooperative kinship network stood a better chance of succeeding, and, in turn, household size was an important determinant of resource availability. More recently, Vietnamese American family networks have been described not as pooling but as patchworking. Pooling implies sharing economic resources, while patchworking refers to many different kinds of resources, in addition to money, such as information, services, and education (Kibria 1993).

Vinh's family provides one example of how this process worked. In 1980, the family comprised four people: Vinh, his wife, and their two young children. He describes how the growth of his family, from four to nine persons, increased their ability to succeed economically:

> When it was just me and my wife, it was hard to save because we had kids. My wife had to stay home and raise the kids. Then when my two brothers, two sisters, and my wife's sister came to live with us, it was easier for us to save money. They could also help us take care of the kids. There was enough money to survive, and everyone could save some, too. My youngest sister went to school, and she learned English fast. She could help us with any papers or bills we had. It was nice to have everyone help.

Many other families described using extended family networks during their first years in the United States. Most agreed that if they had not had the help of family members, it would have been more difficult to succeed. Family networks, coupled with a steady improvement in occupational and economic well-being, helped the Vietnamese American family progress (Zhou and Bankston 1998). The growing financial wealth of the Vietnamese American community enabled its members to send more money with greater frequency to their relatives abroad. For example, Van Nguyen's family came to the United States in 1978. When they arrived, they had no money and found only menial jobs; Van worked as a janitor at a factory, and his wife worked as an assembler in a plastics company. They had three children and were not able to help their families in Vietnam. By 1985, Van was making a good living as a machinist, and his wife had learned English and become a manager at the plastics company. The Nguyens could now send money to their needy families in Vietnam. Today, Van is a software analyst, and his wife is the floor manager of an egg roll factory. They have traveled to Vietnam several times, and they send money home in larger amounts and on a regular basis. The case of the Nguyen family reflects many Vietnamese American families across the United States.

With improvements in technology, by the 1980s Vietnamese Americans were able to fax letters and phone relatives in Vietnam and even travel there, often staying up to three months. As travel to Vietnam became more frequent, the most trusted route for remittances became personal delivery. Travelers could bring a maximum of $10,000 in cash and check two packages with up to seventy pounds of merchandise with the airline. All but two of my respondents had either traveled to Vietnam or knew someone in their immediate family who had done so at least once. A majority of those who had once made the trip had been back multiple times, each time taking money and goods for needy relatives.

Travel to Vietnam is big business. The owner of one of the oldest and the most successful Vietnamese-owned travel agencies specializes in travel to Vietnam, accounting for more than 75 percent of his business. In his words,

> We started doing travel to everywhere, but people want to go to Vietnam. Vietnamese people do not take vacations anywhere except Vietnam. When we started over ten years ago, it was good business, maybe a few hundred customers. But now, it is excellent business—thousands of clients. Many travel agencies are on "sold out" status for tickets to Vietnam during holidays like Vietnamese New Year, which usually falls between the last week in January and the first week or two in February. We know this trend, so we purchase as many seats as we can with our buying power; often we sacrifice slots for other destinations. Still, we are often sold out by the end of the year, too. Our waiting list can get as long as two pages.

It should be noted that older Vietnamese American women travel more often than their male counterparts. Historically, these men sponsored their families to migrate to the United States. Older women's families are often still in Vietnam, so they have more reason to go and to send remittances, as one fifty-two-year-old woman explains:

> My husband and I came here in 1977. We left all our family behind. When we had money here, my husband brought over his sisters and brothers. I did not work because I stayed home to take care of the children. I never asked to have my sister and brother come because it costs money to sponsor them. My husband did not ask if I want them here. Now my kids are grown, and I work so I have money. But my sister and brother have family in Vietnam now. I cannot sponsor, so I visit them every year.

Similar stories are repeated by several of the female respondents. In addition, many older men had not returned until recently because they are former soldiers and officers and feared possible mistreatment by the Vietnamese government. A fifty-eight-year-old former Marine talks about his fear:

> I fought against the Communists. That is why I left because I would die if I stayed. So when my wife told me to go back, I didn't want to because I thought they might still want me. So only three years ago, after I heard many other ex-officers went to Vietnam and everything was okay, then I went. But I was still nervous about it.

Among the younger, 1.5 generation, men travel more frequently than their female counterparts. One factor is their interest in acquiring potential mates in Vietnam. Many of these men told me that Vietnamese women in the United States are too "Americanized." They seek women from the old country who are more traditional. A thirty-three-year-old Vietnamese computer analyst explains why he and several of his friends returned to Vietnam:

> I was born and raised in Vietnam, but I came here [America] when I was sixteen. I have a lot of tradition in me, and my friends have the same mentality. So when we see Vietnamese women in America act so controlling and mean, we just don't want them to raise our kids. I think it is important to have a wife who is kind and peaceful. So I went to Vietnam and found a young and beautiful woman who agrees with my ideas about family. Two of my friends did the same thing, too.

A thirty-seven-year-old accountant and divorcee went back to Vietnam to look for a second wife. He tells his story with much enthusiasm:

> Vietnamese women here and Vietnamese women in Vietnam are so very different! My first wife was rude, loud, and controlling. She was lazy, too, and decided that she had no obligation to do chores if she didn't want to. She said that everything must be equal. I don't think so! My second wife from Vietnam is very good. She knows I work hard all day, and she works hard at home to keep everything in order. My kids are happy with their new mom because she takes care of everything for them. That is the way a wife should be!

Vietnamese older women (mostly first generation and usually from the second wave, post-1980) are working and making money now, something they did not do in Vietnam. In Houston, the manicure industry has been a major source of their employment. In the 1999 Greater Houston Southwestern Bell Yellow Pages, there were more than 500 listings for nail salons, almost all owned and operated by Vietnamese. This economic niche has enabled newly arrived Vietnamese women who have few skills, little education, and very little knowledge of the English language to become economically independent and sometimes even wealthy. A thirty-nine-year-old woman states,

> When I came to America, I only knew a little English. My sister was in the nail business, and she helped me get my license. I really wanted to work so I can send money home to my mother and other sisters. I was happy to work and make such good money. Now, I can go to Vietnam and bring home money for my family.

Linh Doan, a nail technician, exemplifies the relationship between these women and Vietnam. She traveled to Vietnam for the first time in 1989. When her travel arrangements were confirmed, she contacted her eldest brother in Vietnam through fax. He received her fax at a government post in Saigon and asked family members in Vietnam to make a wish list, which he faxed back and she received at the *dich vu.* She says that they requested clothes, electronic equipment, batteries, shoes, music tapes, makeup, and toys. When Linh and others like her reached Vietnam, they were shocked and dismayed at their family members' poverty and suffering. Many report that the money and gifts they had brought were never enough. Linh states, "I have been back three times. I always run out of money by the end part of the trip. When I come home, I try harder to save more money to send home."

As Vietnamese Americans began to travel back to their homeland, they began to realize that temporary monetary assistance for food and clothes was not enough. Their families needed to set up businesses in order to be able to support themselves in the long run. Many respondents reported that they gave money to their families to set up food stands, tailor shops, clothing stores, jewelry stores, and restaurants. In Mai Nguyen's case, her only sister in Vietnam had been a seamstress for a clothing shop before the war. After the war, she was sent to the rice fields for harvest. Her husband died soon thereafter, and she could not regularly feed her children. Mai sent money to her sister, but over the span of six months to a year, her sister would write again to say that the money had run out. Mai decided to travel back to Vietnam to help her sister set up a tailor shop. She paid all the necessary start-up costs and even periodically sends her sister fabric from America. Mai's sister has been very successful and makes enough money to send her youngest child to school. Many people in Vietnam, like Mai's sister, have had the help of their relatives in America and have started to be able to take care of themselves.

Helping the Needy Back Home: Organizational Attempts

After their families in Vietnam had established a regular income and become self-supporting, Vietnamese Americans began to shift their focus from helping individual family members to concentrating on how to help their homeland more broadly. Campaigns to help the needy and poor in Vietnam began to surface in the early 1990s, including fund-raising parties and dances sponsored by Vietnamese American associations. The Vietnamese Professional Society, the Vietnamese Culture and Science Association, and the National United Front for the Liberation of Vietnam are examples of groups that were originally formed for social, cultural, or political purposes. As the need for organizationally based charity networks became increasingly apparent, they extended their missions to incorporate aid to Vietnam's needy. The community in Houston was quick to respond, and networks were set up between organizations in Houston and Saigon. A member of the Vietnamese

Professional Society (VPS) describes how he and other members of the VPS traveled to Vietnam to set up charity networks:

> Most of us had traveled home for personal reasons, but we saw the poverty that the people were suffering from. When we returned, we discussed these issues at the VPS meetings. We decided that there were a lot of well-off people in Houston who could make a difference by donating to charities in Vietnam. We wanted to be the group to organize large-scale charity projects, so we raised money for the homeless, the orphans, and the poor. We went back to Vietnam to find the most needy social services. Arrangements were made to send the money through the *dich vu* centers. We have been successful, but we have not yet reached the goals that we set out. The people aren't sure if they can trust our organization yet.

Other associations also raised money for orphanages, flood and drought victims, the homeless, the elderly, and the disabled, but they were unable to sustain regular remittances. Community members were willing to give once or twice, but they were not donating on a regular basis. A thirty-year-old software analyst stated, "I'd love to help, and I have given donations once or twice. But if they [the associations] keep asking for more money, I have to wonder why they are always asking and what exactly are they doing with the money? How can I be sure that the money is getting to the right places? I just don't know."

In the attempt to aid the needy back home, Houston's Vietnamese community also had to deal with the Communist regime there. The Vietnamese in the United States are a displaced population, and their diaspora resulted from war. Consequently, Vietnamese Americans' perception of the current government is one of mistrust, anger, and resentment. One clear example of this can be seen in downtown Houston, where the Vietnamese business district lies. There is a large yellow banner that hangs on a wire fence and reads, *"Dung nghe nhung di Cong Sang noi. Hay nhin ky nhung di Cong Sang lam"* (Do not listen to what the Communists say. Watch carefully the things the Communists do). Members of the community are not shy about voicing their opinions on issues such as human rights violations, corruption, poverty, and suffering in Vietnam. Local Vietnamese-language radio and television shows often feature community leaders taking phone calls from listeners or viewers who want to help the people of Vietnam but are not sure of the best way to do so. They are afraid that the government will reap all the benefits and that little or none of the money will reach the people in need. The current president of the Vietnamese Community of Houston and Vicinity, a nonprofit organization that acts as a liaison between Houston's Vietnamese community, other ethnic communities, and local government, says that members of the community want to help the Vietnamese people very much, and they frequently inquire about specific associations and groups. "The people want to know if association A or organization B has a good reputation so they can donate money through those services. We often have to tell them that there is no way to be sure that the money you give gets in the right hands unless you deliver it yourself."

Many of my respondents express the view that the Communist government is evil and corrupt. In the words of a thirty-three-year-old man,

> I do not trust Vietnam's government. They will take everything they can from you. When I went to Vietnam, they tried to take all my possessions at the airport. They made me fill out all these forms stating that I was not in Vietnam to overthrow the government, and I had to write down everything that I had brought with me and for what reasons I brought them. I am so sick of the Vietnamese government watching the *Viet Kieu* so carefully. They need our money, but they treat us like we are spies.

Many Vietnamese Americans have learned that the best way to deal with Vietnamese officials is through bribery, as the comments of one middle-aged woman show:

> I went to Vietnam and had a lot of gifts inside my boxes. I also had some music tapes and videotapes for my family. The customs people took my tapes and made me wait for them to listen and view the tapes to make sure there was nothing against the government in the tapes. I waited for almost one hour, and then I got tired. The officer told me that if I gave him some money, he could make the process faster. So I gave him twenty American dollars. Five minutes later, my tapes were returned, and I was allowed to go. Many of my friends who went to Vietnam had to do the same thing.

Another woman, who has been to Vietnam six times since 1993, is very frank about the system:

> People who go to Vietnam for the first time, and especially young people, do not know that giving money to Vietnamese airport officials will make the paperwork go faster. Vietnam is about money. All they want is money from you. If you give them American money, they will leave you alone.

It seems that young people are special targets of government harassment. A twenty-seven-year-old Vietnamese American computer analyst speaks about his first trip back to Vietnam since he left in 1978:

> It was like a nightmare. I went with two of my friends, and they split us up when we got to the customs area. They asked each of us why we were going to Vietnam and why each of the other persons with us was in Vietnam. They told me if they found out I was lying, they could arrest me and keep me here. Then they asked about the things we brought back and how much money we brought back and told

us we had to claim everything. If they checked and found something that we didn't claim, we could get arrested for that, too. When it was over, two hours had passed, and my relatives who were waiting to pick me up left because they thought we didn't make it. It was terrifying.

The Religious Connection

Given their hostility toward the government, Vietnamese Americans sought charitable and social service groups in Vietnam to fund directly. They soon came to realize that there is one type of charitable institution that could be trusted: religious institutions. Many of the respondents who had traveled to Vietnam report that they had given money directly to a church or temple there. As one describes,

> When we were in Vietnam, we saw how all the temples were rebuilding after they had been burned to the ground. We were glad to see that they were coming up so that people had a place to go besides their home. I gave money because I hoped that it would help the temple to help others. I trust monks will use the money for good, like food for the hungry.

Minh Tran provides another example. He went to Vietnam to run a small business and, at the same time, helped the temple in his hamlet build a dining area for the monks. Tran wanted the decor to be modern and different from other temples, so he bought tables and chairs from a designer furniture store in Vietnam rather than the traditional benches and long wooden tables. His temple also added pews, which are nonexistent in Vietnam. Another respondent describes the same sense of trust when she donated money to the Catholic church that she attended while in Vietnam visiting her parents. Yet another woman returned to Vietnam and wanted the church in her parents' village to have a piano for the choir. When she returned the next time, she was astonished to find that the church had no established choir. After she purchased a piano, she was able to recruit several men and women who have started and maintained a choir group. Other churches and temples have started counseling groups for youth with funds sent by members' relatives in Houston. The senders are youth group leaders at a Vietnamese Catholic congregation and a Buddhist temple in Houston.

While Vietnamese American visitors were donating money to their religious institutions in Vietnam, temples and churches in Houston were establishing transnational connections to Vietnam of their own. Beginning in the early 1990s, monks at the Vietnamese Buddhist Center in southwest Houston have traveled to Vietnam to meet with monks and visit temples. Many temples had been destroyed during the years after the war, and the monks from Houston took an interest in rebuilding these structures. As one states, "It was devastating to see that so many temples were burned down and the rebuilt ones were run down. The monks and laypersons at the temples in Vietnam were in bad shape, too. I want to ask our community in America to help these temples in Vietnam." Vietnamese Catholic priests at Notre Dame Church were also traveling to Vietnam to make connections with parishes there. In Sullivan's (2000) study of this Houston church, she discovered that the congregation established an Orphan Sponsorship Program in conjunction with a parish in South Vietnam in 1997. The program helps these children attend school and acquire the skills necessary to improve their lives. The Vietnamese Martyr's Catholic Church in southeast Houston has started a program to bring priests from Vietnam to the United States. Much of the motivation behind this effort stems from the decreasing number of seminary students in the United States. As a member of this church states,

> In the younger generation, there are no kids that want to grow up and be a priest anymore. They want to do something to make money, not to make their parents proud. In Vietnam, a priest is more respected than a doctor or a professional, but here in America, kids want to make money to get respect. There is a need for Vietnamese priests, but the church must get them from Vietnam, not from here.

A fresh supply of new priests is needed to sustain the church, but also important to the future of both temples and churches is a new supply of volunteers. Volunteers at both types of religious institutions usually come from among first-generation immigrants from Vietnam, but those who have been in the United States for a long time tend no longer to volunteer. A youth leader at a Vietnamese Catholic church explains this:

> I came to America eight years ago, and I am just starting to get comfortable speaking English. But my Vietnamese is very good, so the church asked me to help with kids and teach them Vietnamese stories. I am one of only a few volunteers here. My friends help me, but they just came to America, too. And the people who have been here a long time do not help. They say they're busy, but I think they just don't want to help.

A twenty-five-year-old youth leader from the same church notes the same problem:

> In our volunteer groups, I would say only about four or five out of about thirty volunteers have been in America longer than ten years. All the other people I know who help have just come from Vietnam maybe less than five years. These are the only people who will help when there is a church event. Most of the people who have been here for a long time seem too busy to help, or I think they just don't care about volunteerism. They only come here once a week as required, and then they leave. When we have festivals or celebrations, the newcomers do most of the work, and the long-timers enjoy the party. I really don't know how to explain it

for older people, but I think the young kids might feel uncool if they volunteer for the church.

Monks from the Vietnamese Buddhist Center share the same concerns about the second generation. The youth do not want to become monks, and the temple may eventually have to seek clergy in Vietnam. Unlike the Catholic sponsorship of Vietnamese priests, however, the monks in Houston are still paying off loans that were required to buy land and build the temple, so they lack the funds to establish a program to train overseas monks.

Traditionally, religious institutions in Vietnam were not social service centers or fund-raising organizations. They were places where members could pray, worship, and socialize with friends. The role of Vietnamese churches and temples in Houston has had to change and adapt in order to meet the needs of an immigrant population (Ebaugh and Chafetz 2000). Many adults from the first generation report that they trust their religious institutions as the best place for their children to learn Vietnamese culture since "traditional ways often extolled by the elders are followed and understood by fewer and fewer Vietnamese" (Freeman 1995). Language schools and programs to teach the younger generation about their culture and heritage arose from the concerns of first-generation parents. The Vietnamese Buddhist Center offers language classes for Vietnamese youths. The *Linh Son* Buddhist Temple in north Houston has facilities for the *Vo Vi Nam* Vietnamese group that trains youth in martial arts. There is also a volleyball court on the temple grounds for tournaments and picnics. The Notre Dame Catholic Vietnamese Community and the Vietnamese Martyr's Catholic Church also offer language classes for youth and house a youth organization modeled after the Boy and Girl Scouts. On Sundays after Mass, the churches provide rooms for the elderly, who meet to have lunch and socialize with one another. Each also sponsors a women's support group. These programs enable the community to re-create their ethnic identity. The Vietnamese religious community in Oklahoma has done the same (Rutledge 1985). Some respondents in the 1.5 generation admit that during their years in college and a few years thereafter, they lost touch with their heritage; however, as they establish families, they want their children to go to church or temple, which they see as the best place for their children to learn Vietnamese culture and customs.

Vietnamese religious institutions in Houston began to realize that the local Vietnamese community is doing well and that most have adapted successfully to the new society. As community members had earlier, religious leaders began to realize the enormous need for social services in Vietnam. They were already well into the process of setting up transnational networks with temples and churches in Vietnam. The orphan sponsorship program, the sponsoring of priests from Vietnam, and the consistent donations of money to temples in Vietnam were all programs sustained through transnational networks. The support provided by American religious institutions meant that temples and churches in Vietnam could now offer more than worship services. They were able to begin providing social services.

While the roles of temples and churches in both Houston and Saigon were changing, so was the relationship between the U.S. and Vietnamese governments. After a twenty-year hiatus of severed ties, President Clinton announced the formal normalization of diplomatic relations with Vietnam on July 11, 1995 (U.S. Department of State 2001). Corporations such as Nike set up factories there, and hotels for tourists established by Hilton and Ritz Carlton were built in Hanoi and Saigon. In the summer of 1998, Vietnam opened its insurance, banking, and other financial service industries to outside competition, and soon international banks, such as Chase and Citibank, had opened branches. As a result, religious institutions were able to set up accounts in the United States to which their liaisons in Vietnam had access. The frequency and intensity of ties between religious institutions in Houston and Vietnam had become sufficiently strong to justify an international account. There are many advantages to this type of financial transnational linkage between religious groups in Houston and Saigon. Travel expenses are decreased, and the money saved can go into the account for use by religious organizations. There is no way for the funds to get lost. Access is immediate in case of emergency. Finally, records are kept so that doubts about theft and misappropriation are abated.

As members of Houston's Vietnamese community sought trusted ways to send remittances to help Vietnam's needy, religious institutions became the most popular conduit. When the 1999 floods in central Vietnam killed hundreds and left tens of thousands homeless and hungry, the Vietnamese community in Houston turned to the church. The Notre Dame and Vietnamese Martyr's Catholic Churches announced that they would accept donations for flood victims, and they raised tens of thousands of dollars. Other community organizations, such as the Vietnamese Students Association and the Vietnamese Community Civic Group, were also soliciting funds for the flood victims, but they were not very successful. As Tri Nguyen, a third-year law student, states,

> There are a lot of organizations that want to help our country [Vietnam]. But it is hard to really know where the money is going exactly. Sometimes people in organizations can get greedy. But people put their trust in the church. They believe that the church is an honest place and the money will not be spent for the wrong reasons.

Clearly, Houston's Vietnamese religious institutions have become, over time, major pathways for remittances to Vietnam that local community members feel they can trust. However, these trusted pathways have to be situated within the larger context of church–state relations in Vietnam, institutional ties that also impact the story of remittances sent by immigrants to Vietnam.

Both the constitution and the government of Vietnam provide for freedom of worship. However, the government controls religious activities because it fears that organized religion may turn people against it. The Vietnamese government requires that religious groups be registered, a process that allows for monitoring them. Religious organizations must check with the government before they undertake any organized activity. They "must obtain government permission to hold training seminars, conventions, and celebrations outside the regular religious calendar, build or remodel places of worship, engage in charitable activities or operate religious schools, and train, ordain, promote, or transfer clergy" (U.S. Department of State 1999). The government officially recognizes Buddhist, Roman Catholic, Protestant, *Cao Dai, Hoa Hao,* and Muslim religious organizations. However, some Buddhists, Protestants, *Cao Dai,* and *Hoa Hao* believers do not recognize or participate in the government-approved institutions and, in turn, are not considered legal by the authorities. The Vietnamese government's Office of Religious Affairs also requires all Buddhist monks to operate under the Central Buddhist Church of Vietnam and opposes the Unified Buddhist Church of Vietnam, which wants to operate independently. The law also prohibits foreign missionaries from operating in the country. Visiting immigrants and noncitizens alike must comply with the law when practicing their faiths. Catholic and Protestant foreigners can exercise leadership only in worship services that are reserved specifically for foreigners. For example, when a Catholic priest from Houston returns to give a service in Vietnam, foreigners only, not citizens of Vietnam, attend his Mass.

The Houston Vietnamese want their donations to reach the right people in Vietnam. They rely on personal delivery, *dich vus,* and their religious institutions for sending money and goods. If the government recognizes only some specific religious institutions and if they have to obtain permission from the government to participate in or organize events, the question arises as to how much the government runs economic matters at these institutions. And if the immigrants' money is going to institutions that are not recognized by the government, are these institutions operating in secrecy from the government and participating in underground networks? These questions being raised by Vietnamese immigrants in Houston can be answered only if transnational links between the Vietnamese religious organizations in Houston and those in Vietnam are traced in detail: To precisely which churches and temples in Vietnam is the money going? Does the government officially recognize these institutions? How do they manage and operate their finances? Such data can be collected in Vietnam only at considerable risk to the researcher.

As described earlier, the Vietnamese American community is staunchly anti-Communist and suspicious of Vietnam's government. In Vietnam, both the constitution and government decrees provide for freedom of worship; however, the government continues to restrict significantly those organized activities of religious groups that it declares to be at variance with state laws and policies (U.S. Department of State 2000). Although Vietnam's government maintains that its constitution guarantees religious freedom, Vietnamese Americans realize that this is not the case in practice. A member of Notre Dame Catholic Church in Houston who travels to Vietnam at least once a year and visits the Notre Dame Catholic Church in Ho Chi Minh City, states that "the Vietnamese Communist Party either replaces the whole leadership of a religious faith or runs a parallel organization to dilute the authority of that faith's leaders." Thus, the Unified Buddhist Church of Vietnam has been banned and replaced by the state-sponsored Buddhist Church of Vietnam, while the Vietnamese Catholic community is subsumed by the state-run Patriotic Catholic Association. According to one interviewee,

> Vietnamese Catholics in the southern part of the country are leaderless. After the death of Archbishop Nguyen Van Binh, the Vietnamese government has repeatedly rejected the replacement appointed by the Vatican. Also, the training and ordaining of new clergy are still extremely restrictive. It is difficult to fill in the positions that are left open by priests who have passed away.

Authorities must approve the appointments of all new religious leaders, including Buddhist monks and Catholic priests; the construction and renovation of all churches, temples, and pagodas; the publishing of all religious materials; and the training of novice and apprentice church leaders.

The Vietnamese Bishops' Council of the Catholic Church has written several letters to Vietnam's prime minister asking the government to reduce its restrictions on religious activities. Following its annual meeting in 1997 in Hanoi, the council sent a letter to Prime Minister Phan Van Khai similar to the fruitless letters sent to previous prime ministers. In its most recent letter, the council's first request was to reduce restrictions on bishops' and priests' travel for religious purposes. In order to travel, they must apply for permission, which involves many forms and several seals of approval. Another request was to reduce the administrative difficulties confronting young men and women who wish to enter a monastery or seminary. In addition, the council requested permission to open two more seminaries, or at least branches outside the existing facilities, so that the need for training new clergy can be met.

One other important request made by the council was for permission to increase the church's participation in the provision of social services. Part of the letter reads as follows:

> Many religious orders of our Church also wish to be allowed to work with the government to serve in the public health and social services areas, such as taking care of patients, the poor and orphans. Currently, our participation is greatly restricted.

This proposal is of special interest to the immigrant church in Houston, where a priest states,

> Dioceses, parishes, and religious orders need to be open to contribute to the education of young people and to support the poor, the sick, the elderly, and the homeless. These goals can be achieved by setting up schools and by opening social institutions like hospitals, shelters, and rehabilitation and retirement centers. We would like to see Vietnam's Church expand its services like we have in America.

Although Vietnam's religious institutions are limited in their ability to provide social services, there are Catholic ministries from outside the country that aid in social service delivery. Maryknoll missionaries from the United States sponsor self-help projects for poor families, village craft workers, and youth. In 1992, Father Thomas Dunleavy, a missionary in Cambodia, was asked whether he would be willing to set up a mission in Vietnam. He accepted, he secured a visa, and Maryknoll became the first long-term Catholic foreign ministry in postwar Vietnam. Maryknoll is not permitted to work as a partner with the local church, only as a member of a nongovernmental organization (NGO) that funds and monitors humanitarian projects. Some of its projects include Small Business Development and Assistance to Traditional Handicraft Artisans, Skills Training for the Poor Youth in the Son Soc District, and Assistance for Free Treatment of Vietnamese Children with Disabilities. Maryknoll's success, as well as its reputation for not violating the terms of its government contract, enabled it to easily obtain permission to help boys in a detention center. The Vietnamese Catholic churches in Houston also work through this type of channel. They are restricted to providing aid to Vietnamese social services as an NGO and must not affiliate with any local churches. A representative from the church meets with government officials and NGO officials, and a contract is written up. Funds raised in the Houston churches are used to support the NGO. Some of the programs that Houston's Vietnamese Catholic community helps through this mechanism are vocational training and education for poor youth, flood relief, and medical treatment for orphans, the elderly, and the homeless.

Regardless of the myriad controls government exercises over religion, because there is now some level of religious freedom, the number of Catholics has grown. There are an estimated seven million Roman Catholics in Vietnam, making this the second-largest Catholic country in Asia after the Philippines (U.S. Department of State 1999). Another way in which the government has improved the situation for religious groups concerns its restrictions on travel. In November 1997, Vietnam eliminated the need for its citizens to obtain exit visas from the government in order to travel abroad. In the 1980s, only senior Communist Party officials were permitted to travel abroad. Within the past several years, an increasing number of business people, students, and tourists have begun to travel outside of Vietnam. Since the inception of this new* policy, it has become easier for Vietnamese students to come to the United States. According to a Vietnamese priest in Houston, Vietnamese coming to the United States for religious training do so under student visas. This has made it easier for the Vietnamese American community to obtain students of theology from Vietnam as well as clergy for their parishes and missions.

Catholic seminarians in the United States who come from Vietnam do so with one of two hopes: either returning to Vietnam to serve a parish there or staying in the United States to serve in a Vietnamese American parish. This is important for the Catholic community in the United States, where the number of priests has declined significantly in recent years. According to the Diocesan Vocations Office, most men who become priests today come from minority communities. In 1998, the Roman Catholic Diocese of Galveston–Houston ordained four priests who were born in four different countries; one was Vietnamese. He is one of the many Vietnamese studying for the priesthood in the United States who decide to remain, although others decide to return to Vietnam.

Conclusion

Clearly, characteristics of Houston's Vietnamese American community have changed in many ways over the past twenty-five years. Its population has increased considerably, as has its socioeconomic status, and relations between the U.S. and Vietnamese governments have improved. Initially, postwar ties to the homeland were scant, but over time they have amplified greatly. In its early stages, Vietnamese immigrants' transnational links consisted of micro-level family connections. Over time, they developed into community liaisons. These ties initially enabled Houston's Vietnamese to aid relatives and friends, but eventually they were able to help whole villages and communities, including temples and churches. Vietnamese religious bodies have become one of the most highly trusted conduits for channeling resources between Houston and Vietnam, a transnational linkage that enables the former community to increase its aid for the needy in the latter.

The future of transnational connections to Vietnam is questionable because Houston's Vietnamese American community continues to change. As the second and third generations replace the first, the number of Vietnamese Americans with relatives and friends in Vietnam will diminish. In addition, their experiences and opportunities for social mobility in America differ from those of the first generation. Whether the coming generations of Vietnamese Americans will sustain ties to Vietnam is yet to be seen.

References

Ebaugh, Helen Rose, and Janet Chafetz. 2000. *Religion and the New Immigrants: Continuities and Adaptations in Immigrant Congregations.* Walnut Creek, CA: AltaMira.

Faist, Thomas. 2000. "Transnationalization in International Migration: Implications for the Study of Citizenship and Culture." *Ethnic and Racial Studies* 23(March):189–222.

Freeman, James. 1995. *Changing Identities: Vietnamese American, 1975–1995.* Needham Heights, MA: Allyn & Bacon.

Glenn, Charles. 1996. *Educating Immigrant Children: Schools and Language Minorities in 12 Nations.* New York: Garland.

Haines, David. 1989. *Refugees as Immigrants: Cambodians, Laotians and Vietnamese in America.* Lanham, MD: Rowman & Littlefield.

Kibria, Nazli. 1993. *Family Tightrope.* Princeton, NJ: Princeton University Press.

Levitt, Peggy. 1998. "Local-Level Global Religion: The Case of U.S.–Dominican Migration." *Journal for the Scientific Study of Religion* 37:74–89.

Pike, Douglas. 1998. *Viet Kieu in the United States: Political and Economic Activity.* Lubbock: Texas Tech Vietnam Center Study.

Rutledge, Paul. 1985. *The Role of Religion in Ethnic Self-Identity: A Vietnamese Community.* Lanham, MD: University Press of America.

Sullivan, Kathleen. 2000. "St. Catherine's Catholic Church: One Church, Parallel Congregations." In *Religion and the New Immigrants: Continuities and Adaptations in Immigrant Congregations,* edited by Helen R. Ebaugh and Janet S. Chafetz. Walnut Creek, CA: AltaMira.

U.S. Bureau of the Census. 1972. *U.S. Census of the Population: 1970 Detailed Characteristics, Texas.* Washington, DC: U.S. Government Printing Office.

———. 1983. *1980 Census of the Population: Social and Economic Characteristics for Social Racial Groups, Texas.* Washington, DC: U.S. Government Printing Office.

———. 1993. *1990 Census of the Population: Social and Economic Characteristics for Social and Racial Groups, Texas.* Washington, DC: U.S. Government Printing Office.

———. 1999. *American Community Survey: 1997.* Washington, DC: U.S. Government Printing Office.

U.S. Department of State. 1999. *1999 Annual Report on International Religious Freedom: Vietnam.* Released by the Bureau of Democracy, Human Rights, and Labor. Washington, DC: U.S. Government Printing Office.

———. 2000. *2000 Annual Report on International Religious Freedom: Vietnam.* Released by the Bureau of Democracy, Human Rights, and Labor. Washington, DC: U.S. Government Printing Office.

———. 2001. *Countries, Background Notes: Vietnam.* Released by the Bureau of East Asian and Pacific Affairs. Washington, DC: U.S. Government Printing Office.

Zhou, Min, and Carl Bankston. 1998. *Growing Up American: How Vietnamese Children Adapt to Life in the United States.* New York: Russell Sage Foundation.

Chinese Christian Transnationalism   7
Diverse Networks of a Houston Church

FENGGANG YANG

D
iversity is the most notable feature of the transnational ties characteristic of the Chinese immigrant churches in the United States. These congregations commonly maintain transnational ties with people, churches, and parachurch organizations in several societies across the Pacific and elsewhere. The most dense and important connections are with Taiwan, Hong Kong, mainland China, and Southeast Asia; ties also extend to Canada, South and Central America, Australia and New Zealand, Europe, and even Africa. This is in clear contrast to the biregional or binational connections documented in other chapters and other writings (Levitt 1998, 2001; Menjívar 1999). Vietnamese and Indian immigrant congregations, given their wide spread of the recent migrants across various parts of the world, may also maintain some multinational ties.

The diverse transnational ties characteristic of Chinese Christian congregations is due mainly to the fact that most such churches in the United States have a cosmopolitan membership (Yang 1998), including immigrants from different Chinese provinces, Hong Kong, and Taiwan and ethnic Chinese from various countries in Southeast Asia and elsewhere. These immigrants often sojourn in other places in Southeast Asia and North America before settling down. Moreover, the tendency of Chinese churches to remain independent in organization and their evangelical theological orientation allow and promote multiple transnational ties (Yang 1999). About half the Chinese churches in the United States today are nondenominational, and a large proportion of denominational ones are affiliated with nonhierarchical denominations that grant substantial independence to local congregations, such as the Southern Baptist Convention. Such independence enables a church to open its doors to receive people from diverse denominations, many of which are associated with particular geographic locations.[1] The evangelical orientation drives

Chinese Christians to strengthen old ties and develop new ones in other parts of the world for the purpose of gaining converts.

In the multidimensional, multilayer, and multitype networks of Chinese Christian transnationalism, a large church, a major organization, or a leader with charisma may serve as a nexus node. The Houston Chinese Church, which is called the Chinese Gospel Church in the RENIR I project (Yang, in Ebaugh and Chafetz 2000),[2] is one such active node. In this chapter, I first describe this church and its membership and then develop a typology of transnational ties in order to provide a framework for describing its complex ties and networks. This is followed by descriptions of the transnational ties that link the Houston Chinese Church with Hong Kong, Taiwan, mainland China, and other parts of the world. I conclude the chapter with further reflections about Chinese Christian transnational networks.

Data in this chapter come from my ethnographic fieldwork in Houston in 1997–99 and in Taiwan, Hong Kong, and mainland China in the summer of 2000.[3] In Hong Kong, an informational and organizational center of the Chinese diaspora, I interviewed leaders of major Chinese Christian organizations that have strong connections with Chinese churches in the United States, conducted participant observation at Sunday services at three churches that have a sizable number of returned immigrants, and interviewed some returned immigrants at these churches. The three churches include a Mandarin-speaking nondenominational church whose members are originally from Taiwan and mainland China, a Cantonese-speaking Alliance church that has a Mandarin service, and an English-speaking Anglican church that had just set up a Mandarin-speaking congregation for mainland Chinese who have either returned from Western countries or come directly from the mainland. In Taiwan, I visited Taipei, the capital, and Xinzhu, a newly developed city with a concentration of highly advanced technologies that has attracted many returned immigrants. In Xinzhu, I attended the Sunday service of a Lutheran church with a majority of returned immigrants. In Taipei, I attended worship services at three churches, one Presbyterian, one Ling Liang, and one Libaitang; all are Mandarin-speaking. In Taipei and Xinzhu, I interviewed former members of the Houston Chinese Church and other Christians who once lived in the United States. I also interviewed leaders of major Christian organizations and churches that are known to have strong connections with the United States. In mainland China, I visited five cities and talked with many Christian believers and leaders. Supplementing the ethnographic data are my longtime observations of Chinese Christian churches in other parts of the United States and information from Chinese Christian newsletters and magazines.

The Houston Chinese Church

The Houston Chinese Church (HCC) has three characteristics that are common among Chinese Christian churches in the United States: It is evangelical in theology, it is independent in organization, and its members are from different nations (Yang 2000). The membership of HCC, however, is bigger than most Chinese American churches, with about 2,000 to 2,500 in the original and daughter churches in the Houston area, which allows it to have more extensive transnational ties than most of its counterparts.

The HCC grew out of a fellowship group that first met in 1972 and was officially incorporated in 1975 with about eighty founding members. Sunday attendance increased fast, reaching 250 by the end of 1976 and about 600 in 1982. After fluctuations during the rest of the 1980s due to a major economic downturn that drove many immigrants to leave Houston, growth resumed in the 1990s; the congregation numbered more than 800 in 1993. In 1979, HCC planted a church in a southeastern suburb of Houston, in 1991 another in west Houston, and in 1997 yet another church in a southwestern suburb. The mother and three daughter churches all maintain large attendances, ranging from 300 to 800 adults. The HCC has also planted or aided in the establishment of several Chinese churches in other Texas cities, including College Station in central Texas, Port Lavaca and Corpus Christi in southern Texas, and Lubbock in northern Texas. Moreover, in 1997, HCC started a mission church in Kazakhstan, a former Soviet republic in central Asia. The HCC remains at the center of these local, regional, and international networks.

The HCC is not a transplanted church originally organized by a congregation or denomination in another country. It was formed by a group of Chinese immigrant professionals and students attending educational institutions in Houston, and from the very beginning, the origins of its members have been diverse. Some came from Hong Kong (a British colony until 1997), some from Taiwan (the Republic of China), and some from various Southeast Asian countries. Among them, many were born in mainland China and had fled from the wars and the Chinese Communists. What united the founding members was the desire to have a Chinese church of their own that would meet their needs and reach out to other new Chinese immigrants.[4] Beginning in the 1980s, many immigrants and students from China (the People's Republic of China) and American-born Chinese who moved to Houston from other states have joined this church as well, increasingly expanding its cosmopolitan scope.

The acceptance of members from diverse origins is encouraged by the independent nature of the church. Most of the founding members had been Christians before coming to the United States but belonged to different denominations, those reflecting either Western missionary influences or indigenous Chinese sects. Before the incorporation of the church, fellowship gatherings were held at a Chinese Baptist church. However, when the church was officially incorporated, the founding members decided to become nondenominational so that any Chinese Christian, no matter what the denominational background or geographic origin, could join. In fact, throughout North America, Chinese Christians have a strong tendency toward antidenominationalism. Their desires for both Christian unity and Chinese unity augment each other (Yang 1998), resulting in greater cosmopolitanism among church members.

Since its very beginning, HCC has been an evangelical church with a strong missionary commitment. Local evangelism has been very successful as witnessed by its growth in membership and the planting of daughter churches in the Houston area and elsewhere in Texas. The HCC also has dedicated a significant proportion of its resources to overseas missions. Two years after its establishment, in 1977, a Missions Committee was formed, which later evolved into a Missions Department with its own separate budget. The Missions Department constantly explores new opportunities for overseas missions while maintaining existing operations. Since the beginning, the church has provided financial as well as spiritual support to missionaries and Christian organizations outside the United States. Between 1975 and 1995, sixty-four church members gave up their professional careers and entered seminaries; some of them later became missionaries to other countries. The HCC has sent out its own missionaries who were supported completely or mostly by HCC. The drive for overseas evangelistic missions has promoted transnational ties to places both with and without previous connections.

Meanwhile, the turnover rate of HCC membership has been high because of the highly mobile nature of contemporary Chinese migration. Many immigrant members came to Houston after first studying and living in other parts of North America, and many have moved elsewhere after a few years of studying or working in Houston. Some have moved back to Asia. One of the most mobile groups within the church is the Student Fellowship for international students, composed of a Mandarin Student Fellowship group and a Cantonese Student Fellowship group. Taken together, the Student Fellowship has remained one of the largest fellowship groups in the church throughout its twenty-five-year history, although individuals come and go every year. These students, and the transient immigrants as well, did not come from one particular place, nor do they return to one particular place. However, no matter where they go, they usually take one invisible tie with them. Because of its various strengths, many former members of HCC are proud of having been a member and try to maintain some ties with the church or its members.

Given the large and diverse membership of HCC, it is impossible to trace all its ties to one particular church, village, city, district, or province in one home country. Nor is it possible to trace all the transnational ties HCC and its members maintain. To facilitate the description and understanding of its diverse and numerous transnational ties, a classification of various types of ties is useful.

Four Types of Transnational Ties

There are four types of transnational ties that the local Chinese immigrant church and its members maintain: individual to individual, individuals to organizations, the church to individuals, and the church to organizations (see table 7.I).

The transnational ties between individual members of HCC and individuals in other parts of the world are the most numerous. These ties are informal, fluctuating, and yet resilient. As long as a member maintains contacts with family members, relatives, or friends on another shore of the Pacific, a string is stretched out. Of course, these strings vary in strength and intensity. However, given the ease of communication and transportation, many such ties are indeed well maintained through postal letters, e-mail, long-distance phone calls, and mutual visits. Many church members take business or vacation trips to the home country, and at any given time there are no fewer than a dozen temporarily visiting relatives attending HCC along with church members. These visitors are usually the parents of immigrant professionals who either do not want to live permanently in the United States or cannot stay long because of U.S. immigration restrictions. Some of these visiting parents have converted to Christianity during their visit, then returned to

Table 7.1.   Types of Transnational Ties between the Houston Chinese Church (HCC) and Other Nations

	Individuals (Overseas)	Organizations (Overseas)
Individual members (HCC)	Family members and relatives Former church co-members or co-workers Former colleagues Fellow school alumni Friends Missionaries	As donors/supporters As speakers (in private capacity) As authors As board members or trustees As regional representatives
Church (HCC)	Supports missionaries Supports seminarians Supports ministers Supports returned immigrants	Supports Christian organizations Supports seminaries Supports churches Supports associations Supports special task forces

Taiwan, Hong Kong, or mainland China. Some church members have also helped bring their siblings, relatives, or close friends to study or work in Houston. Of course, some people have all their family members and close relatives in Houston or in the United States and thus do not actively maintain transnational ties any longer. However, such families are few at this young church. Even these people, driven by a sense of mission and/or evangelistic church programs, may develop or renew transnational ties.

Some persons maintain more than one string across the Pacific. Among post-1965 Chinese immigrants, some have sojourned in several places before settling down in Houston. Many immigrants from Taiwan and Hong Kong were born in mainland China but fled from the wars and the Chinese Communists in the 1940s and 1950s, wandered around Southeast Asia, and then came to North America for higher education or jobs. In each of the places they once studied or worked, they may have left family members, relatives, good friends, or Chinese churches they once attended.

Many HCC members also maintain relationships with churches and parachurch organizations[5] in other places. They might have belonged to a church or worked at or benefited from a parachurch organization's ministries before coming to Houston. They often continue to contribute money, knowledge, time, organizational skills, and other resources to these Christian organizations. Some lay leaders, as well as clergy, frequently travel to Asia to preach, lecture, or participate in board meetings in their private capacity (not as a representative of HCC), and the clergy sometimes use their vacation time for such trips without receiving financial subsidies from HCC. Occasionally, parachurch organizations in Asia send solicitation letters or representatives to Houston, where some members may be inspired to contribute money and other resources to them. The church may or may not be formally involved in this process. Like ties between individuals, this type of tie between individuals and organizations is informal from HCC's perspective.

The formal transnational ties are those that HCC officially supports, often through its Missions Department. First, HCC supports many individual missionaries, ministers, and staff members of Christian organizations in Asia and other parts of the world. Most often, HCC provides partial financial support and requests that those they support provide regular reports about their ministries. The HCC has also sent out missionaries to Asia and South and Central America and provided full financial support. Second, HCC provides financial support to Christian parachurch organizations, seminaries, churches, and transnational Christian associations in Asia, Europe, and the Americas. These formal relationships between this church and overseas individuals and organizations are established through formal procedures. A church member may propose to the Missions Department that it support an individual or organization, or an individual or organization may initiate the contact with the Missions Department to seek support. After the Missions Department reviews the applications and consults the pastors, it makes recommendations to the Church Council, the decision-making body. The decision of the Church Council then is sent to the congregation for confirmation. Given this structure of procedures, formal ties between the church and overseas individuals and organizations are limited in number but relatively stable. In order to maintain a sense of intimacy, the Missions Department always designates particular individuals to keep in regular contact with the supported individuals and organizations. These designated persons encourage other church members to write encouraging letters to the missionaries or missionary organizations. In return, the missionaries respond with prayer letters to the church and/or to individual members.

The transnational ties may shift from one type to another. For example, an informal connection between a pastor and his missionary friend can be transformed into a formal one when HCC officially supports him. Similarly, the formal ties between the church and individuals can be assigned to church members who, in turn, may nurture more personal relationships. These multidimensional, multilayer, and multitype transnational ties are interwoven to form thick transnational networks around this local church. The HCC thus serves as a very active node in the myriad Chinese Christian transnational networks that link a number of countries and regions, with the densest ties in Hong Kong and Taiwan, and somewhat dense ties in mainland China and Southeast Asia; there are also some ties with other parts of the world.

Hong Kong

The most prominent transnational ties between HCC and Hong Kong are those linking pastors. The senior pastor, Rev. David Chan, was born in Macao during World War II, grew up in Hong Kong, and was an active youth leader in a Baptist church there. He studied at the Christian and Missionary Alliance Seminary in Hong Kong and earned a bachelor's degree. Later he went to Singapore to teach at the Singapore Bible College. During his tenure there, he took a leave and spent some years studying at a Baptist seminary in the United States. He was the dean of the Singapore Bible College before becoming HCC pastor in 1978. The associate pastor, Rev. William Hsueh, a few years younger than Rev. Chan, was born and grew up in Hong Kong and attended the same Baptist church. He went to Japan for college study; earned a Ph.D. in chemical engineering in the United States; worked in Taipei at a medical school; returned to the United States to attend a seminary; ministered to a Chinese church in St. Louis, Missouri, for fourteen years; and joined HCC in the mid-1990s. These two pastors maintain personal ties with some members of that Hong Kong church where they were youth members.

These individual transnational ties between HCC pastors and Hong Kong Christians have become more formal. Both pastors have been invited back to lead evangelistic meetings, retreats, and workshops at this church, their *mu hui* (original, or mother, church). Reverend Chan taught some intensive courses for a couple of years at the Hong Kong Alliance Seminary, his alma mater. This seminary has become one of only a few prestigious seminaries with graduate programs in Southeast Asia. Its students come not only from Hong Kong but also from Taiwan and Southeast Asian countries. Some seminarians and graduates who once took Rev. Chan's course like to claim to be his students; as a consequence, this expands his individual ties throughout Southeast Asia. In 1999, the vice president of the Alliance Seminary came to North America on a fund-raising tour on which Houston was one of about a dozen stops. As an alum of the seminary and personal friend of the seminary vice president, Rev. Chan hosted the delegation, provided a platform at HCC for their fund-raising activities, and helped assemble interested Christians in other Chinese churches in the Houston area to hear the delegation. The HCC also officially supports the Hong Kong Alliance Seminary with regular donations.

While the flow of money is mostly from North America to Asia, including Hong Kong,[6] the flow of Christian publications is mostly in the opposite direction. Among numerous theological and pastoral books, the most notable is a bilingual hymnal book. The *Hymns of Life (Shengming Shengshi)* was published in 1986 by the Alliance Press in Hong Kong. This has become the most popular hymnal book in Chinese Christian churches in the United States and Canada, including HCC. The HCC has a library and an in-house bookstore that sells Christian books to its members. Four-fifths of the books are in Chinese, and the vast majority of those are published in Hong Kong and Taiwan.

An important tie also exists between Rev. William Hsueh, the associate pastor of HCC, and his brother Theodore, the president of Hong Kong–based Christian Communications Ltd (CCL). The CCL was formed in 1971 and has been one of the major publishers of Christian books and magazines in Hong Kong. It also provides leadership training and pilgrimage tours to Israel and sends missionaries to mainland China. The CCL established regional offices in Taiwan (1973), the United States (1982), Canada (1989), Singapore (1990), and Malaysia (1994) and subsequently became Christian Communications International (CCI). As CCI president, Theodore Hsueh frequently travels to the United States and other countries. The Hsueh brothers also co-host a monthly column on a website discussing Christian ministries. Interestingly, this column is maintained by someone whose e-mail address is in Singapore.

The U.S. regional CCI office was originally located in Chicago. In the mid-1990s, about the time William Hsueh came to Houston, some HCC lay leaders took the initiative to move its major operations to Houston. Elder Lee, a high-ranking manager at an oil company and a lay leader at HCC who is originally from Hong Kong, is the president of the CCI USA board of trustees. Under his leadership, CCI USA runs a Christian bookstore in a big shopping mall, has a full-time minister to provide leadership training to local churches, and has organized pastors to go to China to train leaders of underground churches. Besides the personal connection between HCC and CCI through Rev. Hsueh and Mr. Lee, HCC also organizationally supports CCI USA. In fact, CCI USA's full-time minister was on the pastoral staff of HCC for many years and is now considered an HCC missionary with full financial support. In addition, a former interim pastor of HCC during the 1970s whom HCC continues to support as an evangelist in the United States sits on the international CCI board of directors.

Besides the formal connections and personal ties between HCC leaders and Hong Kong individuals and organizations, ordinary HCC members also have various ties with Hong Kong Christianity. Some former HCC members returned to live in Hong Kong, although they do not go to one particular church there. Because HCC does not keep a record of such members, I was unable to follow any such ties and meet Hong Kong returnees. Some of these people move back and forth across the Pacific repeatedly. One example is HCC's music minister, who was hired in 1999. Reverend Jonathan Ling was born and grew up in Hong Kong, immigrated to the United States along with his parents, worked as a youth pastor at a Chinese Baptist church in Houston for several years, and then returned to Hong Kong to work as the music minister at a church. His parents have been members of HCC for many years, and eventually their son moved back to Houston to be with them. In such cases, constantly shifting personal and formal ties are mixed and hard to separate.

The HCC's informal and formal connections with Hong Kong also include other major parachurch organizations, seminaries, churches, and their staff members. Among them, the most active include those with the Fellowship of Evangelical Students (FES), the Breakthrough Organization, the China Graduate School of Theology (CGST), and the Chinese Coordination Center of World Evangelism (CCCOWE). The FES is a campus Christian organization affiliated with the InterVarsity Christian Fellowship International. Its ministries are mostly with middle school and high school students. Most HCC members who came from Hong Kong had once participated in some of its activities and programs. The Breakthrough Organization, a spin-off from FES, is a Christian social service organization. Its president is a Canadian-trained physician and has mobilized conservative Chinese Christians across the Pacific to engage in social services. The CGST was established in 1975 as a result of a Chinese indigenous movement, initiated in the 1960s, by a group of Chinese seminarians attending Westminster Theological Seminary in

Philadelphia. All its more than twenty faculty are ethnic Chinese who had studied, lived, and worked in the United States, Canada, or Britain. The HCC has sent some seminary students to CGST, the latest being a woman who was born and grew up in Hong Kong and then immigrated to the United States. While working as a professional in Houston and attending HCC, she dedicated herself to Christ and became a missionary to central Asia. In 1998, HCC sent her to study at CGST. The CCCOWE is the most encompassing worldwide Chinese Christian association and was also a result of a movement started first in the United States. In 1972, the first North American Congress of Chinese Evangelicals was held in California, and it called for united evangelical efforts. It subsequently expanded to Asia and other parts of the world, and the first Chinese Congress of World Evangelism was held in 1976 in Hong Kong. Following this, headquarters were established in Hong Kong, and a U.S.-based, Chinese Christian leader, Rev. Thomas Wang, became the general secretary for ten years. Now CCCOWE has fifty-five district committees around the world. Reverend David Chan, the senior pastor of HCC, is the chair of the Southwest U.S. District Committee.

Taiwan

For many years, about two-thirds of HCC members had migrated from Taiwan, although some had originally been born in mainland China. Taiwanese remain about 50 percent of the current HCC members. The young Chinese pastor, Rev. Paul Hu, is a native Taiwanese. In the early 1990s, he came to the United States to attend graduate school, converted to Christianity, and then entered a seminary. The HCC supported him as an evangelist ministering to Taiwanese immigrants in other Texas cities until 1998, when he became an HCC pastor. Reverend Hu's parents are still in Taiwan, as are family members of many other HCC members. As mentioned earlier, Associate Pastor Rev. Hsueh worked in Taipei for several years in the 1970s before returning to the United States for seminary education.

Many of the most important connections between HCC and Taiwan involve immigrants who have returned to live in Taiwan. Among the people whom I interviewed in Taiwan, I found three types of returnees. Some came to North America to study for a graduate degree and did not want to settle down there. On receiving their degree and sometimes some work experience, they returned to Taiwan. For them, the United States had always been considered only a sojourning place for education and work. They usually do not have much emotional attachment to the United States, although many do maintain some contacts with people in the United States. The second type of returnees are those who have physically and psychologically settled down in the United States, consider it their home, and regard Taiwan as only a sojourning place for temporary work. Holding

American passports and maintaining regular contacts with relatives and friends in the United States, they plan to retire in the United States. Some hope that within a few years their company will open a branch in the United States so that they can move back. They definitely want their children to go to American universities, and to prepare for that they send their children to American schools in Taiwan that follow American curricula. The third type of returnees are transnationals in the literal sense who simultaneously maintain homes in Taiwan and in the United States. Some leave their wives and children behind in the United States, and some bring their families with them to Taiwan but return to their U.S. home for holidays and vacations.

In Taiwan, I visited a returned family, the Wangs, whom I befriended when I did my initial fieldwork at HCC. This family represents the second type of returnees. Both Dr. and Mrs. Wang, in their forties, were born and grew up in Taipei, came to the United States for graduate study in the 1980s, and settled in Houston. At HCC, they served as advisers to the Mandarin Student Fellowship, whose international students called them "big brother" and "big sister" or "sister-in-law." In 1998, responding to a call from a close friend who had returned to Taiwan, Mr. Wang quit his job at a research lab in Houston, sold their house, and returned to Taiwan to join his friend at a start-up company. Before going to the United States to attend graduate school, the Wangs had belonged to different churches in Taipei. Now they attend the wife's church, where, despite a very busy work schedule, Mr. Wang has become a member of its church council. Their two American-born children attend an American school in Taipei that teaches in English but offers Chinese lessons. Before my visit to Taiwan, I asked the HCC senior pastor to give me a list of former HCC members in Taiwan. He told me that he did not have such a list and that I did not need one. "You know Mr. Wang well, right? Contact him. He should be able to get all the people together." However, when I asked about other former HCC members in Taipei, Dr. Wang told me that they did not really keep in touch because they were scattered all around and everyone was very busy. He told me that when the senior pastor had visited Taipei about a year earlier, a dozen or so former HCC members/families did manage to come together to receive him. However, the dinner reception at which this occurred took considerable effort to organize.

Although I did not see many former HCC members, I was able to interview about a dozen people at a Lutheran church in Xinzhu. Located in the center of this new high-tech city developed by the government to attract investment from overseas Chinese, the church has a membership of about 300 adults, more than half of whom are highly educated professionals returned from North America. Some had been Christian before going to North America, and others had converted at a Chinese church in North America. Almost all keep some contact with their former churches or at least with close friends from their North American churches. The format of the Sunday service at this Lutheran church in Taiwan struck me as very similar to that in the Baptist and independent Chinese churches in the United States. Some Sunday school classes for children and youth were held in English. The pastor received a seminary degree in the United States, and in his preaching he frequently referred to his living and studying experiences in North America, inserting English words and phrases here and there in his Mandarin sermon.

Mr. Hiah, who represents the third type of returnees, was a member of the Chinese Christian Church of Greater Washington, D.C. (CCC) (see Yang 1999). Dr. Hiah and his wife were born in mainland China and left for Taiwan in 1949 as small children. In the United States, after studying in the Midwest and working in the South, they settled in the Washington, D.C., area. They were active at the CCC and its fellowship groups. In 1992, having been laid off because of the economic downturn, Mr. Hiah left for Taiwan, where he started his own consulting firm. However, Mrs. Hiah and their school-age children stayed behind so that their education would not be interrupted. After resisting the idea of resettling in Taipei and finding it difficult to locate a suitable job in the United States, Mr. Hiah has finally routinized his transnational life—having long phone calls with his wife and children every week, flying back once every few months, and flying his wife and children to Taiwan during summer or winter breaks. As part of this process of settling down as a transnational, Mr. Hiah finally agreed to accept a council chair position in his Taipei church. This is the church where he was baptized as a youth. His experiences in the United States are respected, and his leadership abilities are put to use. In the summer of 2000, when I visited him, he was trying to reorganize the congregation according to the model he had learned in Chinese Christian churches in the United States.

Although both the Wang and Hiah families are from Taipei and living there now, they do not know each other. However, they are well acquainted with the parachurch organizations whose leaders I was interviewing. They told me that they had both benefited from and contributed to the Campus Evangelical Fellowship (CEF) and the Cosmic Light Christian Organization (CL).

The CEF was formed in 1957 in Taiwan with the goal to evangelize and spiritually nourish college and high school students. It holds winter and summer camps, evangelistic meetings, and gospel lectures; organizes Bible study and fellowship groups; and publishes evangelistic magazines and newsletters. In 1966, responding to the needs of people who had gone abroad, CEF started a newsletter specially designed for overseas Chinese students, and later it organized a board of directors in North America in order to keep in contact with people and to mobilize support resources for itself. In 1992, CEF launched the magazine *Overseas Campus* in Los Angeles, especially targeting students and scholars from mainland

China. The CEF general secretary in Taipei now goes to North America and Europe several times annually to lead evangelistic meetings. A founding member of HCC, now an elder at a daughter church in Houston, was a former staff member of CEF in Taipei. Some members of HCC and its daughter churches had participated in CEF activities in Taiwan before immigration, more have read CEF magazines and newsletters, and they continue to support it by donating money and introducing new readers to its publications.

The CL was founded in 1973 with two goals: reaching youth through social services and organizing scholarly research on Chinese church history. Both ministries have received financial and other support from North American Chinese Christian individuals and churches. Its general secretary, Dr. Chih-ping Lin, has made several preaching and lecturing tours in North America. Since 1999, he has visited Houston a couple of times, during which he gave talks at HCC. While his visits followed preexisting ties between CL and some church members, closer ties have been forged since his son came to Houston as an international student in 1999 and began attending HCC. The preexisting and new informal ties thus have been transformed into formal ones, nourished by personal relationships.

Since 1998, the senior pastor of HCC, Rev. David Chan, has made several official trips to Taiwan. Although he is not from Taiwan, his knowledge, experience, and the success of HCC are well known there, thanks in part to the returned immigrants who used to attend HCC. Subsequently, Rev. Chan was invited to direct leadership training workshops at churches there and to teach intensive short courses at the China Evangelical Seminary (CES).

The CES was established in 1970 in Taiwan as an evangelical, nondenominational, graduate seminary. Two American-trained Chinese Christians became the first CES provost and dean. The first president was Hudson Taylor III, the grandson of the man who established the China Inland Mission, once the largest missionary organization in China. Since 1980, three consecutive CES presidents have been ethnic Chinese who have had extensive experience in the United States. Two of them, on completing their terms at CES, returned to the United States to minister to Chinese churches. Like CGST in Hong Kong, almost all CES faculty members received their theological education in North America or Europe, and many are American citizens. By 2000, a total of 960 people had graduated from CES. Among them, 120 came to the United States to pastor Chinese churches or to work for Christian organizations. The CES has boards of trustees in the United States and other countries, and in 1986, CES began to offer extension programs in Los Angeles; New Brunswick, New Jersey; and Philadelphia. In 1998, CES established a permanent North American campus in the Los Angeles area. Every year, CES sends its faculty to teach courses in the United States. People from more than 130 Chinese churches in North America have taken courses at the Los Angeles campus and at other extension programs.

In addition to the fact that Rev. Chan teaches short courses at CES in Taipei, HCC financially supports the seminary and has sent seminarians to it. One of them is Elder Chiu, who was born in China; grew up in Taiwan, where he earned an engineering degree; and then immigrated to Brazil, where he and his family converted to Christianity at a Chinese church. Later they immigrated to Houston, joined HCC, and soon became lay leaders. In 1996, the Chius sold their business and house and became full-time missionaries to Kazakhstan, a central Asian republic of the former Soviet Union. After three years, they took a leave from the mission to spend a year in Taiwan attending CES as well as caring for their aged and ailing parents there. When I visited Taipei in the summer of 2000, the Chius had just left to return to Kazakhstan.

The HCC's transnational ties with Taiwan were further extended after the earthquake on September 21, 1999, that killed hundreds of people and devastated central Taiwan. Responding to calls from Taiwan, HCC joined the relief effort by sending teams of volunteers as well as donations of money and clothes. Several HCC volunteer teams were hosted by a local church. While helping in rescue and evangelic efforts alongside the local church, some HCC volunteers became fascinated by the liveliness of such new-wave charismatic practices of the host church as spiritual singing and spontaneous prayers. Some HCC team leaders were so moved that they brought back to Houston the fresh ideas and worship practices that they had just learned in Taiwan and put them into practice. Again, while money flows mostly from HCC to Taiwan, new ideas and practices are apparently two way.

China

While it was difficult to meet many returnees in Taipei, it was simply impossible to do so in mainland China. The HCC members from the People's Republic of China, about 20 percent of the current membership and increasing rapidly, come from different provinces in the vast land of China. Moreover, because of political reasons, many mainland Chinese who converted to Christianity while in the United States do not want their Christian faith known to others; some were actually baptized without the presence of the congregation. These converts include people who came as visiting scholars and international students and their spouses. Because of U.S. immigration restrictions, most of these people had to return to China after a few months or years in the United States. The converts also include the visiting parents of immigrant professionals, visiting scholars, and international students. After their return to China, they maintain contact with HCC through their family members and/or close friends who may send or bring them audio- and videotapes of sermons and Christian books and magazines. However, these returnees in China are so widely scattered that in no way can they form a group or community.

Many people from China have also settled down in the United States as permanent residents or naturalized citizens, and they commonly have relatives in China whom they visit often. With the increasing globalization of capital, some also make business trips to China on behalf of American companies. In the summer of 2000, I interviewed several people who were stationed in big cities in China. These people attended universities in the United States and then found employment with an American company. When these companies opened an office or plant in China, they were sent to work there, taking advantage of their knowledge of the local language and culture. These returnees commonly said that they would return to the United States after completing their assignments. The Christians among them often bring their evangelistic zeal to China with them in the same manner as those going back to Taiwan to work.

The transnational ties between HCC and China also include some older people who were born in mainland China but came to the United States as immigrants from Taiwan or Hong Kong. An old couple in their seventies who grew up in China and lived in Hong Kong before immigration have visited their original hometown in Fujian several times, where they have contributed money to build a new church. Another longtime member of HCC who migrated to Taiwan and then the United States has also visited mainland China many times. During one such visit in the early 1990s, he saw some issues of *Tian Feng*, the official magazine published in Nanjing by the government-sanctioned China Christian Council. He was excited by its reports of rapidly growing churches throughout China and was moved to share that information with fellow Chinese Christians in America. After returning to Houston, he began to periodically reprint selected articles from *Tian Feng* and send them to Chinese churches throughout North America. After a couple of years of this one-man operation, his resources were exhausted, and he failed to win enough support from HCC or other churches to continue.

Many American-born children of immigrants from Hong Kong, Taiwan, and other places have visited China as well. Since the 1980s, HCC has sent college students to China during the summer to learn the Chinese language, to teach English, and to discreetly evangelize. Some of these young people have extended their stay in China for a year or two. When they return to Houston, they bring transnational ties with new friends made in China. Some youth have dedicated themselves to evangelism and attended a seminary in preparation for a missionary career. A church member has established a memorial fund at HCC specifically designated to support this and similar missions to mainland China.

There are also "tent-making" missionaries to China. Such missionaries are Christians who go to China as ordinary workers or business owners, not as professional missionaries, but are motivated primarily by the desire to save souls. These are not necessarily people who originally came from China. For instance, one young couple in their thirties have gone there this way. This couple came from Hong Kong and Singapore to study in Houston, met at HCC, married, found professional jobs, and settled down. However, in 1998 they gave up their jobs and moved to China, where they found jobs in an American company. The HCC does not officially provide them with any financial support, although they received a send-off ceremony by the congregation before leaving for China. They did not want to be designated as missionaries in any official records in order to avoid suspicion by the Chinese authorities. While working in China, they travel to Houston, Hong Kong, and Singapore every few months, and their prayer letters are sent regularly to close church friends in these places. Their friends and others regularly pray for them, and some are encouraged and inspired to follow suit.

An additional transnational connection that dates to the mid-1980s involves pastors and lay leaders of HCC's daughter churches going to China to provide theological training to leaders of underground churches. These trips are usually organized and arranged by Christian organizations and individual contacts. From the standpoint of HCC, such trips are private and informal.

Apparently, the transnational religious ties between HCC and mainland China remain mostly informal in nature. This is primarily because the Chinese government is highly suspicious of Christians and Christian churches. It tries very hard to control all religious groups and strongly discourages unsupervised exchanges between Christians in China and those in the United States. When China opens up, however, the existing informal ties that HCC and its members have developed may be easily transformed into formal ties with Christian leaders, churches, and parachurch organizations there.

Other Places

The cosmopolitan membership of HCC also includes ethnic Chinese from Southeast Asian countries, especially Singapore, Malaysia, the Philippines, and Vietnam, but also from Indonesia, Thailand, Cambodia, Burma, Korea, Japan, and so on. Some other members are ethnic Chinese from Europe (England, Germany, and France), from South and Central America (Brazil, Peru, and Panama), from Australia and New Zealand, and from South Africa. Depending on the size of the ethnic Chinese community in those countries and depending on their personal situations, these HCC members maintain varying transnational ties with their places of origin.

The transnational ties with Singapore are many and active. As mentioned earlier, a Singaporean managed a website in Hong Kong that posted sermons by

Associate Pastor Rev. Hsueh. Reverend Chan, the senior pastor, used to teach at a seminary in Singapore. Every couple of years, he goes back to Singapore to preach, lecture, or lead retreats. At one retreat camp in the 1990s, a young woman came up to him to ask for help in going to the United States to study music. A few months later, Rev. Chan welcomed her at a Houston airport. She quickly joined the church's music worship team and became an active leader of a fellowship group. She met a young man from Hong Kong at the church, and subsequently Rev. Chan married them. Before long, he sent this young couple away as tent-making missionaries to east Asia. Because of the attraction of the successful English and Chinese ministries, some ethnic Chinese from other Southeast Asian countries who came to the United States as international students have also joined HCC.

The HCC supports missionaries in other parts of Asia, including Macao, Thailand, and Burma, and tent-making missionaries to Islamic nations; and, as mentioned earlier, in 1998 it established a mission church in Kazakhstan. In the mid-1990s, in cooperation with a Chinese Christian missionary organization (the Great Commission Center, then based in Dallas, Texas, but now in San Francisco), several HCC leaders went to the former Soviet Union to explore mission opportunities. They visited Russian Siberia and central Asia and eventually chose Kazakhstan, where a sizable Chinese community existed and seemed open to the Christian gospel. The HCC sent one of its lay leaders as a full-time missionary, and every year several short-term mission teams go over to help him out. After a few years of hard work, and in part because of continuous Chinese immigration to that region, the mission church has grown in size and become stable. Some converts there have been sent for seminary education in preparation for indigenous leadership. Reverend Chan envisions that from this core more churches can be established in central Asia to evangelize not just ethnic Chinese but other people as well.

Closer to home in South and Central America, Chinese communities exist in a number of countries. Soon after its founding in 1975, HCC began sending missionaries to Panama and other Central American nations, and during the 1990s the church annually sent short-term mission teams to Central America and sometimes also to South America. Connections with South America have been frequent since the 1980s. Elder Chiu, the missionary to Kazakhstan, and his family were longtime immigrants in Brazil, where they had converted and joined a Chinese church. Later, following a close friend from that church who had immigrated to Houston and liked HCC, the Chiu family came to Houston, where he became a very active lay leader. These immigrants from Brazil maintained contact with their former church there, and since becoming missionaries the Chius have been invited back to preach at the Chinese church in Brazil.

Analysis and Reflection

The HCC maintains diverse transnational networks—personal and organizational, formal as well as informal—with many parts of the world. This chapter provides only a brief account of some of the transnational ties that were visible to me during short periods of fieldwork in Houston, Hong Kong, Taiwan, and mainland China. Many more transnational ties exist on various levels in various forms with various effects. Three factors are especially important for the ability of this church to maintain such rich and varied transnational networks: cosmopolitan membership, organizational independence, and theological evangelism. The HCC members are from various parts of the world, and many people had previously migrated to various places before moving to Houston; in addition, some have moved from Houston back to Asia. These personal connections make diverse transnational ties possible. The HCC is a nondenominational church, and therefore decisions are made solely by the congregation to maintain or develop formal ties with other parts of the world; it does not have to channel resources through a denomination. Because the members are of diverse origins and religious backgrounds and because all can participate in the decision-making process, diverse transnational ties become necessary. Finally, evangelicalism drives the church to actively maintain and seek transnational ties with various parts of the world.

How typical is HCC in its transnational networks? Do other Chinese churches maintain similar numbers and types of transnational ties? My observations of and research in numerous Chinese churches in the United States indicate that HCC is not an exceptional case. Like HCC, most Chinese immigrant churches in the United States are cosmopolitan in membership, independent in organization, and evangelical in theology (Yang 1999), making diverse transnationalism both possible and necessary. Because HCC is bigger in membership than most other Chinese churches in the United States, however, it is a more active node in Chinese Christian transnational networks; midsize and small churches may not be as active as HCC in maintaining and developing transnational ties. Nevertheless, the diverse nature of transnationalism is quite common today in Chinese churches in the United States. For example, even a very small Chinese church in Maine, with a Sunday attendance of only about twenty adults, has a cosmopolitan membership; some members are from Taiwan, some from Hong Kong, some from mainland China, and one is an ethnic Chinese from Malaysia who married a Caucasian and produced three biracial children. One Taiwanese-born woman was sent by her parents to Singapore for school and came to the United States for a college education. Her parents, who fled from mainland China to Taiwan in 1949, intentionally scattered the family. They maintain a home base in Taiwan and have "planted" their sons and daughters in Malaysia, Singapore, Hawaii, California, and New

England. The cosmopolitan membership of this small church maintains diverse transnational networks on the individual level, but the church has also extended formal financial support to missionaries and organizations in Taiwan, Hong Kong, mainland China, and even Africa.

In most Chinese churches in the United States today, the great majority of members are well-educated, middle- or upper-middle-class professionals. This means that they possess important resources in the form of social, cultural, and economic capital, making it possible to maintain diverse transnational networks. However, some Chinese immigrant churches may be exceptional in that they insist on being monolingual or monodialect, using a language that has limited appeal, such as Cantonese, Taiwanese, or Chaozhou (Swato) (Chuck 1996). Some churches in Chinatowns or in isolated communities in which members may be mostly lower-middle or working class may maintain merely biregional transnational ties. However, based on the information I have, such churches are few.

The HCC is only one of many nodes in the numerous worldwide Chinese Christian networks. In order to see the whole picture or gain a more comprehensive understanding of such networks, it would be necessary to trace transnational ties that emanate from other types of nodes, such as those of the parachurch organizations, seminaries, or influential individuals, but this is well beyond the scope of this one project or chapter.

Notes

1. The many American and European denominations had different missionary territories in China and Southeast Asia; indigenous Chinese sectarian or denominational groups formed and developed in particular regions.

2. This church was given the pseudonym "Chinese Gospel Church" in Yang (2000). I decided to use real names in this chapter because most of the organizations and its leaders in HCC's transnational network are unique or distinctively recognizable, so pseudonyms fail to protect the subjects but do obstruct the description. I keep pseudonyms for persons who have not been in key leadership positions in HCC and other Chinese Christian organizations.

3. For a discussion of the fieldwork in Houston, see Yang (2000).

4. There had been a Chinese Baptist church in Houston before the establishment of HCC. The members of that Chinese Baptist church were mostly earlier immigrants and their descendants who differ in social and cultural background from the post-1965 immigrants (see Yang 1999, 2000, 2001).

5. A parachurch organization is an independent organization with a specialized Christian ministry or ministries, such as a Christian music group or a group with the specialized mission to evangelize on a university campus. Wuthnow (1988) calls parachurch organizations "special-purpose groups."

6. When facing the uncertainty of the 1997 turnover of Hong Kong from Britain to the People's Republic of China, many Hong Kong residents migrated to Canada and the United States. Many brought out money as investment capital or bought houses with cash and may have contributed to the immigrant churches they attend.

References

Chuck, James. 1996. *An Exploratory Study of the Growth of Chinese Protestant Congregations from 1950 to Mid-1996 in Five Bay Area Counties: San Francisco, San Mateo, Contra Costa, Alameda and Santa Clara.* Berkeley, CA: American Baptist Seminary of the West.

Ebaugh, Helen Rose, and Janet S. Chafetz. 2000. *Religion and the New Immigrants: Continuities and Adaptations in Immigrant Congregations.* Walnut Creek, CA: AltaMira.

Levitt, Peggy. 1998. "Local-Level Global Religion: The Case of U.S.–Dominican Migration." *Journal for the Scientific Study of Religion* 37: 74–90.

———. 2001. *The Transnational Villagers.* Berkeley: University of California Press.

Menjivar, Cecilia. 1999. "Religious Institutions and Transnationalism: A Case Study of Catholic and Evangelical Salvadoran Immigrants." *International Journal of Politics, Culture and Society* 12, no. 4: 589–612.

Wuthnow, Robert. 1988. *The Restructuring of American Religion.* Princeton, NJ: Princeton University Press.

Yang, Fenggang. 1998. "Tenacious Unity in a Contentious Community: Cultural and Religious Dynamics in a Chinese Christian Church." In *Gatherings in Diaspora: Religious Communities and the New Immigration,* edited by R. Stephen Warner and Judith G. Wittner. Philadelphia: Temple University Press.

———. 1999. *Chinese Christians in America: Conversion, Assimilation, and Adhesive Identities.* University Park: Pennsylvania State University Press.

———. 2000. "The Chinese Gospel Church: The Sinicization of Christianity." In *Religion and the New Immigrants: Continuities and Adaptations in Immigrant Congregations,* edited by Helen Rose Ebaugh and Janet S. Chafetz. Walnut Creek, CA: AltaMira.

———. 2001. "PRC Immigrants in the U.S.: A Demographic Profile and an Assessment of Their Integration in the Chinese American Community." In *The Chinese Triangle of Mainland-Taiwan-Hong Kong: Comparative Institutional Analyses,* edited by Alvin Y. So and Nan Lin Dudley Poston. Westport, CT: Greenwood.

Transnational Religious Networks among New York's Fuzhou Immigrants

8

KENNETH J. GUEST

Since the early 1980s, as many as 200,000 Chinese from the towns and villages outside Fuzhou, in southeast China, have made their way to New York. This massive international migration, spurred by economic restructuring in both China and the United States and facilitated by a vast and highly organized international human smuggling syndicate, has uprooted whole segments of Fuzhounese communities, dislocating people economically, culturally, and legally, and placed them in a receiving country for which they are unprepared and which is unprepared to incorporate them. The undocumented status of many of the new immigrants further complicates the picture.

Their primary destination is Chinatown, New York, a densely populated ethnic enclave on Manhattan's Lower East Side where these new immigrants reconstruct kinship, village, and other social connections to begin the process of adapting to an unfamiliar environment. The street corners where East Broadway passes below the Manhattan Bridge are crowded with young Fuzhounese waiting for jobs to be posted in the myriad employment agencies. The jobs may take them temporarily across the United States to work in "all-you-can-eat" Chinese buffets or to garment sweatshops, take-out restaurants, and construction sites in the New York area. But for most recent Fuzhounese immigrants, New York's Chinatown is home base, the place to which they return to recuperate, reconnect with family and friends, and find their next job.

Over the past fifteen years, Fuzhounese have established a number of their own religious communities in Chinatown, fourteen by the end of 2000. These include Protestant and Catholic churches as well as Buddhist, Daoist, and Chinese popular religion temples. Within the complex economic, political, and social environment of Chinatown's ethnic enclave, these religious organizations have become central locations for a transient Fuzhounese population where they can build a community; activate networks of support built on kinship, region, and faith; and establish transnational links to their home churches, temples, and communities in China.

The data for this chapter are drawn from ethnographic fieldwork conducted over a four-year period, 1997–2001, in New York's Chinatown and in Fuzhou, China, and its surrounding towns and villages (Guest 2001, in press). A street-by-street mapping of the more than sixty Chinese religious communities in China-town revealed the recent emergence of Fuzhounese churches and temples and their prominent location in the migration and immigrant incorporation processes. Re-search in Fuzhou and its environs quickly revealed the significance of the New York Fuzhounese religious communities in the religious revival sweeping Fuzhou as remittances flow back to build towering new religious edifices and fund the rapid revitalization and expansion of religious programming. This chapter exam-ines the particular position of the two Fuzhounese Protestant churches in China-town as access points to nascent transnational Protestant networks connecting New York and Fuzhou that serve the spiritual and material needs of recent im-migrants and build direct links between churches in the two places.

The Church of Grace, founded in 1988, and the New York House Church, which split from it in 1998, are independent congregations created with distinct Fuzhounese identities. Despite the recent schism, both congregations are thriving, filling their worship spaces, and rapidly expanding programs and services for their immigrant constituents. Juxtaposed to this, most Protestant congregations in Chi-natown are small and struggling to survive.

For many native-born Americans, visiting New York's Chinatown feels like en-tering a foreign country. Yet even for those grown accustomed to the "foreignness" of Chinatown, the Fuzhounese sections of the enclave still seem like another re-ality, and the Church of Grace and the New York House Church embody that dis-tinctiveness. Entering either of these churches, embedded in one of the world's most intensely urban cities, is strikingly reminiscent of walking into a church any-where in rural China, more specifically, the churches around Fuzhou. The language changes. The clothing changes. The food changes. Personal kinship and village net-works become revitalized. Using a framework inspired by Turner (1969), the foy-ers of the Church of Grace and the New York House Church are liminal spaces for these Fuzhounese Christian immigrants, places of transition between one re-ality and another, places that remove them, even if temporarily, from their day-to-day reality of often grinding labor and afford them a glimpse of something dif-ferent. Immigrants who outside these churches are foreigners in a very strange land are transformed into insiders. Outside, they cannot speak the dominant U.S. lan-guage, English, or even the dominant Chinese dialects of Cantonese and Man-darin spoken in Chinatown. Inside, their language, Fuzhounese, predominates.

Outside, they are defined by earlier Chinese immigrants as "country bumpkins" (*tubaozi*) and derided as uncultured and uncouth. Inside, they celebrate a common cultural heritage of an exploring people. Outside, they may be undocumented workers, constantly aware that the next moment may bring arrest, detention, and deportation. Inside, they are accepted members of the "Body of Christ" and valued contributors to families and churches in the United States and China. In the midst of an isolated and marginalized community, the churches are locations for mobilizing the social capital necessary for surviving in the ethnic enclave: to exchange information, seek emergency financial assistance, and receive legal advice. And they are places to reterritorialize familial, regional, and religious networks and stay connected to the home country, a service of particular importance to undocumented workers whose transnational mobility is restricted by legal status as well as finances.

The New York House Church

The New York House Church, a congregation of several hundred members, meets on the ground floor of a renovated tenement building, located a block off East Broadway, the main Fuzhounese business district in Chinatown. Formed from a schism with Fuzhounese Protestants at the Church of Grace over theological, regional, and political conflicts, today the New York House Church relies on its own unique network of religious connections, both in New York and between New York and China, to serve its immigrant members' needs and to support the rapid growth of Protestant Christianity in China.

In theology, organization, and politics, the New York House Church largely follows the traditions of an indigenous Chinese Protestant denomination, the Little Flock, founded in Fuzhou in the 1920s and now spreading rapidly across China. A Sunday morning at the New York House Church could just as easily be a Sunday morning in any rural Little Flock church in the Fuzhou area.

The History of Little Flock

The Little Flock was founded in Fuzhou in 1922 by Watchman Nee (Ni Tuosheng) as a completely indigenous and autonomous Chinese Christian movement based on strict biblical literalism, ardent nationalism, and rejection of missionary influence. By 1949, it had grown to include more than 700 congregations and meeting places with 70,000 members, located primarily in China's coastal provinces, rivaling in size even the largest denominations introduced by missionaries (Wickeri 1988).

Following the Communist victory in 1949, the Little Flock encountered difficulties. Many of its leaders had openly supported the failed Nationalist cause in the civil war, fearing the atheist ideology of the Communist Party. Others openly opposed the Communist's signature land reform campaign in 1950–51. As a result, many Little Flock leaders and members were arrested, charged as "counter-revolutionaries," and sentenced to varying terms of "reeducation" to assist in their conversion to socialist principles. Nee himself died in a labor reeducation camp in 1972, a martyr for the faith in the eyes of his constituents.

Since 1979, Little Flock congregations have reemerged and flourished, fueling much of the significant growth of Christianity in Fuzhou and rural areas of Zhejiang and other provinces. Yet many Little Flock members today still bear the scars of their confrontation with the government, and the network of Little Flock churches carries its institutional memory. A network of home meeting places developed outside the sanction of the state and grew during the Cultural Revolution. Today, that rapidly growing network extends throughout much of China. Church leaders in Fuzhou estimate that more than half of local Protestants may be members of the Little Flock. Drawing on their own history of conflict with the state in the 1950s and the collective experience of Christians during the Cultural Revolution, the vast majority of Little Flock congregations in rural areas operate as house churches, fiercely independent of the state and antagonistic to its efforts to monitor and regulate them.

While the Little Flock is not organized as a denomination with a hierarchical structure, a clear network among congregations exists, both in China and elsewhere. Despite government regulations prohibiting Christians from traveling from one locality to another to proselytize, Little Flock Christians regularly exchange visits with other congregations across China, sharing information, training local leaders, and maintaining an extensive intercongregational network. Moreover, despite government prohibitions against visits from Christians outside the mainland for religious purposes, it is not uncommon to find Christians affiliated with Hong Kong and Taiwanese Little Flock groups visiting local Little Flock congregations in China.

The New York House Church

For Fuzhounese Christians related to Little Flock churches, the New York House Church is the New York nodal connection to a transnational network. While not officially declaring itself to be Little Flock, the congregation's ritual and polity reflect Little Flock patterns, and its very name, House Church, places it within the tradition of independent congregations that are reluctant to cooperate with the Chinese government and China's officially recognized Protestant churches.

Worship begins between 9:00 and 9:30 with prayers and hymn singing and lasts well past the noon hour. About thirty people are present at first. Women, roughly 70 percent of the congregation, sit mostly on the right side of the aisle, men mostly on the left, although this tradition becomes impractical as the sanctuary fills to capacity, with nearly 100 worshipers later in the morning. A few women wear a black net hair covering called a *mentou*, following Paul's admonition in Corinthians that women cover their heads in church.

Communion is held every Sunday. Eschewing ordination of ministers, churches related to the Little Flock in principle practice a radical leveling of organizational hierarchy. Unpaid brothers and sisters share leadership. In that tradition, at the New York House Church, shortly before 11:00 every Sunday, the core group of sisters and brothers begins the *bai bing hui*, or communion service. First, flat unleavened bread, most likely matzo purchased at one of the few remaining Jewish stores in the neighborhood, is crumbled in a plate and passed among the congregation. Members stand in their place, break off a small flake, and eat at their discretion. Afterward, a clear glass mug of sweet grape-colored punch is circulated. Most core members drink directly from the cup. Others accept the offer of a plastic spoon for dipping. From the leadership style to the plastic spoons, the ritual is an exact replica of *bai bing hui* in Little Flock churches throughout the Fuzhou area. By 11:00, the hall is packed and the preaching begins, usually in Fuzhou dialect, occasionally in Mandarin translated into Fuzhou dialect by one of the members.

When the worship service concludes well after noon with a few more hymns and prayers, the somewhat subdued congregation comes alive. A huge pot of Fuzhou noodle or rice soup is brought from the back room, which serves as a church kitchen and as a living space for one of the brothers. Hot steamed buns, plain and with meat filling, appear as well. The eighty to ninety people in the room gather their luncheon repast and settle into small groups scattered around the room, drawing their chairs into circles for conversation.

As the smells of Fuzhounese home cooking and the sounds of Fuzhounese dialect fill the room, an elderly gentleman in the front row emerges as a focal point of the congregation. For much of the morning ritual, he participates as an equal among the brothers and sisters. For much of the afternoon, he will be the center of activity. He will remain in the hall late into the day, talking with a long line of parishioners who, despite the pressures of work and family, take the time to approach this pillar of the Fuzhounese Protestant community, a symbol of religious virtue and a source of encouragement and assistance.

Reverend Liu Yangfen, born in 1915, plays a central role in the story of Fuzhounese Protestants in New York City, just as he played a central role in the history of Protestantism in Fuzhou for more than forty years prior to migrating in 1985. The son of Methodist converts, Liu studied for two years at Vanderbilt University after World War II under the sponsorship of the Methodist mission board. On his return to China, Liu pastored the main Protestant church in down-town Fuzhou from 1950 to 1966, helping guide Fuzhou's Christians through the early years of uncertainty under Communist rule. During the Cultural Revolution (1966–76), he was severely persecuted for his Christianity and his Western links and was sent for reeducation to the remote mountains of northeast Fujian Province.

In 1979, Liu was declared "rehabilitated" and allowed to return to Fuzhou, where he worked tirelessly to reopen churches, restart the provincial seminary, re-claim church buildings nationalized by the government, and train new leaders for their congregations. In 1985, Liu left Fuzhou for New York, following his daugh-ter, born in Nashville during his student days, who earlier had been able to leave China and establish U.S. citizenship. Since arriving in New York, Liu has played a central role within Fuzhounese Protestant Christianity, where his spiritual biog-raphy has had a particularly sanctifying effect.

On Sunday afternoon, it is clear that people know that Rev. Liu is well con-nected and that he will help church members if he can; he knows doctors, people with places to stay, and sometimes job possibilities. He also knows a good deal about the legal system and even a few trustworthy Christian lawyers or perhaps someone who, for a reasonable fee, will deliver an undocumented couple's infant back to China to be raised by grandparents. And so people take turns talking to him, sharing with him their troubles, concerns, and hopes. On Sunday afternoons and at times throughout the week, the New York House Church becomes a Fuzhounese Christian community center, with Rev. Liu as the focal point of the network.

Many of those who seek out Rev. Liu and the New York House Church are newly arrived immigrants because Rev. Liu's reputation is well known in Fuzhou, too. Fuzhou churches, particularly Little Flock–related churches, often tell their parishioners that on arrival in New York they must visit him and the New York House Church. When new arrivals, both legal and undocumented, make their way there on Sundays, their first task is to share news of home. How is their church? Their pastor? A well-known brother or sister? Has the church had any problems with the government? Then people discuss their current conditions and ask whether there is anything Rev. Liu or the church can do to help. Sometimes, help is just a prayer, words of encouragement, and a sense that their problems have been heard and understood; they are not alone—an important feeling as one sinks into the travails of the ethnic enclave. Later, as opportunities arise, word may come of more material forms of assistance.

On occasion, Rev. Liu has become actively involved in supporting recent im-migrants' applications for political asylum based on claims of religious persecu-tion. His assistance takes several different forms, among them providing letters of support for members' asylum applications, verifying church membership in New York and China, and accompanying members to court appearances where he may testify on their behalf. He is well informed about church–state relations in Fuzhou. Even the most subtle conflict or controversy eventually reaches his ears. He also has more than half a century of personal experience of religious life in China. An elderly, well-spoken (in English as well as Mandarin and Fuzhou dialect), ordained minister, he has proven to be an ideal expert witness for cases involving claims of religious persecution.

Also visiting Rev. Liu on Sundays at the New York House Church are Chinese Christians who are planning to return to China on short-term missions to underground house churches. Throughout the year, small groups of Chinese U.S. citizens travel as tourists to Fuzhou and other places in China, smuggling in Bibles, audiotapes of sermons, inspirational Christian messages, and a wide variety of other written material. They quietly visit house churches and their leaders, delivering these materials and illegal financial contributions from Christians in the United States. Many represent Chinese Christian churches in the New York area that have assumed as their particular concern the growth of Christianity in China. Most are ardently anti-Communist, which feeds directly into a desire to support Chinese Protestant house churches, typically portrayed as severely persecuted in a country lacking religious freedom and seen as valiantly resisting the godlessness of the Chinese state.

A rich repository of information about the history and contemporary reality of China's house churches, Rev. Liu is a valued resource to many a traveler. A letter from him can open many Chinese doors. He himself produces tapes of sermons and purchases quantities of books and pamphlets with the support of New York House Church members. He sends these materials to China, often with representatives of these short-term mission groups. Although he does not travel, his son is a regular visitor to Chinese house churches, bringing greetings from his father and delivering not insignificant resources. Those returning from China stop by the New York House Church to see Rev. Liu and report on their activities and findings as well as to receive his blessing for a mission successfully accomplished.

Remittances and Religious Revival in Fujian

For centuries, Fuzhou, the capital of Fujian Province, has been a leading port city not only for coastal China but for Southeast Asia as well. The Min River flows east through Fuzhou before emptying into the Pacific Ocean. As it nears the sea, it passes towns and villages that for generations have been home to rural farmers and fisherfolk and a fair number of seafaring people. Today they are emigrant communities, their young and middle-aged members having gone to New York over the past fifteen years to seek their fortune in its garment, restaurant, and construction industries. Their streets are lined with new five-story homes and rebuilt religious edifices, but they are eerily quiet. Many of the houses stand empty; others are occupied primarily by grandparents and young children.

Despite this exodus, a religious revival has swept across the Fuzhou region during the past twenty years. Beginning in 1979, religious practices, including traditional religiocultural practices such as village festivals, funeral and wedding ceremonies, grave building and sweeping, *feng-shui* (geomancy), and fortune-telling, have been reestablished and religious traditions reinvented. The region has been recovering from the devastating effects of the Cultural Revolution and returning religious activities to a prominent role in both urban and rural life. Since 1980, the Chinese government has reinstated the constitutional provision of freedom of and freedom from religion. While applied unevenly, the gradual implementation of this policy has created a religious environment significantly more relaxed than the antagonism and repression of the 1950s through the 1970s. With the rapidly receding influence of official Marxist-state ideology, religion has raced into the vacuum to reclaim a central role in public discourse about ultimate meaning and values, a discourse ever more vibrant as the rapid pace of socioeconomic change compels a reconsideration of what matters in life. Although recent evidence suggests that the pattern is spreading across China, this extraordinary renaissance of ritual activity has been most intense in southeastern China, particularly in Fujian, Zhejiang, and Guangdong Provinces (Dean 1989, 1993, 1997, 1998; Pas 1989; Yang 2000).

Since the 1990s, money has also been flowing back into the Fuzhou area from the tens of thousands of people working in the United States. Just as Fuzhou's overseas garment and restaurant workers remit hard-earned money to build new homes for children and aging parents, roads for local villages, and shops for the local economy, so too do they underwrite the building and rebuilding of religious edifices in their hometowns and support professional and lay religious practitioners and activities. It is quite common for Fuzhounese workers who have arrived safely in America to express their gratitude to the divine power that guided them by returning a portion of their earnings as an offering of thanksgiving (Langfitt 2000). Although many will not be present for ceremonies and rituals in their home communities, they hope their gifts will enhance their good fortune as well as their status in the community.

Fuzhounese Protestants in New York are key sources of the remittances used to build and rebuild churches in the Fuzhou area. The New York House Church (and the Church of Grace) serve as key locations for fund-raising. For example, in an interview conducted in 2000, Mrs. Li Jiande, a key lay leader of the New York House Church, described the network accessed to build a new church in her home town of Houyu, located on the Min River east of Fuzhou:

My grandmother founded the church after her conversion by missionaries in the late 1910s. Over the years it continued to meet in our home, even during the severe repression of the Cultural Revolution when we only dared to meet at night. I left Houyu in 1979 . . . but I kept in very close contact with people at home and especially in the church. In 1989 the congregation contacted me in New York. They had received permission from the local government to build a new church, but they needed financial support from fellow townspeople in the U.S. By that time there were already quite a few of us from Houyu in New York, so I thought we could probably help out. In New York, there was me, and another woman . . . and we organized the brothers and sisters from Houyu. I was in charge of receiving and sending the money. She was in charge of making the contacts. At that time there were many families in Houyu whose husbands were here working in New York or parents with sons in America. They all contributed. Also many of the young people still in China contributed their labor. We collected tens of thousands of dollars.

With a sanctuary that seats 500, the new five-story church today stands prominently on a steep hillside in full view of the Min River, a testimony to the presence of Christianity in Houyu and in New York City.

The Church of Grace

The thriving Church of Grace, now in its third location, meets in a converted public bathhouse built in 1904 on what is today the northeastern edge of Chinatown. Purchased at public auction in 1992 for $300,000, it was renovated for a matching sum. Three full-time ministers serve a membership of more than 700, with a weekly attendance averaging more than 300. Christmas Day is one of the few days of the year that Chinese garment and restaurant workers are guaranteed to have off and when Fuzhounese employed across the United States return to New York City to visit friends and relatives. The Church of Grace's worship attendance then soars to more than 600. The sanctuary is packed, and the second-floor social hall and the basement classrooms are flooded with people watching the service on big-screen televisions. Noisy crowds spill out the front door and into the street.

The theologically conservative Church of Grace adheres to an American evangelical congregational model. Fellowship programs serve youth, women, and the elderly. Weekly prayer meetings draw heavily from the neighboring restaurants and garment shops. Sunday school is available for children of all ages, and in 2001 an English-language service was instituted to serve the handful of teenagers and college students fluent in English and the many immigrants who wish to become so. The monthly newsletter reaches 2,000 constituents across the country, including a number in Immigration and Naturalization Service detention centers. A branch church has been established in the Chinatown satellite neighborhood of Sunset Park Brooklyn, and another is in formation in the recently established Fuzhounese enclave in Philadelphia.

Like the New York House Church, the Church of Grace serves as a Fuzhounese Christian community center on Sunday. Over bowls of noodles served after worship, the conversations roar. News of home is spread by new arrivals. News of jobs and places to live and discussions of recent events in China or in the U.S. media abound. A member of the Board of Deacons passes along a videotape from his home church in Min An that describes its building project and solicits funds from overseas compatriots. The president of the Women's Fellowship collects money from members for emergency relief for a middle-aged garment shop seamstress whose husband just died of cancer in a Lower East Side hospital. She collects more than $2,000 by the end of the day. The evangelists gather together first-time visitors for a discussion of basic principles of the Christian faith and invite them to join the baptism and new membership class that will be starting in a few weeks. A group of college students meets in a corner to discuss their upcoming exams. The Church of Grace lacks the focal point provided by Rev. Liu at the New York House Church, but the decentralized interactions are wide ranging and have their own style and order.

One key to the congregation's allure among recent immigrants has been its identification with and commitment to the use of the Fuzhou dialect in worship and church programs. From its beginning, the congregation has conducted worship services in this dialect, with simultaneous translation into Mandarin. Board meetings are conducted in it, and Fuzhounese is the language of most informal conversations. Among the older members, it is often the only language they speak, although they may understand some spoken Mandarin. For the mostly rural immigrants from the Fuzhou area, the use of Fuzhou dialect has provided a significant unifying factor in the midst of an ethnic enclave dominated by Cantonese and Mandarin speakers, providing the church with a distinctive identity as the "Fuzhounese church."

The Fuzhounese population is highly transient, and church attendance reflects this. The pews may be consistently filled, but the participants change from week to week. A significant portion of the Church of Grace congregation are young, undocumented workers. Approximately 40 percent are under the age of thirty, and another 25 percent are between thirty and thirty-nine years old. Many are "seekers," visiting the church to explore Christianity. As a result, highlights of the Church of Grace liturgical year come in October and at Easter, when converts are baptized. In recent years, more than forty have become Christians on each occasion.

An Immigrant's Tale

Liu Ai Zhu's story exemplifies the role of this church in Fuzhounese immigrant life. When not working on Sunday, this twenty-seven-year-old man is a regular fixture at the Church of Grace, singing in the choir and attending youth group activities. In 1994, at the age of nineteen, Mr. Liu decided to leave Ting Jiang, a town located on the bank of the Min River, and head to America. He arranged the journey with a local snakehead (smuggler) for $24,000, a reasonable price in 1994. Passage today costs more than $50,000 per person. As part of a group of young people from his hometown, he made the grueling four-month trip by bus, fishing boat, freighter, motorboat, foot, car, and airplane. He tells the following story of his migration experiences and subsequent life in New York:

> I wasn't on very good terms with my family when I left Ting Jiang. In fact, I hadn't told anyone in my family that I was leaving. When we finally arrived in Los Angeles the smugglers wanted their money. Twenty-four thousand dollars. I didn't have it. So I called home and told my family. My father couldn't believe it was me. He couldn't believe that I had already reached America, and he didn't really recognize my voice on the telephone. I think he thought it was a trick. The smugglers told my father that they would kill me if they didn't get the money, and then they hung up. They began to beat me with copper piping. They beat me on my back, on my legs, and on my chest. I will have the scars the rest of my life. I was beaten unconscious and left lying bloody on the floor. The next time I called home, thank God, my father had already made arrangements for the money, borrowing from friends and family in China and the U.S. The plan was for my father to pay the snakeheads back in Ting Jiang, but I could tell he still didn't trust them. . . . That was a long night waiting to find out if he had actually paid. I was really scared. I didn't want to be beaten again. But he paid, and after a week, the smugglers let me go.
>
> I was young, and I had finally made it to the "Land of Beauty" as we call America. At the beginning I found a good job in a restaurant. I worked very hard. The boss liked me and even raised my pay. But after several months I came down with a very serious illness that affected my legs. I still think it had something to do with the beating by the snakeheads. This was the beginning of my great hardship in America. I had difficulty standing for any length of time, the pain was too intense. I couldn't keep a job. For more than four years this went on. I saw doctor after doctor, both Western and Chinese. But because I was illegal and I didn't have any money I didn't have many choices. I went to emergency rooms when it was really bad, but I was always afraid someone at the hospital would turn me in. I went to many different Chinese health clinics, which were illegal just like me. But nothing seemed to work. It was so bad I started to think about how to kill myself. If life was going to be this hard I couldn't keep it up. I thought about going home to Ting Jiang. But there was nothing for me there—not after five years away.

Miraculously, in April 1999, I started to feel better, a little bit at a time. I think this was the work of God. I had been living next to the Church of Grace. The people there had been helping me, sometimes paying my medical bills, visiting me in the hospital, and praying for me. One day when the pain was so bad I didn't know what to do; I went to the church and prayed. I asked God what to do, and then I gave my life to Jesus. I think that's when things started to turn around. I've decided to stay in America. The pain still comes and goes, but it's bearable most of the time. I'm able to work again, at least for short stints. But I'm not as strong as I used to be. These jobs in the restaurants are so grueling I can usually only work for a week or two, and then I have to take time off to rest. When I do, I spend as much time as possible around the church. At least I don't think about committing suicide anymore.

Spanning the Continents

The Church of Grace, like the New York House Church, has many links to churches in the Fuzhou area, although its ties are more eclectic, reflecting its own theological, political, and economic diversity. Unlike the New York House Church, which draws its members primarily from the Fuzhou Little Flock networks found along the Min River, the Church of Grace's members come from the wide range of Protestant traditions and regions in the Fuzhou area.

Pastor Chen, now in her early seventies, is not on the staff of the Church of Grace, but she regularly attends its Sunday worship, Bible studies, and Women's Fellowship meetings. Her primary role in New York is as shepherd of an informal network of immigrants from Ting Jiang, where she served as pastor of one of the Protestant churches for twenty years, as did her mother-in-law before. Pastor Chen immigrated to New York with her husband in 1999, leaving her family's church in the hands of a recent graduate of the Protestant seminary in Fuzhou. Her six children all preceded her to the United States, the first coming in 1984, and have opened restaurants in the New York area.

Pastor Chen chose the Church of Grace because of theological and political factors. Her church in Ting Jiang is officially registered with the Chinese government and actively participates in a system of "open" or "public" churches in the Fuzhou area. In a split oddly prescient of the split among New York's Fuzhounese Protestants several years later, a Little Flock group within Pastor Chen's congregation broke away in 1994 and built its own church on the other side of Ting Jiang. Given this history, Pastor Chen chooses to worship at the Church of Grace in New York rather than the New York House Church.

Perhaps her most important role is as liaison between Fuzhounese Christians in New York and the towns and villages along the northern bank of the Min River east of Fuzhou, particularly the open churches there. I interviewed her shortly after her arrival when she told me,

After we get our green cards I want to be able to go back and forth between New York and Ting Jiang. My family is here. I haven't seen them in many years. But no one is there in Ting Jiang. One by one the people are leaving to be with their families in New York. So long as I am able to move about I will go back and forth to help with the church there.

One Sunday at the Church of Grace in New York, Pastor Chen withdrew from her bag an artist's rendering of a new church being built in Mawei—just upriver from Ting Jiang—beautifully reproduced in color on small, wallet-size cards with the church's address printed on the back. Members of that church had assisted her congregation in Ting Jiang when it was constructing a new building in 1998. Now she was returning the favor, but across the Pacific Ocean:

> The Mawei church is rebuilding. They have raised a good bit of money but are hoping to raise more, altogether $250,000. I often went there to preach, sometimes twice a month. So when they found out we were coming to New York they asked us to help spread the word among people here about their project. They asked us to encourage people we meet to contribute money and send it to them. We can't take the money, but you can send it directly. Here's the name and address.

Transnationalism and the Fuzhounese Religious Community

Recent studies of Chinese transnationalism (e.g., Ong and Nonini 1997) focus primarily on economic elites who have the financial resources and legal status to live and work in multiple locations. Transnational identity as part of an overseas Chinese diaspora is a by-product of economic privilege. However, Fuzhounese transnationalism is represented primarily by the global human smuggling syndicates that transport thousands of undocumented workers from Fuzhou to New York. The vast majority of Fuzhounese immigrants are poor and typically portrayed by scholars as objects of action by transnational flows and processes. The activities and networks of the two Fuzhounese religious communities examined in this chapter, however, reveal immigrants and their congregations as determined, ingenious agents and actors engaged in constructing transnational networks of support and communication.

Many contemporary studies of transnationalism and diaspora tend to obscure the fact of structured inequalities of class and race confronting minorities in the United States. The lives of Fuzhounese immigrants within these religious communities must be contextualized within the exploitative and highly stratified ethnic enclave of Chinatown. Some Fuzhounese who arrived prior to the 1986 and 1989 amnesties or who have successfully applied for political asylum may be able to participate in a more extensive set of transnational practices and identity building. They may have the legal status and financial stability to travel between New

York and Fuzhou and engage in activities that span the two locations. But for the majority of Fuzhounese, disciplined by the economic regime of Chinatown and the permanent resident criteria of the U.S. government, their transnationalism is much more nascent, grassroots, and fragile, an ocean-borne transnationalism of the working poor, not the jet-set transnationalism of the elite. It is a transnationalism of the common folk, not of highly organized institutional structures or well-to-do transnational migrants in the Chinese diaspora described by Ong and Nonini. Unlike the transnational entities so often discussed that transcend the state, most Fuzhounese immigrants mobilize small-scale transnational networks from a local position deep within and vulnerable to state structures on both sides of the Pacific.

Despite the fact that religious communities are arguably the oldest transnational networks, with a few exceptions (e.g., Levitt 2001), recent discussions of the role of religious communities in transnational processes have focused largely on the transnational institutions and global structures of world religions that transcend state boundaries (Rudolph and Piscatori 1997). The transnational religious networks being established by Fuzhounese immigrants are more independent, multifaceted, decentralized, and opportunistic. Nonetheless, their influence spans the migration process between China and the United States, the immigrant incorporation process, and changing economic, political, social, and religious conditions in Fuzhou. While clearly in the early stages of formation, these networks are strong enough that events in one place affect the people in the other. When the split occurred between the Church of Grace and the New York House Church, word spread quickly among churches in Fuzhou. Local congregations and leaders, especially those of the Little Flock orientation, soon took sides and aligned themselves with one New York congregation or the other. In recent years, the transnational religious networks have further increased immigrants' influence in the Fuzhou area. The most visible signs are the large, new religious structures that dot the Fuzhou countryside. These serve as symbols of a revitalization of local ritual practices enabled by a relaxation of local government restrictions and fueled by significant international support from overseas Fuzhounese. In the discourse of transnational processes and globalization theory, the Church of Grace and the New York House Church should be considered nodes of access to an intertwined web of social and economic relations that spreads from this New York entry point throughout the city, across the country, and eventually back to China.

For undocumented workers, denied the rights of citizenship and excluded not only from the mainstream U.S. economy and culture but also from the centers/structures of power within the ethnic enclave, Fuzhounese religious communities serve as sites for establishing alternative identities to the dominant hegemonic structures and discourses. Many Fuzhounese in New York find themselves unable to establish full citizenship rights in their new context. Despite actively participating in the U.S. economy, including paying taxes, the most basic rights of U.S. citizens are denied them: legal status, suffrage, labor protection, health care, and a social safety net. Through participation in the religious community's varied activities—religious, social, and institutional—immigrants enact an alternative construction of their role in U.S. society. In addition, the religious community serves as a liminal space, a transitional place, a place in between that touches both New York and China. It re-creates physical surroundings, kinship and village networks, rituals, language, and food that recall life in China. It reconnects to cultural and religious traditions back home, yet it is in the midst of America. Religious communities allow Fuzhounese immigrants to imagine themselves differently in the midst of a hegemonic discourse that describes them in unflattering and dehumanizing terms and to participate differently as well, moving beyond the circumscribed role of immigrant, undocumented laborers.

References

Dean, Kenneth. 1989. "Revival of Religious Practices in Fujian: A Case Study." In *Turning of the Tide: Religion in China Today*, edited by Julian F. Pas. Hong Kong: Oxford University Press.

———. 1993. *Taoist Ritual and Popular Cults of Southeast China*. Princeton, NJ: Princeton University Press.

———. 1997. "Ritual and Space: Civil Society or Popular Religion?" In *Civil Society in China*, edited by Timothy Brook and B. Michael Frolic. Armonk, NY: Sharpe.

———. 1998. *Lord of the Three in One: The Spread of a Cult in Southeast China*. Princeton, NJ: Princeton University Press.

Guest, Kenneth J. 2001. "Walking on Water: Fuzhounese Immigrant Religious Communities in New York's Chinatown." Ph.D. diss., City University of New York.

———. In press. *New Gods in Chinatown: Faith and Survival in New York's Immigrant Community*. New York: New York University Press.

Langfitt, Frank. 2000. "Faith, Power Collide in a Changing China." *Baltimore Sun*, August 27.

Levitt, Peggy. 2001. *The Transnational Villagers*. Berkeley: University of California Press.

Ong, Aihwa, and Donald Nonini, eds. 1997. *Ungrounded Empires: The Cultural Politics of Modern Chinese Transnationalism*. New York: Routledge.

Pas, Julian F., ed. 1989. *The Turning of the Tide: Religion in China Today*. Hong Kong: Oxford University Press.

Rudolph, Susanne Hoeber, and James Piscatori. 1997. *Transnational Religion and Fading States*. Boulder, CO: Westview.

Turner, Victor W. 1969. *The Ritual Process: Structure and Anti-Structure*. Chicago: Aldine.

Wickeri, Philip. 1988. *Seeking the Common Ground: Protestant Christianity, the Three-Self Movement, and China's United Front*. Maryknoll, NY: Orbis.

Yang, Mayfair. 2000. "Putting Global Capitalism in Its Place: Economic Hybridity, Bataille, and Ritual Expenditure." *Current Anthropology* 41:477–95.

The Variety of Transnational Religious Networks 9

JANET SALTZMAN CHAFETZ AND HELEN ROSE EBAUGH

Immigrants and the religious institutions they create or join in Houston are involved in ongoing relationships with individuals and institutions in other nations within which religiously relevant resources circulate. This rather broad and somewhat vague statement encompasses the substantial variation in the structure and functioning of transnational religious networks described in the preceding seven chapters. In this chapter, we use some of the concepts provided by the theoretical approach known as network analysis to examine the preceding case studies for tentative answers to the following questions:

1. What kinds of *actors* are involved in religiously relevant, transnational networks, and what kinds of *ties* describe the relationships that these networks assume?
2. What kinds of religiously relevant *remittances* flow between transnational network members, and what are their major flow *paths and directions*?
3. What variables might *explain* why religiously relevant, transnational networks *differ* in the ways they do?
4. What kinds of *changes over time* do religiously relevant, transnational networks undergo?

Network analysis focuses on patterns of relationships, called *ties*, between points, called *nodes* (for more sustained discussion of network theory, see Berkowitz 1982; Burt 1980, 1982; Wellman 1983; Wellman and Berkowitz 1988; for a general overview of terms, see Turner 1998: chap. 38). Nodes can represent virtually any kind of unit, including individual persons, groups, organizations, and even nation-states. Ties, in turn, are conceptualized as routes through which *resources* flow between nodes. These resources can be material (i.e., money or goods) and/or nonmaterial (e.g., information, services, innovations, influence, or prestige) and refer to many of the same phenomena as the concept *material and social remittances* used by scholars examining the ways that immigrants affect their home country kin, communities, and nations (Levitt 1999, 2001:chap. 2; Menjívar 2000:99–100; Glick Schiller 1999:110). Network analyses typically attempt to trace all nodes and ties for given networks. Obviously, none of our case studies was able to do so, nor was this the purpose of the research. Rather, each of our studies focuses on the predominant types of nodes and ties characteristic of a given case and includes only samples of the populations of potential nodes and ties.

The nature of the relationships between nodes vary along a number of dimensions, several of which are important to our discussion of transnational religious networks (the terms and definitions in this and the next paragraph come from Turner 1998:chap. 38). Tie *density* refers to the actual number of ties between all network nodes, relative to the logically possible number. In low-density networks, a lot of nodes lack direct ties to one another but are heavily linked to one or a few common nodes. In high-density networks, there are numerous ties between virtually all the various nodes. Many of the transnational networks described in this volume can be described as larger networks composed of subnetworks—*cliques* in network analysis parlance—in different nations, communities, and congregations. The network analysis term *bridges* refers to the nodes that link these smaller networks to one another as parts of an overarching one. Ties also differ according to variables that describe the flow of resources between nodes. The first issue is the *direction* of flow for each type of resource involved in a network's ties (e.g., monetary remittances most typically flow from immigrants and their congregations in Houston to religious personnel and institutions abroad). Related to this is flow *reciprocity*, or the extent to which only one versus both flow directions characterize network relationships. The immigration literature uses the term *remittances* to speak of flows between immigrants and their communities of origin. This term, however, generally refers to only one flow direction: from host to home country. The network concept *resources* and allied concerns with direction and reciprocity alert us to the possibility that transnational flows may be two way. Finally, the relative *strength* of network ties refers to the volume and frequency of flows between nodes. Strong ties are characterized by sustained and high levels of flow, weak ties by infrequent and low-level ones.

The Diversity of Network Actors and Ties
The diversity of actors involved in transnational religious networks, as described in the case studies, can be divided into three broad types, representing three different levels of analysis. At the micro level, individual persons or married couples

are often direct participants in religiously relevant networks. Local-level religious organizations, such as churches, temples, and seminaries, constitute the meso level, participating in transnational networks as corporate entities, not simply as congeries of individuals. At the most macro level, religiously relevant networks also sometimes include international religious bodies that are designed to control and integrate local congregations and/or to provide services and advice to member congregations.

Individual actors (including married couples) can also be meaningfully described in terms of three types, each of which serves as nodes in at least some of the networks described in this volume. Clergy, often immigrants themselves, are the most obvious candidates to serve as important nodes in transnational religious networks, although that is not the case everywhere. Lay religious leaders, including missionaries, congregational elders, founding members, and elected officers, as well as wealthy benefactors, play important roles in several cases. In almost every case, ordinary laypeople constitute a large percentage of transnational religious network nodes, underlining the extent to which religion across borders is substantially a grassroots phenomenon.

In most of the case studies, one or a few specific religious institutions in Houston constituted the starting point(s) for the examination of transnational religious networks, which are given privileged position as the core nodes from which network ties are traced. Stated in network theory terminology, these institutions constitute the *focal actors* in *ego-centered* networks (Wasserman and Faust 1994:42). In what follows, we therefore focus on briefly summarizing those transnational ties that directly link Houston nodes with nodes in other nations.

Summarizing the Case Study Network Configurations

LUZ DEL MUNDO HOUSTON–GUADALAJARA NETWORK. The *Luz del Mundo* Houston–Guadalajara network is part of an overarching religious organization whose leader, the apostle Samuel, heads both the international organization and the main church, *Hermosa Provincia*, located in Guadalajara. There are dense personal ties within each congregation and between members of the Magnolia Church in Houston and their kin, one-time neighbors, and friends in the Guadalajara churches from which many came and to which virtually all return annually. These dense ties across the border include all three types of individual-level nodes: clergy, lay leaders, and ordinary members. In addition, the religious institutions constitute directly connected nodes, largely because of the control exercised by Samuel, as denominational head, over all "promotions" into leadership and clerical roles in all congregations.

THE ARGENTINE BRETHREN TRANSNATIONAL NETWORK. Numerous individual and institutional linkages connect the Houston Argentine Brethren congregation (*Iglesia Cristiana Evangelica* [ICE]) and its members with churches, retreat camps, and their participants in three other nations. The Houston congregation serves as a bridge that indirectly links congregations and retreat centers in at least three locations in Argentina and one each in Spain and Honduras to one another. Dense interpersonal networks within the Mendoza, Lujan, and Houston congregations are linked to one another by family and kinship ties that span the border. In addition, lay missionaries, including the Gastons, Lopezes, and Sabbatinis, constitute important nodes in this transnational network. Regardless of the fact that they were born in Argentina, it was the Houston congregation that sponsored their missionary activities, even back to Argentina. Missionaries link the institutions they established in other countries to ICE in Houston as corporate bodies. In addition, they also maintain individual-level ties to fellow ICE members and leaders as well as to individuals in the Mendoza congregation. Further, as a corporate body, ICE provides direct support for several of the camps and congregations in other nations, thereby participating in institution-to-institution ties.

The Guatemalan Evangelical Maya Network
The network ties that link Guatemalan Maya evangelicals in Houston with their home community of San Pedro are entirely interpersonal. The primary actors are ordinary laypersons, clergy in San Pedro and to a lesser extent in Houston, and couriers. Churches in the two communities are not tied to one another institutionally, nor are their clergy. Rather, members of each of the three Houston congregations maintain ties to individuals in a variety of the churches in San Pedro; clergy in San Pedro have former members and/or the offspring of current members spread through all three Houston congregations with whom they often maintain contact; and the couriers accept consignments from members of all three churches in Houston for members in any of the numerous San Pedro churches. There are dense individual-level ties within and across congregations and between the two cities, but they are not contained within specific congregations.

THE HOUSTON–MONTERREY CATHOLIC CONNECTION. The Houston–Monterrey transnational Catholic network described by Sandoval totally lacks ties at the institutional level. The fact that the Catholic Church is the single largest international religious organization in the world seems all but irrelevant to this case, although the local-level parish involvements of various individuals, especially Houston migrants but Monterrey family members as well, infuse personal networks with religious content. While clergy are not directly involved in this transnational network, the two most important nodes are those represented by lay leaders of Catholic groups (the Herreras and Guillermo) who constitute bridges between cliques composed of religious group members in Houston (e.g., the Catholic Family Movement; a parish youth group) and Catholic family members in Monterrey. Each clique, that in Houston and the one in Monterrey, is comprised of dense ties; however, they are relatively loosely tied to one another across the border. Sandoval describes additional religious ties connecting the two cities, also rooted in dense kinship networks. Numerous residents of *La Fama barrio*, whose parish is St. Vincent de Paul (SVP), have family members residing in Houston who attend St. Jerome Church. Again, although no ties are evident between the parishes, *La Fama* residents attend St. Jerome's while visiting kin in Houston, where they not infrequently run into friends from SVP.

HOUSTON–VIETNAMESE CATHOLIC AND BUDDHIST RELIGIOUS NETWORKS. Networks that link Catholics and Buddhists in Houston with their religious counterparts in Vietnam are notable for the absence of transnational religious ties between individuals; all ties link institutions to one another or individuals to institutions. Immigrants, including ordinary members and lay leaders, along with clergy, directly aid churches and temples in Vietnam, and often their Houston congregations do likewise. The other notable feature in this case is the larger number of transnational ties among Catholics than among their Buddhist counterparts, especially those linking institutions in Houston and Vietnam to one another. Vietnamese Catholic institutions in Houston can and have called on the resources of the huge international organization in which they are embedded (the Catholic Church) to expedite the development of their own parishes. Therefore, they are likely to have more resources available to provide their overseas brethren. In contrast, Buddhist temples in Houston, which are largely independent entities, have had to rely largely on their own members to finance buildings and to support staff, and most are still paying off debts incurred as they developed their temples. While there is no reason to believe that individual Catholic and Buddhist immigrants differ in their personal level of resources available to donate to home country religious institutions, their congregations do differ in this way because of the presence or absence of an overarching denomination. Thus, while Catholic institutions appeared to play no role in the transnational network spanning Houston and Monterrey, they play an important role among the Vietnamese.

THE HOUSTON CHINESE CHRISTIAN CHURCH'S TRANSNATIONAL NETWORK. More so than any other case described in this volume, the Houston Chinese Church (HCC) is involved in ties at all three levels of analysis (micro: personal;

meso: local institutional; macro: international organizational), both as an institution and as the location of clergy, lay leaders, and ordinary lay members who participate as individuals in religiously relevant, transnational networks that involve a variety of other nations. Several of HCC's transnational ties are the direct result of its evangelistic commitment, most notably the mission it sent out and supports in Kazakhstan but also several individuals who have moved or returned to Taiwan and other east Asian locations, at least partly in order to proselytize, and other individual foreign missionaries and missionary organizations that HCC supports. Many individual level and institutional ties to Taiwan, Singapore, and Hong Kong link the three HCC clergy with churches to which they once belonged and seminaries they once attended. Each travels to Asia often, teaching, leading retreats, and giving lectures and seminars at a variety of churches and seminaries, especially in Taiwan and Hong Kong. Likewise, HCC is linked to various international Chinese Christian organizations (e.g., Christian Communications Ltd., Chinese Coordination Center of World Evangelism) often through interpersonal ties linking its pastors or lay leaders with organizational leaders.

THE FUZHOU–NEW YORK PROTESTANT NETWORK. Because Guest's study was not conducted as part of the original research design, information concerning specific transnational network linkages is spotty. It appears that the primary transnational network nodes in Fuzhou, China, are religious institutions, both Little Flock underground house churches and officially sanctioned Protestant ones. In New York, Guest focuses on two immigrant clergy (Rev. Liu and Pastor Chen) who play central roles as bridges, linking the tightly interconnected Fuzhou churches with both ordinary lay Chinese immigrants and with the two churches in Chinatown. What is especially interesting about this network is how different it appears from that described by Yang involving a Houston-based Chinese Protestant church and its far-flung and diverse transnational network partners. Nonetheless, in both cases a small number of immigrant clergy appear to serve as especially important nodes linking U.S.-based churches and their members to religious institutions abroad.

Network Institutionalization and Density

What can we conclude about transnational religious network nodes and ties based on these brief reviews of the case studies? In no case are all or most of the ties between corporate religious bodies; the majority of ties link individuals to one another. However, the extent to which individual-to-individual ties predominate varies considerably, as does the involvement of specific types of individuals. At one extreme, both the

Houston–Monterrey Catholic network and the Houston–San Pedro Maya evangelical network depict only individual-level ties. In the former case, all ties that cross the border connect laypersons, although some are lay leaders. In the latter, Guatemalan clergy are involved as well as laypersons. While comprising more institution-to-institution and individual-to-institution ties, nonetheless the complex and far-flung network of the HCC also rests strongly on interpersonal ties. In this case, the three Houston clergy maintain extensive personal as well as institutional ties abroad. The Argentine Brethren congregation's network is similar to the Chinese Christian one both in the mixture of personal and institutional ties and in the central role of lay leaders who, in this faith, are often indistinguishable from clergy. So, too, the *Luz del Mundo* transnational network is comprised of dense interpersonal ties between clergy, lay leaders, and ordinary lay members on both sides of the border as well as tight institutional ties linking the international organization in Guadalajara with its individual congregations in Houston (and elsewhere). The Vietnamese Catholic and Buddhist networks, and apparently that comprising Fuzhou Protestants, represent yet another pattern in that most ties link individuals in Houston with religious institutions in Vietnam and China and, among Catholics and probably Fuzhou Protestants, institutions to one another. These differences between networks can be conceptualized as a variable concerning *the extent to which transnational ties are institutional as opposed to grassroots.* The larger the proportion of institutional or organizational nodes, the more institutional the network is. Likewise, among individual-level ties, the more often clergy and, secondarily, lay leaders serve as individual-level nodes, the more institutional the network. Conversely, the most grassroots networks are those in which ordinary laypersons constitute the greatest proportion of nodes. Smith and Guarnizo (1998) distinguish between "transnationalism from above"—activities directed by institutional actors—and "transnationalism from below"—activities initiated by ordinary immigrants. Our case studies suggest that religious networks uniformly include considerable transnationalism from below but vary substantially on the extent of transnationalism from above.

Another way in which these networks vary concerns the extent to which ties abroad cluster densely in one community and one or a few congregations there or are more far-flung and less densely concentrated. At one extreme are the two Vietnamese religious networks and especially that of the HCC. In these cases, ties abroad are to a large number of religious institutions and/or their members who are geographically dispersed and often unconnected to one another. These ties are therefore relatively low density. The other extreme is represented by *Luz del Mundo*, whose cross-national ties are very densely concentrated in one community and primarily one church there. Argentine Brethren ties are simultaneously densely clustered with the parent congregation in Mendoza yet also widely although thinly dispersed to overseas missions. Although spread among three evangelical churches in

Houston and an even greater number in San Pedro, and in the absence of formal ties linking churches in the two locations, the Maya transnational network still consists of rather dense ties linking co-religionists in the two sites. The Fuzhou Protestant network appears to be similar. The Houston–Monterrey Catholic connection was designed to specifically trace ties between a particular Houston parish and one geographic location in Mexico, although Sandoval did not report dense ties linking members of IHM church in Houston to members of one specific church in Monterrey. Therefore, although this case appears to fall relatively high on a measure of density, that may be substantially an artifact of sampling only those in Houston who had migrated from Monterrey.

Table 9.1 suggests approximate rank ordering of the cases on the two variables. There does not appear to be any relationship between the density and institutional variables. For instance, of the networks with the most institutional ties (Vietnamese Buddhists and Catholics, *Luz del Mundo*), the latter is the most dense, while the former are very low in density. Another way of saying this is that extensive grassroots involvement in transnational religious networks (transnationalism from below) is not predictive of dense network ties and, conversely, that strong institutional ties (transnationalism from above) can occur with relatively dense ties but equally with low-density ties.

Perhaps the most clear-cut finding with regard to network nodes and ties is the great variety of configurations that transnational religious networks assume. There simply is no dominant form. Moreover, there is no reason to assume a priori that

Table 9.1.   Approximate Rank Order on Network Variables

Extent to Which Nodes Are Institutional versus Grassroots

Most institutional:	Vietnamese Catholics/Buddhists
	Fuzhou Protestants
	Luz del Mundo
	Houston Chinese Christian
	Argentine Brethren
	Guatemalan Maya Evangelical
Most grassroots:	Monterrey Catholics

Density of Network Ties to Specific Communities and Congregations

Most dense:	*Luz del Mundo*
	Argentine Brethren
	Monterrey Catholics
	Guatemalan Maya Evangelical
	Fuzhou Protestants
	Vietnamese Catholics/Buddhists
Least dense:	Houston Chinese Christian

economic, political, or any other kinds of transnational networks are any less diverse than religious ones in the kinds of nodes and ties they exhibit.

Resource Flows

When we ask what kinds of resources flow along ties between network nodes, we are asking about the *content* of network interactions, in this case, what resources flow across national borders that have a bearing on religious institutions, personnel, objects, practices, and/or beliefs. Thus, for instance, we are interested only in monetary flows from migrants to their families in the home community when we have evidence that at least some of that money is subsequently used by the recipients to fund religious practices or celebrations (rituals), purchase religious items, or support religious institutions or personnel. Clearly, it will often be the case that some or many of the resources that flow within the networks described in this volume, especially ties linking laypersons, will have no religious content. For instance, remaining with the example of monetary remittances, while some of the money may find its way to a religious purpose, perhaps most will be devoted to more mundane purposes, such as food, clothing, schooling, housing, furniture/appliances, capital to start a small business or buy a farm, and so on. We will ignore all nonreligiously relevant flows that may be occurring alongside religious ones.

Immigration scholars have long studied financial and material remittances that migrants send to their home community and the effects of these on those who remain behind. Indeed, often the major purpose of migration is precisely to gain the economic wherewithal to be able to remit money and goods to kin in the home community. Levitt (1998, 1999) introduced the concept *social remittances* and defined it as the ideas, behaviors, and social capital that flow from receiving to sending communities. She argues that as immigrants adapt to their host society, they often develop new norms and practices and amass social capital, all of which can, and often does, flow back to affect kin, neighbors, and other community members in their place of origin. Levitt makes an important contribution by broadening the concept *remittances* to include nonmaterial as well as financial phenomena. She recognizes that migrants bring with them to the host society a set of norms, practices, and varying degrees of social capital, which she calls their "resources" (Levitt 2001). In the course of their lives in the receiving country, they adapt and effect changes in these resources, which, in turn, become the content of social remittances sent back to their home communities. When we examine the transnational religious networks described earlier, we find not only the variety of material and social remittances of which Levitt speaks but also varying degrees of bidirectionality in flows of different kinds of resources. In what follows, we examine each major kind of resource that flows within the networks described in our case studies along with the direction(s) and relative intensity of the flows.

Monetary and Material Resources

When an immigrant congregation is young and its members mostly new arrivals, money and material goods sometimes flow from home to host country religious institutions. In the prologue to this volume, based on data from the RENIR I project, we noted that at least three congregations received financial help from abroad to build a religious facility. Within several years, however, immigrants usually become financially stable and increasingly able to send money home, at least some of which is devoted to religious purposes. Each of the case studies in this volume documents monetary resources that flow, directly and indirectly, from Houston to religious institutions abroad.

Cook documents the fact that, within a few years of their initial settlement, Argentine Brethren immigrants and the church they established sent money to the pastor of the Mendoza congregation from which they came and in later years financially supported Brethren missions and retreat centers in a number of locations in Argentina as well as in Honduras and Spain. He further cites the Mendoza pastor as remarking that immigrant remittances to impoverished family members constitute indirect contributions to the church inasmuch as they enable the church to save money that otherwise would be given to support the poor. Ha's chapter on the Vietnamese Buddhist and Catholic transnational networks is devoted almost entirely to showing how immigrant members of both religious communities and Vietnamese Catholic parishes have devoted increasing financial resources to rehabilitating homeland temples and churches and supporting their efforts to deliver social services to the needy. In another Communist nation characterized by tight government regulation of religion following years of outright religious repression, Guest shows the enormous importance of Fuzhou immigrant monetary remittances for rebuilding home community churches and supporting their clergy and activities. Likewise, the HCC and many individual members financially support numerous seminaries, missions, and missionaries in a variety of nations in Asia and elsewhere. *Luz del Mundo* does not appear to directly subsidize its parent church in Guadalajara. However, it is clear that it is immigrant dollars that provide much of the funding that makes possible the all-important transnational celebration of *Santa Cena* and especially the ability of impoverished immigrants to attend it. In the process of attending that celebration, immigrants also pump up to $90 million into the local economy, at least some of which likely finds its way back to the church in the form of donations. The Maya evangelicals also return home for an annual religious celebration, which probably has the same kind (although nowhere near the same magnitude) of indirect monetary effect as the *Luz del Mundo* cele-bration. More important, Maya immigrants directly contribute substantial funds to San Pedro churches, and their families there appear to contribute at least some of the money remitted to them to their churches. Hagan documents two cases where immigrants raised considerable sums of money for religious institutions in San Pedro, in one case to build a church and in the other a home for the pastor. Both Maya evangelical and Monterrey Catholic immigrants often celebrate life cy-cle rituals at home community churches and send money home for family mem-bers' ritual celebrations. In both cases, at least some of the money accrues to the church at which the ritual is celebrated. Finally, Sandoval also details the processes by which dollars sent by Houston immigrants to family members in *La Fama bar-rio* find their way, as donations in pesos, into church coffers. We assume that this is a widespread phenomenon (for more examples of monetary flows, see this vol-ume's prologue and Ebaugh and Chafetz 2000a).

Immigrants provide substantial amounts of goods for their home communi-ties, but only a few are religiously relevant. Perhaps the most frequent type is in-formation technology hardware and software. For instance, a few Houston *Luz del Mundo* members supply advanced electronic equipment—and the needed expertise to use it—that makes possible the satellite transmission of the *Santa Cena* to mem-bers everywhere who are unable to attend. Immigrant Maya tape life cycle and re-ligious celebrations to bring or send back to San Pedro, and when visiting San Pe-dro, they tape these types of events to bring back to the Houston community. Likewise, religious tapes flow from immigrant Catholics to their families in Mon-terrey (for more examples, taken from RENIR I, see this volume's prologue and Ebaugh and Chafetz 2000a). Underground churches in Fuzhou, China, receive smuggled books and pamphlets, as well as tapes of sermons produced in New York, from immigrant church members returning to visit or to serve as short-term missionaries.

Like money, technology typically flows from Houston to the home community/ country, but some other types of religious objects continue over time to flow to Houston or flow bilaterally. For instance, Sandoval found that religious images and other artifacts circulate among family members in both directions, from Houston to Monterrey and vice versa, and Yang documented extensive flows of religious books from Asia to HCC (and elsewhere in the United States). Yet other types of material objects are linked to particular practices so that when exported to home country con-gregations, new practices are simultaneously exported. Two examples of this were pro-vided by Ha in her chapter on Vietnam. A Buddhist immigrant wanted to help re-furbish a temple in Vietnam. He built a dining area for its monks in which he placed designer tables and chairs in lieu of the traditional benches and long wooden tables that perhaps symbolize a life of simplicity. He also added pews to the temple, where traditionally people sat on the floor. Likewise, a Catholic immigrant provided the church in her parents' village with a piano, only to discover that no choir existed, a lack to which she then turned her energies. In these instances, the introduction of material goods served also to alter religious norms and/or practices.

Social Resources

Far more than monetary flows, early in the history of most immigrant congregations religious norms and practices are imported and reproduced as faithfully as possible (see Ebaugh and Chafetz 2000a). The issue here, however, concerns the extent to which this importation process continues at more mature stages of institutional development and the extent to which innovations, often developed as part of the process of adaptation to the host community (see this volume's prologue and Yang and Ebaugh 2001b), are exported back to religious institutions in home countries. Recall that Levitt (1999, 2001) posits three types of social remittances—normative structures, practices, and social capital—that we use to structure our discussion.

NORMATIVE STRUCTURES: THEOLOGICAL IDEAS, VALUES, AND BELIEFS. The clearest case of ongoing importation to Houston of a religious normative structure is the *Luz del Mundo*. Fortuny-Loret De Mola asserts that the virtual one-way flow of religious doctrine from Guadalajara to Houston is explained by the highly authoritarian nature of the denominational organization whose leader, Samuel, directly controls the leadership of all individual churches and insists on the faithful reproduction of doctrine everywhere. In addition, by drawing nearly all members back to the parent church in Guadalajara at least once a year and involving them collectively in a highly emotional set of rituals, members' commitment to Samuel's version of Christian doctrine is renewed at regular intervals.

The HCC is both an exporter and an importer of religious doctrine. It devotes enormous efforts to evangelizing, including in places where there are few if any Christians, thereby exporting its nondenominational brand of Christianity. Thus, for instance, it has funded and staffed a mission in Kazakhstan and encourages, without formal support, lay ("tent-making") missionaries in mainland China, where, in addition to proselytizing, they also provide theological training to leaders of underground churches. The church also exports its religious doctrine through church members' families from overseas who attend HCC while visiting Houston and, not infrequently, convert before returning home. We can probably also assume that the active role of HCC's pastors in teaching, preaching, and running retreats in a variety of east Asian locales includes the exportation of doctrine that may differ in more or less subtle ways from that of the institutions that import them. However, HCC also imports theological ideas from abroad. Recall that it belongs to a variety of Chinese Christian international organizations that are rooted in east Asia, although they may have branches in the United States and elsewhere. For several, their most important role is to provide religious books and other instructional materials to congregational members such as HCC. Thus, for instance, the hymnals and other religious materials that HCC clergy and members consume express the theological ideas of overseas Chinese. In this way, the importation of material objects—books—coincides with the likely importation of theological ideas. The HCC may best be conceptualized as being situated within a Chinese Christian circuit that spans the world and within which religious ideas are constantly flowing from a variety of points (nodes) to a variety of points, with each participant both sending out and receiving new theological ideas, values, and beliefs.

The Vietnamese immigrants have effectively exported to Catholic and especially Buddhist religious institutions in Vietnam the idea that they should provide social services to the needy, not just religious services. In Houston, their churches and temples, like other immigrant congregations (see Ebaugh and Chafetz 2000a:chap. 17, 2000b; Yang and Ebaugh 2001b), have become community centers at which a variety of secular activities occur, thereby broadening their scope of activities beyond the strictly religious. In Vietnam and many other nations, religious institutions traditionally confine themselves to strictly religious activities (Fenton 1988; Rutledge 1992; Warner 1994). Because there are so many needy people in Vietnam and because the immigrants trust only religious bodies to handle monetary contributions to help them, they have urged churches and temples to define their missions more broadly. Clearly, this constitutes both a normative change and the transfer of an innovative practice from immigrant congregations to those in Vietnam.

RELIGIOUS PRACTICES. We have already discussed some examples in which the exportation from Houston congregations of material objects (pews, designer furniture, piano) and religious norms (secular service as religious mission) simultaneously entails the exportation of practice innovations. All these examples were taken from the Vietnamese case study. There are other examples of the export of innovative practices as well. For instance, returned migrants to Mendoza, Argentina, introduced several innovative practices that were routine in the Houston congregation to their original sending church, including a choir, Bible study groups, adult Sunday school, and a weekend Bible school. Immigrant Catholics from Monterrey were typically inactive in their home parish but often became involved in parish life in Houston as part of the process of adaptation to their new community. Some became lay leaders of Catholic groups who subsequently exported their new religious commitment by urging family members to attend church and become active in parish groups. Sometimes they were successful.

Importation of new practices sometimes also occurs. For instance, a group of HCC volunteers who went to Taiwan to help earthquake victims learned and subsequently brought back to Houston practices from a local church with which they worked. Yang called the practices "new-wave charismatic," including spiritual singing and spontaneous prayers. Perhaps the most interesting case of practice innovation is one in which exportation was followed by reimportation. Two Houston immigrant couples who would ultimately become foreign missionaries visited a Brethren retreat center in west Texas. One (the Gastons) subsequently went to Spain, where they established a center based on the west Texas model, while the other did the same in a new Argentine location (Entre Rios). A third couple did likewise in Honduras. Eventually, the Gastons returned to their community of origin, Mendoza, where they again established a retreat center, drawing on their experiences in both the United States and Spain. In fact, they imported to the Mendoza center the practice of structuring a nonprofit organization based on U.S. tax code requirements. Finally, the Gastons returned to Houston to oversee the development of ICE's new family ministries center, which is an urban version of the Mendoza center they had earlier built. Finally, there is one example of an on-the-spot innovation in Houston, combining inputs from both immigrants and home country family members, but it is not clear whether this practice will be exported. Hagan recounted an incident in which a Houston immigrant family threw a nontraditional (and secular) bridal shower that was converted into a quasi-traditional religious event by visitors from San Pedro.

SOCIAL CAPITAL.   Yang and Ebaugh (2001b) suggest that U.S. immigrant congregations become influential actors in other nations because of the core-country status of the United States and the kinds of resources and experiences immigrants in a wealthy nation can amass. Another way of saying this is that immigrants and their congregations often gain considerable social prestige in the home community (and elsewhere) and thus a heightened influence on beliefs and practices elsewhere. In addition, their heightened prestige can transfer to individuals or religious institutions in their home community or elsewhere abroad. In the prologue to this volume, we discussed how both the mosque and the Zoroastrian Center in Houston have become highly influential in international religious bodies. A few examples also emerge from the case studies in this volume.

Fortuny-Loret De Mola explicitly addresses the phenomenon of social capital in her analysis of Luz del Mundo. Unlike in Mexico, in the United States this religious community is a fully legitimate religion, which translates into high social status for immigrant members within the international church. Perhaps one indication of this is the honored location just above the main altar annually provided the U.S. choir during the *Santa Cena* celebration. Because members are loath to perceive themselves as "higher" than other members, Fortuny-Loret De Mola argues that the social capital earned in the United States is used to elevate the status of the church in Mexico. According to Cook, the Argentine Brethren congregation in Houston is perceived as the trendsetter or "established core of the network" by its sister congregations in Argentina, Spain, Honduras, and elsewhere. This is based on the myriad successful projects it and its missionaries have undertaken and is reflected in the central roles played by ICE leaders in international conferences and workshops. Finally, unlike the prior two cases where social capital accrues to congregations, among immigrant Mexican Catholics it accrues to individuals. Sandoval argues that leadership in a Houston parish group assumes symbolic importance among family members and friends in Monterrey who take pride in telling others about it.

Flow Directions and Intensity

The previous discussions in this section were organized according to resource type. Here we briefly examine each case study and trace the kinds of resources that are flowing through their networks and the directions in which the flows occur. We also estimate the relative intensity of flows.

The Magnolia congregation of *Luz del Mundo* in Houston is involved in reciprocal exchanges of different types of resources with its parent church in Guadalajara. Houston provides regular but not frequent material and financial resources and is also involved, along with other U.S. congregations, in the provision of social capital to the Mexican-based denomination. The parent church in Guadalajara provides ongoing normative resources to Houston by centrally controlling all religious personnel and doctrine. This reciprocal exchange is probably mostly latent except in the weeks leading up to and including the annual celebration of *Santa Cena.* Therefore, we conclude that, for much of the year, the transnational religious ties that connect these two religious bodies is moderately strong but grows to a very high level of intensity every summer.

The Argentine Brethren Church in Houston (ICE) is directly linked to a number of religious institutions in Argentina, Spain, Honduras, and elsewhere, all of which receive regular financial support from ICE. Likewise, practice innovations flow outward from the Houston congregation to its transnational network partners. Social capital accrues to ICE and becomes a resource that can also spread outward along its network ties. Indeed, the prestige that ICE and its leaders receive because of the congregation's innovative and active role in the transnational Brethren network is virtually the only reciprocal flow back to Houston. Cook suggests that today this transnational network is in a state of decline (see the final section of this chapter), but at its height it appears to have enjoyed highly intense, albeit substantially asymmetrical, ties, especially with the Mendoza and Luján congregations, from which most of the Houston immigrants came.

For Maya evangelicals, Fuzhou Protestants, Vietnamese Catholics, and Vietnamese Buddhists, resource flows are unidirectional from Houston to the home community/country. In addition, in each case the flow consists of money and material goods, although in both Vietnamese cases the material goods simultaneously involved normative or practice changes in some of the churches/temples that received them. The level of intensity of these flows is relatively high inasmuch as significant sums of money are involved and they flow, especially to Vietnam, quite consistently.

Flows between Houston and Monterrey are almost entirely unidirectional as well. Relatively small amounts of money, minor practice innovations, and some social capital flow from Houston to Monterrey. The only reciprocity results from a two-way flow of religious items. While the flows appear to be regular and ongoing, they involve low levels of each resource. We therefore conclude that the intensity level of the ties that compose the Houston–Monterrey Catholic network is relatively low.

Finally, the HCC is involved in numerous and substantially reciprocal ties to religious institutions, international Chinese Christian organizations, and individuals in diverse Asian locations. Monetary flows, which are substantial, are entirely unidirectional, originating in Houston. Material flows, mostly books and other instructional material, are also mostly unidirectional, but they originate primarily in east Asian locales. Finally, normative flows are reciprocal, flowing east to west and vice versa, in circular fashion. While the total volume of flows throughout the sprawling network appears to be quite high, the volume and frequency along any one tie line is probably modest. Therefore, we rank the intensity level as moderate.

Table 9.2 presents our conclusions about the relative intensity and reciprocity characteristic of resource flows in each transnational religious network. As we found concerning table 9.1, when we examined the relative levels of density and institutionalization of network ties, there appears to be no relationship between the rank orders on the reciprocity and intensity variables. In a few cases, a high level on one is matched by a high level on the other (*Luz del Mundo*), or two relatively low levels are found together (Maya evangelicals), but most cases show no such relationship. However, when we compare rankings on these two variables with those in the last section, there does appear to be somewhat of a relationship between the level of flow intensity and the level of institutionalization/grassroots ties. With the exceptions of the Argentine Brethren and Fuzhou Protestants, those with more highly institutional ties have more intense flows; conversely, the more

Table 9.2.   **Approximate Rank Order on Resource Flow Variables**

Intensity	
High:	Argentine Brethren
	Luz del Mundo
	Vietnamese Catholics/Buddhists
	Houston Chinese Christians
	Fuzhou Protestants
	Guatemalan Maya
Low:	Monterrey Catholics

Reciprocity	
High:	Houston Chinese Christians
	Luz del Mundo
Low:	Monterrey Catholics
	Argentine Brethren
	Guatemalan Maya
	Vietnamese Catholics/Buddhists
	Fuzhou Protestants

grassroots networks tend to have lower-intensity flows. Grassroots networks link individuals, often ordinary laypersons, together, and it is highly likely that the resources that flow along such ties have only occasional and low-level religious relevance. Because the only institutions included within the networks discussed here are religious ones, virtually all resources flowing from or to them will have religious relevance. Thus, it is not surprising that networks composed of a higher proportion of organizations and institutions enjoy more frequent and valuable religiously relevant flows than those composed mostly of individual persons.

The examination of resource flows in transnational religious networks demonstrates that, in addition to money and material goods, there are a number of other resources that circulate along tie lines. While most flows are "remittances" in the sense that they originate among immigrants and their congregations and flow to home communities (and sometimes other foreign destinations), we did find cases of reciprocity. Reciprocity is never financial, but it can be in terms of material goods (religious objects, books), normative structures, and occasionally practices. This underscores the importance of examining ongoing, bidirectional resource flows, not just remittances, when considering well-established, as well as new, immigrant communities and their transnational networks.

Toward Explaining Network Differences

With only seven cases at hand, it is at best possible to suggest some variables that might explain why transnational religious networks differ in the ways that they do, leaving it to future research to systematically explore our ideas using more cases and/or networks defined around institutions other than religion. Most studies of transnational communities to date have examined those whose home countries are in the Western Hemisphere, especially Latin America and some Caribbean nations (e.g., Basch et al. 1994; Levitt 1998; Portes 1996; see also the eight case studies that constitute the special issue on transnational communities, *Ethnic and Racial Studies* 22 [March 1999]). Besides their relatively highly proximate geographic relationship to the United States, immigrants from these countries tend, on average, to be relatively low in human capital and socioeconomic status (SES). Our small sample is quite diverse on both of these dimensions. It includes communities/nations of origin in Asia, South and Central America, as well as Mexico. Moreover, the average human capital and SES of immigrant congregation members in the case studies varies from relatively low (e.g., *Luz del Mundo*, Monterrey Catholics, Fuzhou Protestants, and Maya evangelicals) to one in which a large proportion have college, if not graduate professional, degrees (HCC), with the Argentine Brethren and Vietnamese Buddhists and Catholics falling in between. It is likely that physical distance between the home and host communities becomes meaningful primarily when combined with average SES. To the extent that most community members are poor, they are unlikely to be able to travel home often—or at all—unless home is relatively close. Conversely, those with higher incomes can travel relatively often even if distances are great. Moreover, those with higher incomes and educations are more likely than lower-SES immigrants to own and know how to use (and even purchase for those in the home community) cheap and rapid means of communication, such as computers linked to the Internet and fax machines. This also has the effect of making the relevance of distance significantly a function of SES. The ability to travel home also may be impacted by legal status in the United States. Undocumented immigrants assume a great risk of not being able to reenter the United States if they go home for a visit. Thus, we expect to find that physical distance between the home and host communities, average congregational SES, and proportion undocumented influence aspects of transnational network structure and functioning.

Two other variables are also hypothesized as affecting transnational religious networks. Because in some of our cases (those involving Vietnam and China) the governments in the nations of origin, until recently, have been overtly hostile to religion and continue to strongly control it, the nature of the political regime is expected to have some effect on religiously relevant transnational networks. However, even where the government does not repress religion, we found in RENIR I (see Yang and Ebaugh 2001a) and some of the studies in this volume that minority faiths often suffer at the hands of majority religions in their homelands. For instance, members of *Luz del Mundo*, Argentine Brethren, and Guatemalan Mayans have all reported significant persecution at the hands of the Catholic majority in their homelands. Finally, the degree to which members of immigrant congregations originate in one local community or region of one nation, versus a more diverse, cosmopolitan set of home communities and nations, should also affect the nature of the transnational religious networks in which they participate.

In the remainder of this section, we explore the effects on three network variables (institutionalization, density, and intensity) discussed earlier in the chapter of (1) relative proximity of home and host communities, (2) average immigrant congregation member SES, (3) relative proportion of undocumented congregational members, (4) degree of religious persecution in home country, and (5) degree of immigrant congregational membership diversity. Before we do this, in table 9.3 we approximate the rank order of our case studies for each of the five variables based on information from RENIR I as well as the case studies presented in this volume.

Given such a small sample of cases, the only way we can begin to see whether these hypothesized variables do indeed impact how networks are configured is very crude but, it is hoped, suggestive. We will take the five variables in table 9.3 one at a time, collapse their rank orders into two levels, and see whether their mean rankings on three of the network variables presented in tables 9.1 and 9.2 differ in ways that make sense. Note that a high mean represents a high rank ordering on the variables as they were presented in these earlier tables. In table 9.4, we show mean rankings on three network variables, excluding reciprocity, which exhibited too little variation to be able to rank order the cases. We were able to meaningfully divide the sample into two categories composed of three and four cases in all but one case. In panel E, membership diversity is divided into one category with five cases, which were all fairly to very local, relative to the two remaining cases.

The first three panels of table 9.4 show identical patterns, which is not surprising given that the SES and proportion-undocumented panels group cases identically, and they, in turn, differ by the placement of only one case (Fuzhou) from the proximity subsamples. With the exception of Fuzhou, transnational religious networks characterized by closer physical proximity and lower SES are higher in the proportion of undocumented immigrant members. What these three panels tell us is that, relative to their opposites, networks composed of proximate communities and poorer and more undocumented members tend to be more grassroots and more dense, and religiously relevant resources flow within them less intensely. Earlier we explained that grassroots networks are likely to experience less intense resource flows than the more institutionalized networks because of our narrow focus on religious resources. All organizations and institutions included in these networks are religious, while many of the individual persons are ordinary laypeople whose resource flows typically will be only minimally religiously relevant. Stated

Table 9.3.   Approximate Rank Order of Cases on Explanatory Variables

A. Proximity

Nearest:	Monterrey Catholics
	Luz del Mundo
	Guatemalan Maya
	Argentine Brethren
	Vietnamese Catholics/Buddhists
	Fuzhou Protestants
Farthest:	Houston Chinese Christians

B. Socioeconomic Status

Lowest:	Fuzhou Protestants
	Guatemalan Maya
	Luz del Mundo
	Monterrey Catholics
	Vietnamese Catholics/Buddhists
	Argentine Brethren
Highest:	Houston Chinese Christians

C. Proportion Undocumented

Highest:	Fuzhou Protestants
	Guatemalan Maya
	Monterrey Catholics
	Luz del Mundo
	Argentine Brethren
	Houston Chinese Christians
Lowest:	Vietnamese Catholics/Buddhists

D. Religious Persecution

Highest:	Fuzhou Protestants
	Vietnamese Christians/Buddhists
	Houston Chinese Christians
	Luz del Mundo
	Guatemalan Maya
	Argentine Brethren
None:	Monterrey Catholics

E. Level of Diversity

Highly local:	*Luz del Mundo*
	Argentine Brethren
	Guatemalan Maya
	Fuzhou Protestants
	Monterrey Catholics
	Vietnamese Catholics/Buddhists
Cosmopolitan:	*Houston Chinese Christians*

Table 9.4. Mean Rank Order of Network Variables by Explanatory Variables Divided into Two Categories

	Institutionalization	Density	Intensity
Proximity			
High (*Luz*, Monterrey, Maya)	5.3	2.7	5
Low (Argentine, Vietnam, HCC, Fuzhou)	3	5	3.25
Socioeconomic Status			
Low (Fuzhou, Maya, *Luz*, Monterrey)	4.5	3.25	5
High (Vietnam, Argentine, HCC)	3.3	5	2.7
Proportion Undocumented			
High (Fuzhou, Maya, *Luz*, Monterrey)	4.5	3.25	5
Low (Vietnam, Argentine, HCC)	3.3	5	2.7
Religious Persecution			
High (Fuzhou, Vietnam, HCC)	2.3	6	4
Low (*Luz*, Maya, Argentine, Monterrey)	5.25	2.5	4
Membership Diversity			
Local (*Luz*, Argentine, Maya, Fuzhou, Monterrey)	4.6	3	4.2
Cosmopolitan (HCC, Vietnam)	2.5	6.5	3.5

otherwise, these grassroots networks may enjoy very intense resource flows, but usually not in religious goods. Given this, it seems to make sense to find that immigrants who come from relatively nearby communities of origin, despite being disproportionately poor, will have a relatively easy time maintaining dense, grassroots relationships with kin and friends left behind. It was especially clear in the chapters on *Luz del Mundo* and the Houston–Monterrey connection just how frequently Mexican immigrants return home and their family members visit Houston, often disregarding potential border problems that returning undocumented migrants are likely to face. Wealthier immigrants from communities to which they must fly great distances to visit tend to be involved in networks that include more institutional actors and are less dense as well, although the flow of religiously relevant resources within such networks is greater. Where undocumented status and poverty apparently do not deter proximate migrants from maintaining dense transnational networks, high SES and legal status do not appear sufficient to overcome great distances in order to maintain dense networks.

Turning to panel D, while all the home religious communities except Monterrey Catholics experienced some religious persecution in their home communities, we chose to distinguish the three Asian cases from the others because of the active role of government in their persecution. The HCC has a minority of members from mainland China; a majority came from Taiwan, where they have not been the victims of persecution. However, when we recomputed the means with HCC grouped with the less persecuted subsample, the basic findings in this panel remained the same. First, intensity of religious resource flows is totally unrelated to level of persecution, which is at first surprising. This is probably a result of timing. Specifically, after years of systematically destroying churches and temples, in recent years Communist regimes in both Vietnam and China have begun permitting selected religious institutions to rebuild and specifically to accept money from abroad to foster institutional rebuilding and development. Ha's chapter on Vietnamese Catholics and Buddhists documents how and why money for the redevelopment of that nation is especially likely now to be channeled by immigrants through religious institutions. Guest also describes how immigrant remittances are rebuilding at least the officially sanctioned churches in Fuzhou. Thus, it is not surprising to find that in these cases the level of institutionalization is high. Immigrants and their congregations funnel religious resources directly to churches and temples that are in dire need and that are also defined as trustworthy rather than through some of the more circuitous routes described, for instance, by Sandoval in the case of Monterrey. Finally, the highly persecuted cases are composed of the least dense networks. We believe that this occurs because two of the three cases that experience high persecution are also the most cosmopolitan. When we examine panel E, we find that, not surprisingly, given the way the subsamples overlap with those in panel D, cosmopolitan networks, in which immigrant congregation members do not share a community or even national region of origin, behave like those highly persecuted and more local ones like the less persecuted.

What can we conclude from this discussion? Because, when reduced to only two categories for each dimension, the subsamples overlap considerably, it is impossible to assert confidently how important each of the five variables is for explaining variation in the network variables; however, there are grounds for choosing three of the five as likely most important. We think that among the first three—proximity, SES, and legal status—proximity is probably the most important. Less distance between home and host communities produces more grassroots and dense networks despite travel difficulties associated with low SES and more frequent undocumented status. Conversely, geographically remote home and host communities produce more institutionalized, less dense networks despite advantages of SES and legal status. Between the religious persecution and diversity variables, we believe that both may be important but for different reasons. By the time this research was conducted, in both China and Vietnam officially recognized churches and temples were permitted to receive help from abroad. However, there is still significant control exercised over religious practice in both nations. This helps us understand why the more persecuted cases are far more institutionalized than the less persecuted. Religious resources channeled to these nations will go largely to approved institutions, whether they are supplied by individuals or institutions in the United States. The difference in density is probably best understood as the result of the diversity variable. Especially HCC, whose members hail from numerous nations, but also Vietnamese temples and churches, whose members do not come from any specific cities or even regions, will be involved in far-flung network relationships with their diverse communities of origin. This will result in wide but "thin" (i.e., low-density) networks for their congregations.

Another, more simple way to look at these findings is to note that, with two exceptions, the same case studies always cluster together. *Luz del Mundo*, Monterrey Catholics, and Guatemalan Maya are uniformly in the same subsample; likewise, the HCC and the Vietnamese Catholics and Buddhists are found together in the other. The first of these clusters is characterized by closer proximity, lower SES, a higher proportion of undocumented immigrants, lower levels of religious persecution, and more shared local origins than the second. The characteristic transnational religious network of cluster 1 is more grassroots, more dense, and less intense than cluster 2. The Fuzhou Protestants and Argentine Brethren constitute cases that fit with neither empirically constructed type. The two clusters divide neatly in terms of geography, with the first composed of proximate Spanish-speaking networks, the latter of distant, Asian ones. This fact alone suggests the need to conduct research on transnational networks rooted in communities outside the Western Hemisphere, which may lead to very different conclusions from studies based only on nearby sending nations. That the Argentine and Fuzhou cases fit neatly with neither type underscores the diversity of transnational networks. Not only is Argentina considerably less proximate to Houston than other Spanish-speaking sending nations, but its immigrants tend to have more human capital and higher SES than most other sending nations in the Western Hemisphere. Conversely, Fuzhou immigrants are atypical of Asian immigrants to the United States in having lower human capital and SES and in coming to this country as undocumented migrants. These findings suggest the need to use independent variables rather than types when attempting to explain variation in network attributes.

Network Change and Prognoses for the Future

There is one additional phenomenon that impacts transnational religious networks, namely, the passage of time. More specifically, over time, immigrants, their congregations, and communities change in two broad ways relevant to our interests: (1) The immigrants adapt to their new setting and typically improve their financial situation, and (2) eventually a second generation grows to maturity and assumes adult roles. While collectively the case studies provide little information on the topic of transnational religious network change, Ha's chapter on the Vietnamese provides insights on the first issue, and Cook's analysis of the Argentine Brethren is suggestive of what the future holds for these networks as the second generation comes to re-place their parents as community and congregational leaders.

Ha traces a transition among Vietnamese immigrants of both faiths from re-mitting money and goods directly to kin in the home country to the development of a system through which a significant part of their financial remittances now flow through international financial institutions to congregations in Vietnam. Catholic institutions in the United States, including parishes in Houston, also participate in this mature, transnational network. Besides rebuilding churches and temples, Ha argues that Vietnamese immigrants have come to believe that the best way to help the huge population of needy people in their homeland is to encour-age religious institutions there to assume a new role as social service providers and then fund those activities. The transition from individual to individual/family ties through which money and goods flowed to one in which immigrants and some-times their congregations developed direct ties to channel support to temples and churches in Vietnam resulted from both the improved financial situation of the immigrants and a series of policy changes effected by the Vietnamese government.

The relevance of Ha's findings to the evolution of transnational religious net-works rooted in nations other than Vietnam is twofold. In the relatively small number of contemporary nations where government policy sharply curtails reli-gious institutions and practices, this fact constrains the possible network configu-rations that can exist. When and if policy changes, the nature of network nodes and ties and the quantity and types of resources flowing to religious purposes will change as well. In virtually all cases (but to a variable extent) in the early stages of immigrant community development, monetary remittances are likely to flow at the grassroots level and have, at most, small impact on religious institutions. Over time, immigrants, and often the religious institutions they develop, amass suffi-cient financial resources to contribute to overseas religious purposes without nec-essarily curtailing their ongoing help for kin left behind (e.g., see Hagan's discus-sion of the sizable amount of money sent to kin in Guatemala yet also the money raised in Houston for a church and for a pastor's home in San Pedro by a com-munity of relatively poor immigrants). Variation in this scenario will be primarily a function of the average human capital and SES of the immigrants. Wealthier congregations (e.g., HCC) will likely develop ties through which they funnel ma-terial resources to religious institutions abroad earlier in their immigrant commu-nity's history than congregations whose members are disproportionately poor. In addition, obviously the quantity of financial support to religious purposes abroad will vary by SES, holding constant the level of immigrant community maturity.

Cook set out to explicitly trace change in the Argentine Brethren transnational religious network. The forty-year-old Houston congregation is now the core of a mature immigrant community. What began as a congregation completely dependent on its Mendoza home congregation for theological beliefs and practices developed into perhaps the most influential node in a multinational network, based on a variety of innovations it created. As in other cases, as the congregation and its members became more established in Houston, financial remittances were sent home to support the church in Mendoza and, over time, to an increasing number of churches, retreat centers, and missionaries in a variety of places outside the United States. However, Cook argues that this dense religious transnational network is now in the first stage of decline. For instance, monetary remittances to Mendoza and Luján have all but ceased.

The founders of the ICE now have adult second-generation children, although a steady, if small, stream of Argentines have continued to arrive since the pioneering cohort of the 1960s, and the children of more recent arrivals are naturally younger. Cook recounts the experiences of three of the mature, second-generation church members, whom he thinks represent the main ways members of this cohort relate to the church and Argentina. One, for whom "symbolic ethnicity" as Latin American is important, is only loosely connected to the church and has few ties to Argentina. Another is closely integrated into the church and is being groomed to become a congregational leader. However, his focus is on developing a broad Hispanic ministry in Houston rather than maintaining close ties to Argentina. The third, also an up-and-coming religious leader, is also oriented to Houston and a Hispanic—not distinctively Argentine—ministry. In varying amounts, all three have spent time in Argentina, and all speak Spanish. Nonetheless, not one combines a strong commitment to the church with a strong tie to Argentina, leading Cook to conclude that the days of a transnational religious field in which ICE is involved "are numbered" (although he continues on to discuss circumstances that do not now exist under which this scenario might not come to pass).

The future of transnational religious networks will, sooner or later, be left in the hands of the second and subsequent generations, except in cases where continued large streams of immigration infuse such networks with a steady supply of newcomers (almost certainly ensuring for the foreseeable future the continuation of Mexican transnational networks involving Houston). There is still very little information on the adult second-generation in post-1965 immigration streams (see Portes 1996; Portes and Rumbaut 2001), in part because, for many nationalities, this generation is only now, in the dawn of the millennium, beginning to reach adulthood. However, the little evidence that does exist, along with much more information on the evolution of immigrant communities in the fifty years after the turn of the twentieth century, suggests that transnational networks are likely to weaken substantially as the immigrant generation passes from community and congregational leadership and ultimately from life.

Conclusion

Whether transnational religious networks maintain their strength over the coming decades as immigrant communities age and, increasingly, second- and subsequent generation members become the adult leaders of their communities remains for future research to explore. As is evident in the cases described in this volume, currently, immigrants are still actively involved in creating and sustaining transnational religious ties. We hope that our study, along with other recent case studies (e.g. Levitt 2001; Menjivar 2000; Peterson et al. 2001), demonstrates that religion operates transnationally, along with politics, economics, and family—the social institutions that have been of central concern in the transnationalism literature. It is hoped that religion will soon be included among these institutions as equally important to understanding transnational communities.

Throughout the studies in this volume, the concept *networks* has been used as an organizing framework for describing the pathways, content, and impact of religious exchanges among actors (individuals, groups, communities, institutions) in home and host countries. By including congregations that vary in national origins, religion, proximity to the United States, socioeconomic and legal status of members, and diversity in membership, we were able to suggest factors that influence the ways in which religious networks differ across congregations. We are convinced of the necessity of moving beyond single case studies and incorporating comparative research in order to begin to develop generalizations regarding variations in the ways in which transnational religious networks function.

Immigrants coming to the United States bring with them religious beliefs, practices, and resources that they transplant to and adapt within their American congregations. The myriad immigrant congregations that have arisen in the United States within the past three decades have significantly changed the landscape of American religion. As immigrants maintain contact with their home communities, they export these religious adaptations, often prompting change within the more traditional religious culture and congregational structures of their homelands. The transnational religious networks in which the new immigrants participate, therefore, play a central role in the global, transnational world of the twenty-first century.

References

Basch, Linda, Nina Glick Schiller, and Cristina Szanton Blanc. 1994. *Nations Unbound: Transnational Projects, Postcolonial Predicaments and Deterritorialized Nation-States.* Amsterdam: Gordon and Breach.

Berkowitz, S. D. 1982. *An Introduction to Structural Analysis: The Network Approach to Social Research.* Toronto: Butterworths.

Burt, Ronald. 1980. "Models of Network Structure." *Annual Review of Sociology* 6:79–141.
———. 1982. *Towards a Structural Theory of Action: Network Modes of Social Structure, Perceptions, and Action.* New York: Academic.
Ebaugh, Helen Rose, and Janet Saltzman Chafetz. 2000a. *Religion and the New Immigrants: Continuities and Adaptations in Immigrant Congregations.* Walnut Creek, CA: AltaMira.
———. 2000b. "Structural Adaptation in Immigrant Congregations." *Sociology of Religion* 61:135–53.
Fenton, John Y. 1988. *Transplanting Religious Traditions: Asian Indians in America.* New York: Praeger.
Glick Schiller, Nina. 1999. "Transmigrants and Nation-States: Something Old and Something New in the U.S. Immigrant Experience." In *The Handbook of International Migration: The American Experience,* edited by Charles Hirschman, Philip Kasinitz, and Josh DeWind. New York: Russell Sage Foundation.
Levitt, Peggy. 1998. "Local-Level Global Religion: The Case of the U.S.-Dominican Migration." *Journal for the Scientific Study of Religion* 37:74–89.
———. 1999. "Social Remittances: Migration Driven, Local-Level Forms of Cultural Diffusion." *International Migration Review* 32:926–48.
———. 2001. *The Transnational Villagers.* Berkeley: University of California Press.
Menjivar, Cecilia. 2000. *Fragmented Ties: Salvadoran Immigrant Networks in America.* Berkeley: University of California Press.
Peterson, Anna L., Manuel A. Vasquez, and Philip J. Williams, eds. 2001. *Christianity, Social Change, and Globalization in the Americas.* New Brunswick, NJ: Rutgers University Press.
Portes, Alejandro, ed. 1996. *The New Second Generation.* New York: Russell Sage Foundation.
Portes, Alejandro, and Ruben Rumbaut. 2001. *Legacies: The Story of the Immigrant Second Generation.* Berkeley: University of California Press.
Rutledge, Paul James. 1992. *The Vietnamese Experience in America.* Bloomington: Indiana University Press.
Smith, Michael Peter, and Luis Eduardo Guarnizo, eds. 1998. *Transnationalism from Below.* New Brunswick, NJ: Transaction.
Turner, Jonathan. 1998. *The Structure of Social Theory.* Belmont, CA: Wadsworth.
Warner, R. Stephen. 1994. "The Place of the Congregation in the Contemporary American Configuration." In *American Congregations,* vol. 2, edited by James P. Wind and James W. Lewis. Chicago: University of Chicago Press.
Wasserman, Stanley, and Katherine Faust. 1994. *Social Network Analysis: Methods and Applications.* Cambridge: Cambridge University Press.
Wellman, Barry. 1983. "Network Analysis: Some Basic Principles." In *Sociological Theory,* edited by R. Collins. San Francisco: Jossey-Bass.
Wellman, Barry, and S. D. Berkowitz. 1988. *Social Structures: A Network Approach.* Cambridge: Cambridge University Press.
Yang, Fenggang, and Helen Rose Ebaugh. 2001a. "Religion and Ethnicity among New Immigrants: The Impact of Majority/Minority Status in Home and Host Countries." *Journal for the Scientific Study of Religion* 40:367–78.
———. 2001b. "Transformations in New Immigrant Religions and Their Global Implications." *American Sociological Review* 66:269–88.

Index

About the Contributors

Janet Saltzman Chafetz, chair and professor of sociology, has been at the University of Houston since 1971. She received her Ph.D. from the University of Texas, Austin, in 1969. Her most recent publications include *Handbook on the Sociology of Gender* (1999), a review of feminist theories in *Annual Review of Sociology* (1997), and a paper on feminist theory and social change in *Current Perspectives in Social Theory* (1999). She is coauthor, with Helen Rose Ebaugh, of *Religion and the New Immigrants: Adaptations and Continuities in New Immigrant Congregations* (AltaMira Press, 2000), as well as numerous articles in sociological journals. Her lifelong interest in gender led to the publication of an article in *Social Forces* on women and immigrant religious institutions.

David A. Cook is a doctoral student at the University of California, Los Angeles, where he is a Mellon fellow for Latin American sociology. He received a master's degree from the University of Houston. His research has focused on migration, religion, and ethnicity. He is the author of "Iglesia Cristiana Evangilica: Arriving in the Pipeline" in *Religion and the New Immigrants*, edited by Helen Rose Ebaugh and Janet Saltzman Chafetz. He is currently researching Latin American migration to Spain.

Helen Rose Ebaugh, professor at the University of Houston, received her Ph.D. in sociology from Columbia University in 1975, specializing in organizational sociology, sociology of the family, and sociology of religion. In addition to five books, she has published numerous articles in scholarly journals, including *Social Forces, Journal of Marriage and the Family, Sociological Analysis,* and *The Journal for the Scientific Study of Religion*. She served as president of the National Association for the Sociology of Religion; helped organize and served as the first chair of the American

Sociological Association's section on the sociology of religion; and is past president of the Society for the Scientific Study of Religion. Recently, Ebaugh received two consecutive research grants from the Pew Charitable Trusts to study religion and new immigrants to the United States. The results from the first grant, which focused on the role of religious congregations in the incorporation of new immigrants, is described in *Religion and the New Immigrants: Adaptations and Continuities in New Immigrant Congregations*, as well as a number of recent articles in major sociological journals. She routinely teaches courses at the University of Houston in the sociology of world religions.

Kenneth J. Guest, visiting assistant professor of anthropology at Baruch College, City University of New York (CUNY), received his Ph.D. from the CUNY Graduate Center. His research, to be published in his forthcoming book, *New Gods in Chinatown: Faith and Survival in New York's Immigrant Community*, focuses on the role of religion in Chinese immigrant communities in New York; the transnational immigrant ties being established between Chinatown and southeast China, particularly Fujian Province; and the influence of these ties on the religious revival now sweeping southeastern China. Research for this study was partially supported by a dissertation Fellowship for the Study of Religion and Immigration from the Social Science Research Council with funds provided by the Pew Charitable Trusts.

Thao Ha is a doctoral student at the University of Texas, Austin, where she is focusing on race, ethnicity, and Asian American studies. She was born in Vietnam and grew up in Houston, Texas, where she was active in the Vietnamese community, often serving as a guide and interpreter for visitors interested in the Vietnamese in Houston.

Jacqueline Maria Hagan is associate professor of sociology and codirector of the Center for Immigration Research at the University of Houston. Her research interests include immigration, social policy, community organization, and human rights issues. She is involved in an ongoing study that assesses migrant mortality associated with unauthorized crossings along the U.S.–Mexico border. In a second, related human rights project she is interviewing deportees in Mexico and El Salvador to better understand the effects of deportation on families and communities. Her most recently launched project focuses on the role of religion in the migration process.

Patricia Fortuny-Loret de Mola received her Ph.D. from University College London in 1995. She is a researcher in the Center of Research and Advanced Studies in Social Anthropology (CIESAS–Peninsular) in Merida, Yucatan, Mexico. Since the 1980s, she has studied religious minorities in rural and urban areas in Mexico. She has edited the book, *Creyentes y Creencias en Guadalajara* (Believers and Beliefs in Guadalajara, 2000), as well as numerous articles on conversion, religious change in modern societies, religion and gender, and religion and migration. In 1997–1998, she was a Fulbright scholar at St. Mary's University, San Antonio, Texas. In 2001, she was a Rockefeller fellow at the University of Florida in Gainesville.

Efrén Sandoval has a master's degree in social anthropology at Centro de Investigaciones y Estudios Superiores de Antropologia Social (CIESAS–Occidente). His dissertation is based on Catholicism and nongovernment organizations in Mexico. He has participated in various research projects about international migration through the northeastern border of Mexico.

Fenggang Yang received his Ph.D. from the Catholic University of America, conducted postdoctoral research at the University of Houston, and is assistant professor of sociology at Purdue University. His research has focused on new immigrant religions. He is the author of *Chinese Christians in America* (1999), chapters in various books, and articles in the *Journal for the Scientific Study of Religion, Sociology of Religion, Amerasia Journal, Journal of Asian American Studies,* and *American Sociological Review.*